Forced Passages

Forced Passages

Imprisoned Radical Intellectuals and the U.S. Prison Regime

Dylan Rodríguez

University of Minnesota Press
Minneapolis • London

Cover photograph by the author, taken outside Soledad State Prison in California, December 2004

Chapter 2 is a significantly revised version of "Against the Discipline of 'Prison Writing': Toward a Theoretical Conception of Contemporary Radical Prison Praxis," *Genre: Forms of Discourse and Culture* 35, no. 3/4 (special issue, "Prisoners Writing"; fall 2002/winter 2003): 407–28; reprinted with permission of University of Oklahoma.

Chapter 3 is based on "The 'Question' of Prison Praxis: Relations of Force, Social Reproduction, Points of Departure," in *Radical Philosophy Today. Volume 2: The Problems of Resistance*, edited by Steve Martinot and Joy James (Amherst, NY: Humanity Books, 2001), 46–68; copyright 2001 by Steve Martinot and Joy James.

 Chapter 4 was originally published as "State Terror and the Reproduction of Imprisoned Dissent," *Social Identities: Journal for the Study of Race, Nation, and Culture* 9, no. 2 (June 2003): 183–204.

"Grave Digger," by Viet Mike Ngo, was originally published in *Amerasia Journal*; reprinted with permission. "A Sunny Soledad Afternoon" was originally published in *Words from the House of the Dead: Prison Writings from Soledad* (New York: Crossing Press, 1974).

Published by the University of Minnesota Press
111 Third Avenue South, Suite 290
Minneapolis, MN 55401-2520
http://www.upress.umn.edu

Library of Congress Cataloging-in-Publication Data

Rodríguez, Dylan.
    Forced passages : imprisoned radical intellectuals and the U.S. prison regime / Dylan Rodríguez.
        p. cm.
    Includes bibliographical references and index.
    ISBN 0-8166-4560-4 (hc : alk. paper) — ISBN 0-8166-4561-2 (pb : alk. paper)
    1. Prisoners—United States. 2. Radicals—United States. 3. Prisoners' writings, American. I. Title.
HV9466.R63 2005
365'.450973—dc22

    2005023234

Printed in the United States of America on acid-free paper

The University of Minnesota is an equal-opportunity educator and employer.

12 11 10 09 08 07 06   10 9 8 7 6 5 4 3 2 1

Contents

American Apocalypse

While America is boasting of her freedom and making the world ring with her professions of equality, she holds millions of her inhabitants in bondage.

    —Henry Box Brown, *Narrative of the Life of Henry Box Brown* (1851)

where does it all lead to?
i mean, like where are we going?
and where did we come from?
where did it all begin?
and who started it?

      —raúlrsalinas (Raúl Salinas), "Pregúntome" (1970)

Living Apocalypse, Radical Freedom

Amid the current apocalypse of mass-based punishment and liquidation thrives a political lineage at war with its own disappearance, haunting and shadowing U.S. civil society with earthquake fantasies of liberation and freedom. Resonating the opening epigraph by Henry Box Brown, the onetime slave who escaped Virginia by sealing himself in a mail crate and emerging in Philadelphia twenty-seven hours later, these are visions of displacement and disarticulation, confronting the nonimprisoned "free world" with the sturdy deadly premises of its own definition and self-narration. Fatal unfreedom, historically articulated through imprisonment and varieties of (undeclared) warfare, and currently proliferating through epochal technologies of human immobilization and bodily disintegration, forms the grammar and materiality of American society. I offer this book from within a troubled relation to this American social formation, across its multiple geographies and histories, as a Pinoy scholar-activist who is both a direct descendant and vexed inheritor of

1

the legacies of U.S. conquest, colonization, enslavement, and neoliberal ("multicultural") incorporation.[1] Thus, as with any political-cultural production, my subjectivity, autobiography, and desire are present throughout this text.

I am focusing my theoretical attention on the post-1970s formation of "radical prison praxis," which I fully conceptualize in chapter 2 as an active current of political-intellectual work shaped by a condition of direct and unmediated confrontation with technologies of state and state-sanctioned (domestic) warfare. This political lineage refutes and displaces, confuses and short-circuits the coherent and durable sets of political assumptions that define the commonly enforced limits of public discourse and social intercourse in the United States. In part, the theoretical trajectories and political legacies of this praxis render *essentially unstable and, at times, untenable* the very foundations of such valorized and allegedly universal American entitlements as (1) formal protection under the fundamental ("inalienable") rubrics of constitutional or civil "rights," (2) mediated protection under the rule and dominion of the state's juridical, policing, and (para)military structures, and (3) the everyday presumption of individual and collective bodily integrity, that is, a generalized freedom from anticipated or imminent physical suffering, violation, or obliteration. Departing from this condition of theoretical and material crisis, I am interested in a different philosophy of praxis, one inscribed by the very logic of violence, disappearance, and death that forms the regime from within which it is produced, returning an image (shadow? apparition? echo?) of a world in terror, at war, yet unsettlingly stable.

The following chapters thus attempt a genealogy and political theorization of what I am calling the contemporary U.S. "prison regime." At the same time, this book offers an extended meditation on—and critical engagement with—a lineage of praxis that awakens the constitutive antagonism between (1) technologies of bodily immobilization and programmatic violence that enact through the particular institutionality of the prison, and (2) the creative new languages and embodied spaces, visions, and fantasies of liberationist political struggle generated by imprisoned insurgents, insurrectionists, and (proto)revolutionaries.[2] I argue that, in its most creative renditions and theoretical elaborations, this living lineage of radical captive intellectuals conceptualizes and provokes the disarticulation of the sociohistorical formation—plainly, the "United States of America"—that operationalizes our living apocalypse of unfreedom. Imprisoned radical intellectuals critically envision (and sometimes strategize) the displacement or termination of the epochal American production of biological and cultural genocides, mass-based bodily violence, racialized domestic warfare, and targeted, coercive misery. At its most ambitious, this book is attempting to generate a modality and momentum of political articulation that elaborates the possibility, currency, and necessity of *centering the antisystemic:* I proceed from the premise that we must enunciate new languages and philosophies of liberation and freedom that envision radical opposition to—and liquidation of—the current structural entanglements between the normative localization of white-supremacist patriarchal violence (including advanced forms of warfare and genocide) and the globalization of militarized empire.

Lineage and "Social Truth":
Distinguishing "Imprisoned Radical Intellectuals"

I have chosen the conceptual designation "imprisoned radical intellectuals" for reasons that should be clarified. First, my choice of designation foregrounds the term "imprisoned" in order to bring attention to the conditions of possibility, that is, the changing regime of rituals, practices, and juridical procedures, that structure this category of intellectual and cultural production. As I argue more thoroughly in chapter 1, the terms "prison intellectual," "prison writer," or "radical prisoner" (terms that I freely used until the last revisions of this manuscript) tend to reinscribe and naturalize the regime of imprisonment, as if it were a natural feature of the social landscape and an irreducible facet of the "prisoner's" identity and historical subjectivity.

Second, I am addressing while exceeding current juridical and progressive activist/human rights categorizations of "political prisoners" and "prisoners of war (POWs)." Progressive and leftist definitions of these terms, despite their subtle (and hotly debated) variations, often address a specific telos of incarceration that privileges the existence of the liberationist/radical insurrectionist/revolutionary political subject *prior to* her or his encounter with formal juridical criminalization, police bodily apprehension, and state captivity. According to these definitions, political prisoners and prisoners of war are imprisoned as a direct result of their political activities in civil society—community organizing, political education, public speech, armed self-defense, artistic production, guerrilla warfare—that foster or manifest insurrection against socially embedded forms of domination and subjection. Activist attorney Jill Soffiyah Elijah, who has worked on behalf of U.S. political prisoners for more than two decades, outlines the broadly accepted international standard of definition:

> Political prisoners are men and women who have been incarcerated for their political views and actions. They have consciously fought against social injustice, colonialism, and/or imperialism and have been incarcerated as a result of their political commitments. Even while in prison, these men and women continue to adhere to their principles. This definition of the term "political prisoner" is accepted throughout the international community.[3]

Other, less restrictive though still politically centered conceptions focus on the criminalization of those *already imprisoned* who have taken action against systems of national, racial, gender, and/or class oppression during the time of their incarceration. Within these definitions, "common" or social prisoners may *become* "political prisoners" by virtue of their politically articulated actions on behalf of the oppressed, and their frequent subjection to enhanced penal consequences as a result. According to *Can't Jail the Spirit*, a political prisoner is "a person, sanctioned by the movement, evolved in character and deeds, who is held in confinement for support of, or identity with, a people struggling for freedom from an oppressive government or against its oppressive policies."[4]

In addition to personifying the (rather slippery) attribute of an "evolved" political identity, political prisoners and POWs are overwhelmingly understood as having been affiliated with particular organizations, discrete social movements, or specific counter- and antistate uprisings that seek a liquidation of oppressive sociopolitical and economic structures, including (proto)slavery, (cultural and biological) genocide, military occupation, communal displacement, white-supremacist apartheid, and neoliberalism.

Although my conceptualization of "imprisoned radical intellectuals" incorporates (and centers) the political prisoners and POWs encompassed by the aforementioned definitions, it also invites a broader political understanding of the abject categorization of "commonly" imprisoned people. Overwhelmingly poor, black, and brown, "common prisoners" remain broadly unrecognized by the activist public, rendered nameless and nonspecified, while generally presumed to be outside staid and elitist conceptions of the "political." Such politically unrecognized captives compose the vast majority of those who have become activists and political intellectuals *while imprisoned*, many of whom were and are engaged in unprogrammatic (or nonorganizational) varieties of liberationist-directed antisystemic activity prior to, during, and after their incarceration. Some are explicitly radical or revolutionary in their political commitments, and many more are protoradical—that is, committed to insurrection and rebellion against structures of domination, though in the absence of a formal ideological system. Most often, rather than being a product of extant social movements or free-world–based organizations, the unrecognized imprisoned activist is interpellated by the political influence and mentorship of her or his peers and predecessors (including political prisoners and POWs duly "recognized" by activists in civil society), as well as the pragmatic urgency of self-education for legal defense and political and spiritual self-defense.

I follow a dynamic, contextual definition of "the political" within my conception of the imprisoned radical intellectual, following activist and political theorist Marshall Eddie Conway's thoughtful reflections on the sociohistorical transformations he has witnessed over the time of his incarceration (a Baltimore Black Panther imprisoned since 1970, Conway is among the longest-held political prisoners in the United States).[5] During a 2004 interview conducted via speakerphone for an advanced seminar

in ethnic studies, Conway was pressed by one student to offer a redefi-
nition of the "political prisoner" that accounts for the shape of the post-
1970s political landscape.[6] His response proves instructive as a framework
for conceptualizing the current condition.

The seminar had been discussing the juridical, cultural, and military proliferation of the state's racialized domestic warfare techniques,
hallmarked by the 1980s intensification of the "War on Drugs," and
accompanied by a drastic police militarization, punitive juridical shift,
and emergence of the mass incarceration form now known as the prison
industrial complex. The seminar was also critically examining the breathtaking varieties of the state's formal and ad hoc aggression against broad
categories of (poor) black, indigenous, and Third World populations
in the *current* historical moment, a trajectory of domestic warfare that
appears to target "civilian populations" (in addition to radical "activist"
and insurgent groups) for social liquidation and/or political neutralization. Speaking to this shift in sociohistorical context, Conway departs
from static definitions of the "political prisoner" in exchange for a more
multilayered understanding:

> [A political prisoner] in my opinion would be an activist, a person that
> stands up to injustices, a person who for whatever reason takes the position
> that this or that is wrong, whether they do it based on ideology or they do
> it based on what they think is morally right. . . . It's where you're at in
> [terms of] location on the one hand, and it's where you're at historically. . . .
>
> On the one hand, I think that there's a universal classification for
> political prisoners and that's movement related, activity related, ideologi-
> cally related, in the sense that . . . these people were engaged in political
> activity.
>
> But I also have learned over thirty-some years of being in jail that a
> lot of people become political prisoners, become conscious and become
> aware and act and behave based on that awareness after they have been
> incarcerated for criminal activity or other kinds of activities.
>
> That's on one level; on another level I'm also aware [that] there are
> people forced into the position of [becoming] political prisoners because

of some act of the government or some opposition they have presented to the government.[7]

Following Conway's political inventory, I emphasize the *historical and cultural specificity* of the "imprisoned radical intellectual" in order to foreground the counter- and antisystemic, radical and revolutionary materiality of this political lineage. Imprisoned radical intellectuals, as I argue throughout the book, are *politically constituted* by the prison's regime of immobilization and bodily disintegration. The state's (and prison's) technologies of incarceration do not *only* repress or delimit the praxis of imprisoned activists—this programmatic violence inhabits, occupies, and interpellates political and historical subjects within a specific structure of political confrontation. It is precisely this unstable tension—at times an explosive or fatal confrontation—between the oppressive regime of the prison and the materialized political subjectivity of the captive radical intellectual that catalyzes and shapes a pathway of radicalism and insurgency.

Imprisoned radical intellectuals densely articulate, through multiple voices and vernaculars, the proliferation and extension of the prison's regimented technologies of domination into the everyday systems of social formation. The allegedly excessive, exceptional, or abnormal violence of the prison regime's violence is, within this political-intellectual lineage, reconceptualized as a *fundamental organizing logic* of the United States in its local, translocal, and global enactments: as such, this is a body of "radical" praxis in the etymological sense of the term, as a political labor that emanates from and is directed toward transforming or destroying the "roots" of a particular social formation, engaged in critical opposition to its constitutive logics of organization and historical possibility. Truly, this is a lineage that exposes the symbiosis of love and hate, revolution and creative destruction, in the process of envisioning the end of oppressive violence and programmatic human domination.

To appropriate Frantz Fanon's meditation in a different time and place, a *war of social truths* rages beneath the normalized violence of any such condition of domination. It is the Manichaean relation between colonized and colonizer, "native" and "settler," or here, free and unfree that conditions the subaltern truths of both imminent and manifest insurgencies. Speaking to the anticolonialist nationalism of the Algerian Revolution, Fanon writes:

> The problem of truth ought also to be considered. In every age, among the people truth is the property of the national cause. No absolute verity, no discourse on the purity of the soul, can shake this position. The native replies to the living lie of the colonial situation by an equal falsehood. His dealings with his fellow-nationals are open; they are strained and incomprehensible with regard to the settlers. Truth is that which hurries on the break-up of the colonialist regime; it is that which promotes the emergence of the nation; it is all that protects the natives, and ruins the foreigners. In this colonialist context there is no truthful behavior: and the good is quite simply that which is evil for "them."[8]

Truth, for Fanon, is precisely that which generates and multiplies the historical possibility of disruptive, subversive movement against colonial oppression. The evident rhetoric of oppositionality, of the subaltern "good" that necessarily materializes "evil" in the eyes of domination, offers a stunning departure from the language of negotiation, dialogue, progress, moderation, and peace that has become hegemonic in discourses of social change and social justice, in and outside the United States. The native's "equal falsehood" is, in fact, a necessary and ethical response to a regime that renders a hegemonic truth through the regulated death and deterioration of the native's body and society. Perhaps most important, the political language of opposition is premised on its open-endedness and contingency, a particular refusal to soothe the anxiety generated in the attempt to displace a condition of violent peace for the sake of something else, a world beyond agendas, platforms, and practical proposals. There are no guarantees, or arrogant expectations, of an ultimate state of liberation waiting on the other side of the politically immediate struggle against the settler colony.

A similar political vernacular and vision haunts the recent history of radical prison praxis. The reductive conception of the prison as simply a site of "resistance" to state violence vastly underestimates the complexity of political discourse generated by its resident, radical organic intellectuals. This body of knowledge and truth is premised on the utter impossibility of dialogue and communication with the *force*—discursive, embodied, institutionalized—of one's own domination. Longtime U.S. political prisoner Marilyn Buck, imprisoned for assisting in the liberation and eventual political refuge of Assata Shakur, offers powerful testimony from the Dublin (California) women's prison in her 2000 article "Prisons, Social Control, and Political Prisoners."[9] Arguing against the tendency of progressive and radical social movements to institutionalize politics through conservative organizational forms, Buck articulates a form of political commitment that foreshadows a new—though historically rooted—political language:

> There is always room to debate politics, points of view, strategies, and tactics. To confront differences and questions is a good thing. Any struggle for liberation demands free and open debate of ideas and practices. At the same time, active struggles need to support those who act consciously and politically. *To do so is a part of asserting the right to struggle*, as well as defending activism and promoting stronger resistance to the military, financial, and political apparatus that denies our society and the whole world true equality and justice.[10]

Buck's insistence on the necessity of conflict and exchange among and within such "active struggles" begs the question of how *imprisoned* activists might project themselves into the social movements of the free world as well as the ongoing, decentered political skirmishes occurring in civil society. Her conception of a "free and open debate" among activists as the condition of possibility for viable liberation struggle foregrounds the current condition of mass (and political) imprisonment as perhaps *the* fundamental obstacle to an authentic political radicalism: where the categorical status of unfreedom is tolerated or otherwise compromised by activists in the free world, their putative visions of social transformation fall into complicity with the contemporary material symbiosis of punishment and human containment.

Most important in the passage just quoted is Buck's audacious assertion of a moral, political, and historical right to struggle. In addition to offering an incipient, alternate political theory of resistance, opposition, and revolutionary movement that demystifies the state's naturalized monopoly on both legitimate violence and the moral/juridical right to determine the acceptable (noncriminalized) modes of political struggle within its formal domain, the notion of a right to struggle is akin to a transhistorical political mandate. Buck reminds activists and intellectuals in civil society that the genesis of radical, liberatory power hinges on the pronouncement and actualization of this right, compelling the invention of new languages, strategies, and fantasies of struggle against domination and oppression.

White Supremacy and the Prison Industrial Complex: "A Society Structured in Dominance"

In addition to generating a unique vernacular of freedom, liberation, and political struggle this radical intellectual lineage composes an extensive theorization of state and state-sanctioned bodily violence as the central and productive technology of a "society structured in dominance." Stuart Hall's oft-quoted elaboration of racism as a central sociocultural production—and dynamic, politically structuring component—of modern social formations bespeaks the specificity of racist and racial ideologies as they are produced and "made operative" in different historical moments. His essay "Race, Articulation, and Societies Structured in Dominance" rigorously examines the "ideological articulation" between racism and class relations, popular culture, and other modes of social thought and "popular consciousness." Hall is worth quoting at length, for the purposes of situating his theorization within this discussion of the U.S. carceral formation:

> In each case, in specific social formations, racism as an ideological configuration has been reconstituted by the dominant class relations, and

thoroughly reworked. If it has performed the function of that cementing ideology which secures a whole social formation under a dominant class, its pertinent differences from other such hegemonic ideologies require to be registered in detail. Here, racism is particularly powerful and its imprint on popular consciousness especially deep, because in such racial characteristics as colour, ethnic origin, geographical position, etc., racism discovers what other ideologies have to construct: an apparently "natural" and universal basis in nature itself. Yet, despite this apparent grounding in biological givens, outside history racism, when it appears, has an effect on other ideological formations within the same society, and its development promotes a transformation of the whole ideological field in which it becomes operative.[11]

Imprisoned radical intellectuals put a finer point on Hall's conception of racism's multiple (and transformative) articulations within social formation, conceptualizing imprisonment, punishment, and policing as the categorical practices through which hegemonic, overlapping conceptions of "freedom" and "peace"—themselves structured in dominance— cohere U.S. "society." A close examination of these regimes of social ordering—prisons, the law, (domestic/undeclared) warfare, and policing—contextualizes a historicized definition of white supremacy, which is essential to the theoretical framework of this book.

White-supremacist regimes organic (if not unique) to the United States—from racial chattel slavery and frontier genocide to recent and current modes of land displacement and (domestic/undeclared) warfare—are sociologically entangled with the state's changing paradigms, strategies, and technologies of human incarceration and punishment. The historical nature of this entanglement is widely acknowledged, although explanations of the structuring relations of force vary widely and conflict deeply.[12] For our theoretical purposes, white supremacy may be understood *as a logic of social organization* that produces regimented, institutionalized, and militarized conceptions of hierarchized "human" difference. There are three essential components to this theoretical framework.

First, as a historical discourse of power, white supremacy is premised on the conception and enforcement of the universalized white (European and Euro-American) "human" vis-à-vis the rigorous production, penal discipline, and frequent social, political, and biological neutralization or extermination of the (nonwhite) subhuman or nonhuman. Although such hierarchized differences are overwhelmingly constituted through discourses of "race," they are also made through references to and productions of "ethnicity," "nationality," "religion," "biology," and other discursive regimes. It is, however, the fundamental and durable opposition between the white universal human and the peculiar nonwhite sub/semi/nonhuman that reproduces white supremacy as a force of social order.[13]

Second, in order to understand white supremacy as a complex technology of human domination, one need look no further than radical political geographer and abolitionist activist Ruth Wilson Gilmore's conception of "racism" as the primary weapon of white supremacy. Her conceptualization departs from hackneyed definitions of racism (as well as "racial discrimination," "racial inequality," and "race relations") that obscure historical relations of power and domination, and instead magnifies the centrality of race to the programmatic and hierarchical organization of life and death:

> Racism is the state-sanctioned and/or extra-legal production and exploitation of group-differentiated vulnerabilities to premature death, in distinct yet densely interconnected political geographies.[14]

As a logic of social organization, white supremacy is scaffolded by technologies of killing that sediment in Gilmore's definition of racism, recalling histories of militarized mass-based liquidation as well as normalized and institutionalized forms of racial population control and targeted decimation, including coerced inaccessibility to shelter, nutrition, and health care.

Third, white supremacy must be understood as inextricably gendered;

its modalities of articulation and violence are specific to constructions and expropriations of the male/female "biological" and projections of masculine/feminine sexuality and social existence.[15] Critical race theorist Dorothy Roberts, in her study of U.S. judicial aggression against black women's reproductive freedoms, writes:

> Black procreation helped to sustain slavery, giving slave masters an economic incentive to govern Black women's reproductive lives. Slave women's childbearing replenished the enslaved labor force: Black women bore children who belonged to the slaveowner from the moment of their conception. This feature of slavery made control of reproduction a central aspect of whites' subjugation of African people in America. It marked Black women from the beginning as objects whose decisions about reproduction should be subject to social regulation rather than their own will. . . .
>
> All of these violations were sanctioned by law. Racism created for white slaveowners the possibility of unrestrained reproductive control. The social order established by powerful white men was founded on two inseparable ingredients: the dehumanization of Africans on the basis of race, and the control of women's sexuality and reproduction.[16]

Native American scholar and radical antiviolence activist Andrea Smith echoes Roberts in her contention that

> communities of color become pollution from which the state must constantly purify itself. Women of color become particularly dangerous to the world order as they have the ability to reproduce the next generations of communities of color. . . .
>
> Colonizers such as Andrew Jackson recommended that troops systematically kill Indian women and children after massacres in order to complete extermination. . . .
>
> Consequently, Native women and women of color *deserve no bodily integrity* . . . [o]r, as Chicago-based reproductive rights activist Sharon Powell describes it, women of color are "better dead than pregnant."[17]

White supremacy, in this historical and theoretical context, may be conceptualized as a socially ordering logic rather than an "extremist" or otherwise marginal political ideology. By way of illustration, this is to consider the American social formation as the *template for* the Ku Klux Klan (a proudly "white Christian" organization), and to comprehend the complex role of "mainstream" American civil society (in conjunction with its precedent colonial, frontier, and plantation forms) as *simultaneously* the Klan's periodic political antagonist and historical partner in violence.[18]

To consider white supremacy *as* American social formation facilitates a discussion of the modalities through which this material racial logic constitutes and overdetermines the social, political, economic, and cultural structures that compose the contemporary hegemony and constitute the common sense that is organic to its ordering. For the purposes of this text, I conceptualize white supremacy through its fundamental contrapuntality: the inscription of a fundamental relation between freedom and unfreedom, life and death, historically derived from the socially constitutive American production of white life/mobility through black, brown, and indigenous death/immobilization. The contemporary prison regime is, in this context, simultaneously the materialization of U.S. civil society's presumptive white corporate identity (inclusive of its post–civil rights "multicultural" articulations) and the production of a social logic essential to the current social order—a fabrication and criminalization of disorder for the sake of extracting and dramatizing order, compliance, authority.

Thus, whereas Hall references racism as the ideological glue of a given hegemony, I am arguing that in the current era of mass imprisonment, white-supremacist unfreedom—specifically, carceral technologies of human immobilization and bodily disintegration—provides the institutional form, cultural discourse, and ethical basis of social coherence, safety, and civic peace. It is therefore the normal functioning of the prison that bears interrogation, as opposed to its "brutal," "unconstitutional," "racist," "homophobic," or "sexist" excesses, corruptions, and institutional imperfections. The work of imprisoned radical intellectuals traces the contours and continuities of American civil society as a dynamic locality of white freedom, domesticating and proliferating the twinned constitutive logics of white bodily mobility and ascendant white historical/political subjectivity ("freedom") across scales of varying magnitude—from the grandiose racial property and white existential claims of the United States' political and juridical foundations, to the ongoing construction of the white American telos and corresponding material narration of the white nationalist bildungsroman.

Sometimes forgotten in the wash of the current epoch of "globalized" and hypermobile technologies of power are the regimes of bodily immobilization that counterpose social formation and global civil society with the production of new mass-based carceral forms, (undeclared) war zones, and what might be called unfree worlds. Gilmore's body of work closely examines and theorizes this condition, situating California's rapid post-1980s prison expansion amid the multiple political, cultural, and economic crises generated and compounded by the processes of "globalization." Her analysis opens new lines of insight into the emergence of the prison regime as a fundamental and generative, rather than supplemental and static, dimension of local and global American hegemonies. Moving through Gilmore's theoretical lead, we can more easily comprehend the qualitative transformation of policing, jurisprudence, and imprisonment technologies into forms of power that extend significantly beyond their nominally limited juridical, administrative, or punitive functions.

Rejecting the two predominant critical explanations for the emergence of the prison industrial complex—namely, institutionalized racism and "carceral Keynesianism"—Gilmore argues that in the age of globalized capital,

> the expansion of prison constitutes a geographical solution to socioeconomic problems, politically organized by the state which is itself in the process of radical restructuring. This view brings the complexities and contradictions of globalization home, by showing how already existing social, political and economic relations constitute the conditions of possibility (but not inevitability) for ways to solve major problems.[19]

Gilmore argues that the Goldwater/Nixon electoral bloc's serial, reactionary "law-and-order" campaigns fueled an ascendant right wing that recoded domestic political insurrection or dissidence—inscribed most centrally on the movements and collective bodies of radical and liberationist black and Third World people during the late 1960s—as criminality and rogue racial (read "antiwhite") vengeance.

Simultaneous with the genesis of this "moral panic" surrounding racially and politically overdetermined "crime" was a mounting macroeconomic crisis that reached its nadir in the 1973–77 global recession. Widespread racialized "class" displacements followed, as corporations moved investment and structural focus away from industrial production and cast entire regions and populations of the United States into veritable economic obsolescence: in particular, the vital disappearance of domestic "heavy industries" (the factory-based production of auto, steel, rubber, etc.) and "rural extractive industries" (timber, fishing, mining) almost instantaneously obsolesced the labor of masses of people. Gilmore thus argues that the statecraft arising from this socioeconomic crisis materialized in the formation of the "integument of the prison industrial complex," inaugurating a *"modus operandi* for solving crises [through] the relentless identification, coercive control, and violent elimination of foreign and domestic enemies."[20] In resonance with Gilmore's analysis, political prisoner Linda Evans (released in 2001) and activist Eve Goldberg write: "Like the military/industrial complex, the prison industrial complex is an interweaving of private business and government interests. Its twofold purpose is profit and social control. Its public rationale is the fight against crime."[21]

Gilmore's conception of "post-Keynesian militarism" elaborates this nexus of state–corporate alliance, social control, and state violence. As the right wing asserted its hegemony within the legislative and juridical apparatuses in and beyond the 1980s, it was confronted with another basic political challenge:

[H]aving abandoned the Keynesian full employment/aggregate guarantee approach to downturns, the power bloc that emerged from the 1980s onward faced the political problem of how to carry out its agenda—how, in other words, to go about its post-Keynesian state-building project in order to retain and reproduce victories. Capital might be the object of desire, but voters mattered. The new bloc, having achieved power under crisis conditions, consolidated around a popular anti-crime campaign that revived Richard Nixon's successful law and order pitch. Thus the state rebuilt itself by building prisons fashioned from surpluses that the emergent post-golden-age political economy was not absorbing in other ways.[22]

Statecraft under these conditions required a qualitative transformation and expansion of the existing prison apparatus, over and above a mere refinement of its existing juridical or punitive technologies.

The relative (white) public consent to the breathtaking violence underlying this state project was enabled by the fact that the fodder of its production involved the massive social liquidation of human beings who, upon conviction, encountered civil death and de jure slave status vis-à-vis the provisions of the Thirteenth Amendment to the U.S. Constitution: "Neither slavery nor involuntary servitude, *except as a punishment for crime, whereof the party shall have been duly convicted,* shall exist within the United States, or anyplace subject to their jurisdiction" (emphasis added). Further, the overwhelming criminalization of poor black and brown populations saturated this structural expansion with a white-supremacist recodification of the requirements for U.S. civil society's intercourse and reproduction, as well as its very modality of self-articulation (now pitched in contrast or opposition to the social specter of black/brown criminality). To paraphrase the critical theory of white-supremacist policing formulated by Jared Sexton and Steve Martinot, what we see in the American national formation is a production of the prison site as the organized ritualization of gratuitous violence: "It is a twin structure, a regime of violence that operates in two registers, terror and the seduction into the fraudulent ethics of social order; a double economy of terror, structured by a ritual of incessant performance."[23]

The budding structure of mass-based, white-supremacist penality—as both formalized state violence and state-sanctioned articulation of racist domination—spurred the genesis of a new wave of punitive juridical measures (not the other way around). Accompanying these formal juridical innovations was a brilliant wave of state-popular cultural production, encompassing and exceeding the searing and enveloping "War on Drugs" discourse of the 1980s renaissance of white civil society under the political and symbolic stewardship of Ronald Reagan. Providing a commonsense explanation for the new state coercion, this legal and cultural labor generated an overwhelming popular acceptance of—and ideological investment in—the transformation of the prison into a primary apparatus for the maintenance and reproduction of social order.

As the U.S. prison, jail, INS/Homeland Security detainee, and incarcerated youth population approaches the 2.5 million mark, the quantitative evidence only refracts the prison's qualitative transformation.[24] Activist-scholar and former political prisoner Angela Y. Davis has written and spoken extensively of the structures of "invisibility" accompanying the formation of state and corporate alliances through the development of a mass imprisonment regime. Echoing Davis, political prisoner Jalil Muntaqim argues that the elaboration and circulation of a racially coded punitive state discourse assumes a material life of its own, as the constant dramatization of criminality, personal endangerment, and vengeance interpellates civil society's subjects:

> By shaping the collective consciousness and attitudes, the politicians are then able to pass into law draconian sanctions. Sanctions that appease the will of the people demanding a safe society . . . ultimately serve the interest of restructuring the industrial-military complex, by forging an infrastructure for the proliferation of prison building. . . . [I]t anesthetizes the collective consciousness towards the desired end of permitting hundreds of thousands, if not millions more people to be incarcerated *at no moral or psychic detriment to those who constitute the majority of Americans.*[25]

Muntaqim reminds us that the political and economic impetus behind this historical formation has generated a popular ethos of repression that renders criminalized populations and incarcerated people the collective objects of a normalized state violence. The most insidious aspect of this violence is that it is not simply a repressive response to social upheaval, collective disobedience, or criminal activity; that is, the (neo)liberal white-supremacist state is not simply coercive, but is also productive of and symbiotic with the logic and culture of what Gilmore aptly names "industrialized punishment." Carceral state violence is thus the figurative and material nexus of multiple logics of domination and hegemony in the post-1960s era: it is a white-supremacist formation that is simultaneously (though always unevenly) constituted by a vectoring of power trajectories that entwines "race," "gender," "class," "sexuality," "age," and bodily/mental "(dis)ability." To the extent that the state has come to rely on the pageantry of sociopolitical crisis for its various productions of social coherence, it has also reconstructed the political and cultural fabric of policing, punishment, and incarceration. The following section discusses the manner in which a new and necessary exterior to civil society, premised on the rehabilitation and security of civil society's common white-supremacist normativity, has transformed the prison into a constitutive center of the existing hegemony. This new constitutive center reinscribes social formation by consolidating the emergent carceral formation as a new site of structured antisociality and civic death.

Reconstructing the Homeland:
"Law and Order" and the White Atlantic

The historically unprecedented repression of the black, Native American, Puerto Rican, Chicana/o, and other U.S.-based Third World liberation movements during and beyond the 1960s and 1970s forged a peculiar intersection between official and illicit forms of state and state-sanctioned violence. Policing, carceral, and punitive technologies were invented, developed, and refined at scales from the local to the national, encompassing a wide variety of organizing and deployment strategies. Although the notorious Counterintelligence Program (COINTELPRO) of J. Edgar Hoover's FBI remains the most historically prominent incidence of the warfare waged by the state against domestic political movements, the multifarious spectacle of Hooverite repression at times obscures the broader—and far more sweeping—convergence of histori-cal blocs and state formation that defined this era and its legacies.

Spurring a rhetoric that would, within a decade, decisively shape the development of a bureaucratized, exponentially expanded, and widely militarized domestic police force, Arizona senator Barry Goldwater's 1964 acceptance of the Republican Party nomination for the presiden-tial candidacy was a harbinger for white civil society at a moment of amplified political anxiety:

> Now, my fellow Americans, the tide has been running against freedom. Our people have followed false prophets. We must, and we shall, return to proven ways—not because they are old, but because they are true. We must, and we shall, set the tide running again in the cause of freedom . . . freedom—balanced so that liberty lacking order will not become the slav-ery of the prison cell; *balanced so that liberty lacking order will not become the license of the mob and of the jungle.*[26]

Echoing the racial juxtapositions of Joseph Conrad's *Heart of Darkness*, Goldwater elaborated a white populist conception of liberty and security defined through the militarized containment—and ultimate liquidation—of the lurking urban/mob/jungle threat. Goldwater's strident conviction was to defend white civil society from its aggressors—an intimate, racial self-defense that generated a paradigm for law-and-order statecraft that remains a central facet of U.S. political life. Although his bid for the presidency failed, Goldwater's cultural thematic prevailed.

> Security from domestic violence, no less than from foreign aggression, is the most elementary and fundamental purpose of any government, and a government that cannot fulfill that purpose is one that cannot long com-mand the loyalty of its citizens. History shows us—demonstrates that nothing—nothing prepares the way for tyranny more than the failure of public officials to keep the streets from bullies and marauders.[27]

The exponential growth of the police industry in the United States closely followed the dictates of the Goldwater (and eventually Nixon) "law-and-order" bloc.[28] An allegory of bodily confrontation between innocent white vulnerability and black/brown criminal physicality instantiated a binding historical telos for a 1960s and 1970s White Reconstruction, a post–civil rights revival that required the simultaneous and decisive disruption of U.S.-based black, Third World, and indigenous liberation movements and their counterpart urban insurrections. Law and order was essentially an agenda for white liberation, instantiated through white civil society's awakening to the possibility of its own political disarticulation at the hands of black and Third World insurrectionists and revolutionaries. U.S. civil society's invigorated institutionality—shaped by the burgeoning of foundation-funded nonprofit organizations and nongovernmental organizations (NGOs), and mediated by the private sector, conservative and liberal faith communities, and corporate mass media—aligned with the law-and-order state as a virtual recruit and mass participant during the emergence of the Goldwater–Nixon bloc.[29] Elaborating the popular anxieties sprouting around the apparent and imminent displacement of the unique white-supremacist hegemony of the United States, this historical bloc amounted to a broadly based political reconsolidation of a white civil society that had momentarily strolled with the specter of its own incoherence.

The militant reformism of the civil rights movement had not only broken the legal structures of segregation and Jim Crow, but additionally foreshadowed a lapse and spasm within the white-supremacist body politic's historical ascendancy. As it moved to reconfigure around the crisis yielded by this local and national struggle against official apartheid, white civil society was met with blossoming, radical struggles organized through and against historical structures of racial domination and "national" oppression. New forms of organized resistance to racist state violence were hallmarked during this period by the regional and national manifestations of the Black Panther Party and the underground Black Liberation Army, and multiplied through the emergence of the Young Lords, the Weather Underground, the George Jackson Brigade, (U.S. Chinatown-based) Red Guards, Katipunan ng Demokratikong

Pilipino, and other radical self-defense, anti-imperialist, and domestic revolutionary organizations.[30] Along with the upsurge of urban insurrections against police brutality and other forms of state-sanctioned murder, these movements demystified and attacked the primary institutions of white-supremacist hegemony and black/brown premature death: police, military, property, and law. Simultaneously, struggles for Indian sovereignty openly declared and defended liberated territories while valorizing a politics of national treason, disrupting the presumptive juridical monopoly and sanctity of the U.S. Constitution (the legal heart of the white body politic).[31] Similarly, Puerto Rican *independentistas* waged an anticolonial struggle on multiple fronts within the domestic spheres of American empire, culminating in the political trial of fourteen activists who refused to recognize the legitimacy of U.S. law and quickly became prisoners of war.[32]

The emergence of a definitive era of U.S.-based (and frequently internationalist) liberation and revolutionary movements encompassed political and juridical claims that directly antagonized the constitutive logic of the nation's historical formation as a white settler society. Such notions as "black liberation," "Indian sovereignty," and Puerto Rican "self-determination" represented unanswerable demands on the United States of America, blaspheming the sanctity of American white localities. Although examples of political violence committed by people of color against white bodies were few and far between, the culmination of the state's strategic (and self-legitimating) use of unmediated physical force against Third World liberationists—at home and abroad—nonetheless articulated as self-defensive moral, cultural, and material structures of white militarization.[33] White civil society braced at the possibility of a blowback for collective grievances that were gravely historical.

Thus, the politics of law and order entailed a pedagogical refining of a budding white-supremacist desire for surveilling, policing, caging, and (preemptively) exterminating those who embodied the gathering storm of dissidence—organized and disarticulated, radical and protopolitical. Articulated through and against the progressive and radical countercommunities that threatened the disruption and transformation of the American social formation's normative whiteness, this reinvigorated white civil society asserted its essential stewardship of the state through the versatile mechanism of racialized criminalization. In this sense, COINTELPRO's illegal and unconstitutional abuses of state power, unabashed use of strategic and deadly violence, and development of invasive, terrorizing surveillance technologies might be seen as the state's prototyping of the era's broadly revivified (and significantly extrastate) domestic low-intensity warfare techniques against racially pathologized "activist" and "civilian" populations alike.[34]

J. Edgar Hoover's formalization of a venerated racist state strategy—the criminalization of black, brown, and Indian liberationists—simply reflected and foreshadowed the imperative of white civil society's impulse toward self-preservation in this moment.[35] The emergent technology of racialized criminalization was galvanized by Richard Nixon's rise to the executive office and the subsequent massive federal and local investment in militarized police forces.[36] Perhaps most important, this domestic military technology both incorporated and exceeded COINTELPRO's narrower objectives of containing urban uprising and liquidating domestic radicals, (proto)revolutionaries, and sovereignty fighters. Outdoing the FBI's secret counterintelligence campaign, "law and order" constituted a novel discursive technology of domestic warfare that spoke through the reified body of the state executive.

Goldwater's ominous forecast of tyranny's onset shot through a civic consciousness that was absorbing the possibility of white freedom's rollback, and although white self-defense formed the template for an aggressive white-supremacist state, the message remained intensely grandiose and global. His was the foreshadowing of white civil society's globalization, literally the reconstruction of domestic white hegemony and the unmitigated construction of a *white Atlantic:*

> I believe that we must look beyond the defense of freedom today to its extension tomorrow. . . . I can see and I suggest that all thoughtful men must contemplate the flowering of an Atlantic civilization, the whole world of Europe unified and free, trading openly across its borders, communicating

openly across the world. This is a goal far, far more meaningful than a moon shot. . . .

I can also see—and all free men must thrill to—the events of this Atlantic civilization joined by its great ocean highway to the United States. What a destiny, what a destiny can be ours to stand as a great central pillar linking Europe, the Americas and the venerable and vital peoples and cultures of the Pacific. I can see a day when all the Americas, North and South, will be linked in a mighty system, a system in which the errors and misunderstandings of the past will be submerged one by one in a rising tide of prosperity and interdependence. . . . But we pledge—we pledge that human sympathy—what our neighbors to the South call that attitude of "simpatico"—no less than enlightened self-interest will be our guide.[37]

Couched in the rhetoric of civic security and personal safety, this discourse offered white civil society political rescue and a new structure of collective sentimentality. The smooth symbiosis between "racial" and "criminal" discourse was the stuff of the new white civil society, in fact, the central premise of the post-1960s White Reconstruction. Goldwater rendered a white-supremacist populist conception of liberty and security, defined through the militarized containment—and ultimate liquidation—of the lurking "urban threat." His declaration of virtual domestic warfare in this speech, while presumptuous, blueprinted the watershed Nixon victory of 1968 and the onset of the emergent police-prison hegemony in the United States. Policing and criminal justice emerged in this way as socially productive technologies during a crucial historical conjuncture, forging an indelible linkage between the site and scene of the prison and the corresponding world of a consolidated and coherent—though always endangered—normative white civil society.

Whiteness as Property (Interest):
A Note on "Multiculturalism" and White Supremacy

To foreground U.S. civil society as normatively white is not to posit a discrete "ethnic" or "racial" identity as the uncontested or noncontradictory determination of the social. This is to say that civil society is not "white" in the apartheid—that is, official, totalizing, and closed—sense. Goldwater's (and his heirs') normative civil whiteness implies an ongoing and complex relation of hierarchy, discipline, power, and violence that has come to oversee the current and increasingly incorporative "multicultural" modalities of white supremacy, wherein "people of color" are selectively and incrementally solicited, rewarded, and absorbed into the operative functionings of white-supremacist institutions (e.g., the military, police, and school) and discourses (e.g., patriotism). This multicultural turn is effectively the neoliberal and neoconservative assimilationism of a post-apartheid state and civil regime. The social formation of the current epoch is aggressively normatively white, to the extent that multicultur-alism is based on an empirical production of "diversity" fostered and sus-tained by a white-supremacist organizing logic, and, as evidenced in the formation of the prison regime, premised on an astronomically scaled institutionalization of black and indigenous civil and social death (black and Native American imprisonment significantly exceeds all other group-based incarceration rates).

American civil society (in both its local and global articulations) aggressively constructs normative whiteness as biopolitical power, cre-atively transposing the technologies of racism and white supremacy into alternate (putatively "nonwhite") racial identifications and embodiments. The contemporary hegemony of law and order, its materialization into a "way of life," is based on a discursive and material expansion of civil society's normative whiteness, to the extent that "nonwhites" or "people of color" have increasingly invested in the protection of this sanctified property interest: the sustenance of civil society and its reproduction on a scale of globalized magnitude as the United States of America.[38] This identification marks the "multiculturalization" of white supremacy, a paradigm shift that offers promise for the global project of the "white civilian" ontology.

To blur the boundaries and limits of juridically and culturally legit-imated racist state violence is the act at the heart of the American polic-ing modality, and this rearticulation of the state—a political labor that disembodies the formal state while reembodying it in the lives of its subjects—entails more than the institutionalization of police impunity: it calls for the deputization of white civil society itself. President George W. Bush's October 2003 pronouncement regarding the Homeland Security Appropriations Act was enunciated as no less than the extension and elaboration of the Goldwaterist mandate:

> On September the 11th, 2001, enemies of freedom made our country a battleground. Their method is the mass murder of the innocent, and their goal is to make all Americans live in fear. . . . The danger to America gives all of you an essential role in the war on terror. You've done fine work under difficult and urgent circumstances, and on behalf of a grateful nation, I thank you all for what you do for the security and safety of our fellow citizens.[39]

Although white citizens have always served as appendages of the U.S. state as its self-appointed (and juridically sanctioned) eyes and ears, the distinctiveness of the present moment lies in the technologies of interpellation that imbue a new conception of white locality—it is a "here" that is, in practice, entitled (even compelled) to be everywhere.[40]

In contradistinction to civil society's normative whiteness, the carceral formation of the U.S. prison regime, itself generated and reproduced by the white-supremacist logic of targeted, though rigorously mass-based policing, criminalization, and imprisonment technologies, is normatively embodied black, brown, and indigenous. Although many journalists and scholars belabor the black/Native American/Latino "overrepresentation" in census counts of the imprisoned population, this rhetoric of empirical racial inequity or institutional bias—and conspicuous absence of a discourse of "white underrepresentation" among the imprisoned—elides the historical context and legacies of the White Reconstruction. Revising Marx's classical discussion of the "usefulness of crime" to the regime of capital, radical criminologist Nils Christie frames the emergence of this carceral formation as the lifeblood of nationalized, domestic warfare(s). Read in the context of Goldwater's white Atlantic and the Bush/Ashcroft Homeland Security imaginaries, Christie's meditation can be interpreted as an explication of the white-supremacist logic of carceral organization, "law and order's" culminating act:

> Crime does not exist. Crime is created. First there are acts. Then follows a long process of giving meaning to these acts. . . .
>
> The social system has changed into one where there are fewer restraints against perceiving even minor transgressions of laws as crimes and their actors as criminals. . . . *This new situation, with an unlimited reservoir of acts which can be defined as crimes, also creates unlimited possibilities for warfare against all sorts of unwanted acts.*
>
> With a living tradition from the period where natural crimes were the only ones, combined with an unlimited reservoir of what can be seen as crimes in modern times, the ground has been prepared. The crime control market is waiting for its entrepreneurs.[41]

Christie's historicization of the crime-control market as a production premised on access to the limitless raw material of "unwanted acts" resonates with both the circulation of capital and the materiality of ownership. This begs the question of what, under the terms of white civil society, forms the baseline of its putative protection from criminality and disorder, the countless unwanted acts of aggression that threaten to destabilize the "social system." Critical race theorist Cheryl I. Harris's legal-historical theorization of "whiteness as property" responds to this crucial question. Her working answer illuminates the intersection of property and subjectivity, a convergence that articulates through civil society's persistent propositions of universalizing values of collective white (and putatively multicultural) identity—a form of "corporate ownership"—which, simultaneously, invents and remakes material boundaries of racial unassimilability and otherness.

Correctly positing that "the origins of property rights in the United States are rooted in racial domination," Harris exposes the juridical means through which concepts of nationhood, ownership, and civil subjectivity have emanated from the fabricated materiality of whiteness. In the epoch of chattel slavery, Harris writes, *"Whiteness was the characteristic, the attribute, the property of free human beings.*" Far from eroding with the formal abolition of the slave plantation (and constitutional relocation of enslavement to the site of the prison), law and property have continuously intertwined through the reproduction of civil society's constitutive whiteness. In fact, Harris contends, the possession and protection of an ontologically propertied whiteness remains a pillar of contemporary jurisprudence:

> In ways so embedded that it is rarely apparent, the set of assumptions, privileges, and benefits that accompany the status of being white have become a valuable asset. . . . Whites have come to expect and rely on these benefits, and over time these expectations have been affirmed, legitimated, and protected by the law. Even though the law is neither uniform nor explicit in all instances, in protecting the settled expectations based on white privilege, American law has recognized a property interest in whiteness that, although unacknowledged, now forms the background against which legal disputes are framed, argued, and adjudicated.[42]

Conceptualizing whiteness as a form of property, and white civic identity as a collective entitlement to ownership (of property, Others, and propertied Others), implies that when "nonwhites" threaten, attack, or steal the common property of white civil society, they are actually violating the sanctified materiality, and the vicarious and deeply valued collective bodily integrity, of whiteness. Multiculturalism is, in this sense, a keystone for the rearticulation of white supremacy as a simultaneously (and often contradictorily) incorporative and exclusionary regime of social ordering: it bears witness to both the spectacle of "diversity" as showcased through various state and civil institutions and the proliferation of the post-1970s prison industrial complex as the normative whitesupremacist materialization of Goldwater's white Atlantic.

Methodology (or Its Failure): The Terms of Collaboration

The genealogical and theoretical work of this project draws widely from publicly circulated texts, as well as interviews, correspondence, and informal conversations that I conducted or participated in over the course of eight years. Visible throughout this book are passages from the published communiqués, polemics, scholarly articles, essays, memoirs, testimonials, and legal documents composed by such widely recognized radical intellectuals and political prisoners as George Jackson, Angela Y. Davis, Leonard Peltier, Mumia Abu-Jamal, Assata Shakur, Laura White-horn, Marilyn Buck, and others. Equally significant, however, are the unpublished, undercirculated, or heretofore uncirculated texts produced by captive intellectuals who remain largely outside the nonimprisoned public's (and particularly the U.S. left's) fields of political vision or concern. By way of example, the private correspondence, visiting room conversations, legal scholarship, theoretical meditations, creative writing, and scholarly essays of Viet Mike Ngo (as of this writing imprisoned in Soledad Prison in California) have been crucial to the development of this book from its earliest stages through the final revisions.[43] Ngo's status as a common or "social" prisoner, textually prolific yet virtually anonymous to the overlapping "literary," "academic," and "activist" publics, refracts in individualized form the massive and violent social extermination of human beings through current regimes of state captivity and carceral punishment.

Some inherent problems of methodology, conventionally conceived as a relatively stable and closed system (or "discipline") of scholarly inquiry, loom over this book. Moving from the text of a personal correspondence penned by Ngo in 2002, the remainder of this introduction meditates on the propositions, structured violence, and failures of "methodology" as it passes through (and aggresses) the embodied figure of one imprisoned radical intellectual, in this case a putatively "Asian" subject (Ngo identifies as Vietnamese).

Troubled relations of freedom and unfreedom, life and death constantly surface in the moments of political contact and possibility inscribed here, as well as in the *absence* of intimacies rendered difficult or impossible by gendered white-supremacist hierarchies. Even this relation with Ngo, in other words, is a relatively "privileged" one, to the extent that Ngo's subjectivity—not to mention my own, as the "free" and variously identified Filipino, Asian, or "Hispanic" visitor—is not a primary object of the prison's racist hyperviolence ("Asian" prisoners often escape the normative racial classifications of jails and prisons, and are not as massively or eagerly addressed and punished under "prison gang" penalties and institutional segregations). By way of example, Kijana Tashiri Askari (Harrison), another longtime correspondent, is imprisoned in twenty-four-hour isolation in the California Security Housing Unit (Pelican Bay State Prison) under the official rubric of (black) "gang affiliation." Hugo "Yogi" Pinell, a black Nicaraguan, has been imprisoned for more than three decades under similar circumstances, and is incarcerated in the same "unit" as Askari (they often shout communication to one another across closed cell doors). I have had the opportunity to meet with both Askari and Pinell, but our relations manifest within the violence of a particular structure and racial geography of distance and alienation: we are not allowed "contact visits," and our conversations are closely monitored by guards standing within earshot; furthermore, Pelican Bay State Prison is located in a part of California that is difficult to access, six to eight hours from the closest major airport and near the border with Oregon. Finally, neither Askari nor Pinell is allowed phone calls, and their mail correspondence is more frequently denied or censored. This is, to invoke the terms of Orlando Patterson, the very picture of an ultramodern "social death," the virtual liquidation of affective and (extended) familial ties through a historically specific articulation of penal slavery. (I revisit Patterson's work in chapter 1.)

The history of my privileged relation to Ngo, in this sense, reinscribes and amplifies the failure of methodology in the nexus of a white-supremacist continuum of freedom and unfreedom, one that is fundamentally structured by an institutional hierarchy of capture and punishment that reserves and ranks its technologies of violence for deployment on a landscape directly defined by the institutional genealogies of U.S. chattel slavery, an essentially antiblack technology. I am meditating, through the context of this privileged relation to Ngo, on the structured violence of attempts at political collaboration between the broadly structured categories of "free" and "unfree," and am attempting to offer a conception of praxis that fractures the coherence and order of civil society's banal notions of the "political" as well as conventional academic renditions of the "methodological."

Ngo is part of a lineage of social prisoners whose organizing, teaching, and legal work have antagonized the California Department of Corrections (CDC). As of this writing, he has nine pending cases or writs of habeas corpus against the CDC over such matters as racial segregation, institutional retaliation, religious freedom, and sexual harassment. He has said:

> They really don't know what to do with me and my comrades right now. I mean, one minute they want to transfer us, another minute they tell us "We changed our minds," because they don't know what to do with us, because we're thinking outside the box. We're fighting. We're actually standing up, saying, "You know what? I have the right to challenge your policy, challenge the way you run things. Just 'cause you're a pig and I'm an inmate doesn't mean that I have to listen to what you say. That your word is law."[44]

Since the winter of 2000, Ngo and I have developed an ongoing, critical dialogue about the structure of engagement between civil society's activists and those radical intellectuals and activists who live in state captivity.

Ngo has lucidly located his political work within a historical lineage of radical and revolutionary praxis. Variously influenced by such thinkers as George Jackson, Assata Shakur, Che Guevara, Ho Chi Minh, Toni Morrison, Angela Davis, and Frantz Fanon, he speaks to an epochal condition illuminated and enriched by his living encounters with the prison regime. Ngo's written work, which includes published pieces and unpublished notebooks of journal entries and political meditations, moves within a contemporary genealogy of "prison letters" produced by captive U.S. radicals, liberationists, and revolutionaries: consider the examples of Jackson's *Soledad Brother*, public correspondence in Angela Davis et al.'s *If They Come in the Morning*, News and Letters Committees' *Revolutionary Prisoners Speak!* or former political prisoner Ray Luc Levasseur's online compilation "Letters from Exile."[45] A personal note written by Ngo in January 2002 reflects on the history of our critical collaboration and offers a concise philosophy of praxis:

> I wanted to meet you 'cuz I heard you were radical. . . . I was hoping we could collaborate our work—specifically, I was hoping to liberate myself. When I realized this wasn't going to happen, I was comforted by the fact that my writing was being used by someone whose politics were like my own.[46]

For Ngo, the scene of the meeting with the nonimprisoned radical activist provokes a sudden revision of familiar political terms, conditioning the collaborative praxis of the "radical" free and unfree through the desire and political necessity of liberation, suggesting a living freedom that requires (at least) a material end to the condition of imprisonment. Ngo foregrounds the constitutive failure of this meeting by rendering explicit the premises of its political structuring. As he describes it, the possibility of a "radicalism" with integrity—that is, one that does not presume or reinscribe structures of civil and social death—hinges on the liquidation of the essential dichotomy on which the meeting itself is founded.

Failing the persistent test of a radical freedom, mutually obtained and embodied, the meeting becomes a reifying event: the charade of "collaboration" reproduces the violent condition of its genesis, for there would have been no (alleged) collaboration absent the existence of the imprisonment regime, the contemporary formalization of what Fanon terms "systematized de-humanization."[47] In this sense, the only "good" meeting (that is, the only liberatory meeting) is the one that *foments the collapse of its condition*, the disarticulation of what has been, in the American national formation, the necessary linkage between freedom and imprisonment. It is the *methodology of liberation* that remains the central and vexing question here, to the extent that it confronts the nonimprisoned activist/scholar with the physical (as well as political-intellectual) contingencies of insurgency, insurrection, and transformation in relation to their cohorts held captive.

The meeting that matters, then, is the one that displaces the condition of its reification, critically exposing and demystifying the structures and technologies through which "a relation between people takes on the character of a thing and thus acquires a 'phantom objectivity,' an autonomy that seems so strictly rational and all-embracing as to conceal every trace of its fundamental nature: the relation between people."[48] Reflecting Georg Lukács's notion of reification is the commonsense conception of the "free world's" relation (or nonrelation) to the imprisoned world as a "thing," a natural feature of the social landscape, rather than an expansive and mindboggling technology of domination and subjection. This common sense evinces "prisons" as somewhere outside of civil society, when in fact these modes of human capture surround, enmesh, and articulate with the normative everyday of the social formation.

Ngo suggests that our attempt at "collaborative work" is radically insufficient, and that there can be no authentic relation of integrity or equity between those inhabiting the formal and opposed categories of free and unfree. He is, instead, momentarily solaced by the hope that my pedagogical appropriations of his intellectual work (though such appropriations must often go anonymous and unaccredited to minimize further endangerment of the imprisoned) are somehow relevant to his political desires, visions, and fantasies. Perhaps, then, the vernacular of "collaboration" (or coalition, solidarity, partnership, etc.) exaggerates the political and historical possibilities of these meetings between free and unfree, to the extent that one of the "collaborators" is categorically immobilized—not at liberty to move, speak, and practice.

During a May 2002 phone interview that we recorded for a course I was teaching titled "Imprisoned U.S. Radical Intellectuals and Social Movements," Ngo elaborated on the political implications of his January note:

> You have to find people who love you, and that's the biggest problem in here in prison. If we had more access to people who think and feel like us . . . it helps us do the work. Because we're so isolated in here and out there at least you guys have the opportunity to sit down and break bread with

each other. . . . With people who love and feel the way you do. . . . That's where you get your energy from.

We get our energy from our despair and our hate and a lot of things that have to do with love too, and love of wanting to live. But it's overwhelming at times; so you have to use whatever advantages you have; and for a free person, that is your advantage. So definitely utilize it. That's something me and my comrades dream of.[49]

Although uneven, conflict-ridden relations of personal and structural power are inherent to any form of political collaboration, there is a qualitative difference to the engagement Ngo speaks of here. Only in the meeting of the nominally free subject of civil society and the imprisoned subject of the carceral formation is there a bodily confrontation between people juridically and civically defined as *alive* ("citizen") and *dead* ("inmate").

More pointedly, as Sharon Patricia Holland contends, the "free" (nonimprisoned) activist/scholar/theorist's movement into communities of intimacy with death—whatever form or force that death embodies—requires a principled entanglement with institutional, intellectual, and bodily marginality, if not more immediate varieties of clear and present endangerment:

> Speaking about death and the dead necessitates that critics move beyond familiar country and into liminal spaces. These liminal spaces are present whenever a scholar moves between the borders separating nations and communities, disciplines and departments.[50]

To situate Holland's "critic" within the dominion of the U.S. prison regime is to depart from the presumptive mobility of civic (and academic) freedom, the hallmark of the (white) Western professional intellectual subject, and to instead move into zones of conflict and (undeclared/domestic) warfare.

Ngo writes and speaks constantly of being decisively de-linked from the political modalities of civil society. In the following passage from the same January 2002 communiqué, the illicit and subversive work of cultural production reconstitutes a Fanonian "literature of warfare," produced as both means and end, momentarily gratifying writer and recipient, although ultimately incomplete absent the actualized dream of liberation. Self-consciously writing from the contemporary U.S. prison regime, Ngo elaborates a philosophy of praxis that relocates to civil society's carceral underside:

> Over the past year, I've come to terms with the fact that the conditions of my existence dictate my mode of warfare. At this point in time, my warfare *must* entail writing and teaching. I'm disheartened that this mode lacks urgency, but pleased that I may be alive to enjoy my work. And knowing that my work helps your teaching eases my mind. I'm doing what I can for now. Until other options show themselves to me to be worthy of a greater sacrifice, I'll live with what I'm doing now.[51]

Recasting praxis through an open-ended, though nonetheless material conception of liberation's urgency—he is not simply invoking a metaphoric liberation that elides (or purports to transcend) his bodily incarceration—Ngo speaks to a vision of radical freedom that is authentic to its context. Since the time of our initial meeting, he has communicated a theoretical corpus through a variety of strategic gestures, historical allegories, tactical silences, and vernacular codes (including poetry, correspondence, and memoir). Ngo's work refigures the time and context of a methodology that is premised on his imprisonment.

Although a clear vision of freedom in struggle is the defining aspect of Ngo's political intellectual work, he has always been clear that he expects to die in captivity. He insists that even if he reentered the "free world," he would not experience freedom unless his imprisoned "comrades" were to accompany him.[52] Contradicting the individualizing political logic of many current and popular prisoner support organizations and campaigns—most conspicuously, the significant sector of liberal-to-progressive international support magnetized around the cases of Leonard Peltier and Mumia Abu-Jamal—Ngo's conception of radical freedom illuminates the fatal categorical condition of imprisonment. There are no individuals within the regime of imprisonment, only sub-categories of punishment and classification that evaporate the individual into her or his condition of existence. Appropriately, Ngo's principled refusal to individualize his condition (and thus, his "liberation") invokes the radically de-individuating gestures of both Peltier and Abu-Jamal. Peltier writes in *Prison Writings: My Life Is My Sun Dance:*

> This book is not a plea or a justification. Neither is it an explanation or an apology for the events that overtook my life and many other lives in 1975 and made me unwittingly—and, yes, even unwillingly—a symbol, a focus for the sufferings of my people. But *all* of my people are suffering, so I'm in no way special in that regard.
>
> You must understand . . . I am ordinary. Painfully ordinary. This isn't modesty. This is fact. If so, I honor your ordinariness, your human-ness, your spirituality. I hope you will honor mine. That ordinariness is our bond, you and I. We are ordinary. We are human. The Creator made us this way. Imperfect. Inadequate. Ordinary.[53]

Radical intellectuals who are captives of the state, insofar as they are defined and categorized as civically dead, are formally deindividuated upon imprisonment. Their presumptive recognition as "individuals" or legal subjects under the juridical mores of U.S. liberalism erode, displaced by a structure of direct subjection to the punitive state. Further, the continuum of subjection that structures this condition can be conceptualized and disaggregated within the Thirteenth Amendment's signification of a genealogy of antiblack racism, that is, the formative social relations of racial chattel slavery and what Fanon might call the epidermalization of pathology and property.

Imprisoned people have no "right" to exist as political beings or social subjects. Often, the state punishes and preempts the political work and affective labor of its captives through physical violence, forced narcotic sedation, isolation, and relocation (often to prisons that are hundreds or thousands of miles away from family, loved ones, and political supporters).

What, then, is the significance of political praxis for people whose right to exist has been eliminated? What is an appropriate "methodology" of engagement with this lineage of radical, revolutionary, and liberationist political subjects who are, by force of condition, putative "nonsubjects"? Perhaps these are the very questions that underwrite the permanently troubled relation between the free and the unfree (or the imprisoned and the nonimprisoned), as the structure of political-intellectual "collaboration" begs the question of how "politics" happens at the carceral underside of social formation: imprisoned radical intellectuals are practitioners of a qualitatively different "politics," precisely because their field of engagement is defined through a relation of direct violence with the state. This condition of confrontation constitutes a discrete modality of praxis that is incommensurable with the myriad forms of political practice in civil society.

The condition of praxis overdetermines its political significance, particularly when carried out by juridically dead people: that which is reasonably demanded by the free becomes grounds for punitive sanction against the unfree. Prisoners striking and rebelling for acknowledgment of nonexistent human rights—as in the Attica rebellion of 1971—thus amount to far more than "reformist" struggles against fascistic and localized regimes of domination. Assertions of political personhood by the imprisoned are a constrained attempt to decisively delegitimize the carceral formation's official attempts to eliminate them from the realm of the "political," as well as to generate new symbolic and spatial terrain for political struggle against a state regime that consistently militates and militarizes against any such possibility. This is to say that the structuring of unfreedom extinguishes the possibility of legitimate political subjectivity a priori, while constructing a discrete border at which "politics" is presumed subversive in and of itself.

At the risk of stating the obvious, I am arguing that the study of and critical engagement with contemporary prison praxis represents a relation of appropriation and translation, structurally dominated by free world (professional and nonprofessional) intellectuals and activists whose necessarily exploitative use of these texts (for there is little material benefit and much potential punishment in store for their authors) is often endorsed and encouraged by their imprisoned counterparts. The living figure and political specter of the imprisoned political intellectual represents a crisis of meaning for the "methodology" of the nonimprisoned scholar, as well as a fundamental disruption of the free-world activist's operative assumptions (e.g., bodily mobility, political subjectivity, access to civil society). It is through the lens of this failure of methodology that this book must be read and (re)interpreted.

CHAPTER 1

Domestic War Zones and the Extremities of Power: Conceptualizing the U.S. Prison Regime

And then one fine day the bourgeoisie is awakened by a terrific
boomerang effect: the gestapos are busy, the prisons fill up, the
torturers standing around the racks invent, refine, discuss.

—Aimé Césaire, *Discourse on Colonialism* (1972)

Toward a Genealogy of the Prison Regime

The problem of human captivity, a practice that blurs conventional and
clean distinctions between technologies of human immobilization, punishment, and liquidation, initiates this chapter's inquiry into the form
and political animation of the contemporary U.S. prison. Amid the rise
and consolidation of imprisonment as a mass-scale technology of domination, a refreshed and current genealogy of imprisonment—as a practice of statecraft and social (dis)organization—is both theoretically and
politically urgent.

This chapter is structured around two theoretical concerns. First,
by foregrounding a conception of the post-1970s U.S. "prison regime,"
I am examining a historical and political condition that has been materially and figuratively dislocated or disappeared to the underside of the
U.S. social formation and, as such, structured outside the legitimate or
acceptable "political" domains of civil society (including and beyond its
resident activists, professional intellectuals, and most social movements).
A radical genealogy of the U.S. prison regime is necessary because it simultaneously contextualizes and sites the emergence of imprisonment as a
central "constitutive logic" of the American social/racial formation, which
historically—and currently—inscribes its coherence through the durable, white-supremacist institutionality of technologies of immobilization

and bodily disintegration.[1] While others have begun to delineate the "globalization" of these mutually constitutive technologies of domination—for example, into the conspicuously "extradomestic" sites of Guantánamo Bay and Abu Ghraib[2]—I am closely examining the *genesis and prototyping* of this expansive carceral formation at the localized sites of the "domestic."

Second, this genealogy offers an overarching interpretive framework for situating the work of imprisoned radical intellectuals ("radical prison praxis," a term that I will conceptualize more fully in chapter 2) as an irreconcilable political antagonism to that same American social/racial formation, thus displacing the notion that this lineage of political-intellectual insurgency and embodied insurrection is concerned only with addressing the particular or localized site of the prison itself. To understand the prison as a *regime*—that is, to conceptualize it as a dynamic state-mediated practice of domination and control, rather than as a reified "institution" or "apparatus"—suggests the significance of radical prison praxis as a critical, paradigm shaping political lineage. It is also to imply the possibility—even the necessity—of decentering or drastically altering extant political practices that are based in civil society or the putative "free world."

The following sections attempt a historical definition of the U.S. prison regime that traces the emergence of its seminal or prototype technologies of violence. Critically departing from the work of Orlando Patterson and Michel Foucault, the next section distinguishes the scale and analytic scope of the prison regime as a specific mobilization of (state) power that relies on a particular reified institutional form ("the prison") while generating a technology of domination that exceeds the narrow boundaries of that very same juridical-carceral structure. The succeeding section illustrates the genesis and prototyping of the contemporary U.S. prison regime through its pursuit, capture, and punishment of women and men affiliated with the Black Liberation Army (BLA), a clandestine revolutionary organization whose formation was necessitated by the state's waging of relentless and deadly domestic warfare against black and other Third World liberationists during the late 1960s and 1970s.

Survivors' testimonials—the chosen praxis of those whose bodies evade the structured and strategic state violence of domestic warfare, but whose lives and spirits are permanently entangled in the social truth of imminent liquidation—guide this historical elaboration. Following this discussion of the BLA and its legacies, I offer a theorization of the prison regime's essential logics of power, in an attempt to formulate a rudimentary language through which to address the current problematic of mass-based human captivity. The chapter concludes with a discussion of the situated significance of radical prison praxis in the context of its structured confrontation with the regime's militarized production of human subjection.

Capillary Power and Dominium: Conceptualizing the "Prison Regime"

My use of the term "prison regime" differentiates both the scale and the object(s) of analysis from the more typical macroscale institutional categories of "the prison," "the prison system," and, most recently, "the prison industrial complex." The conceptual scope of this term similarly exceeds the analytic scope of prison management, prison policy, and "the prison (or prisoner's) experience," categories that most often take textual form through discrete case studies, institutional reform initiatives, prison/prisoner ethnographies, and individualized biographical and autobiographical narratives. Rather, my working conception of the prison regime invokes a "meso" (middle, or mediating) dimension of processes, structures, and vernaculars that compose the state's modalities of self-articulation and "rule" *across* these macro and micro scales. It is within this meso-range of dynamic, fluctuating articulations of power that the prison is inscribed as both a localization and a constitutive logic of the state's production of juridical, spatial, and militarized dominion.

I consider the range and parameters of the prison regime to encompass both the conventional definition of "dominion" as a discrete territory controlled by a ruling order or state, and its etymological relation to the Latin word *dominium*, a conception of power that posits "absolute dominion in tangible things." The specificity of imprisonment as a regime of power is its *chattel logic*, or structure of abject and non-human objectification: to the extent that the prisoner or "inmate" is conceived as the fungible property of the state (as noted in the introduction, the Thirteenth Amendment designates the "convict's" juridical eligibility for "involuntary servitude," or enslavement), the captive is both the state's abstracted legal property/obligation and intimate bodily possession. Orlando Patterson's explication of the roots of slavery offers a useful framework through which to comprehend the root structure of this carceral-punitive regime:

> [T]he Romans invented the legal fiction of dominium or absolute owner-ship, a fiction that highlights their practical genius. . . . [B]y emphasizing the categories of persona (owner) and res (thing) and by rigidly distin-guishing between corporeal and incorporeal things, the Romans created a new legal paradigm. . . . An object could only be a tangible thing. *More important . . . property was no longer a relation between persons but a relation between persons and things.* And this fiction fitted perfectly its purpose, to define one of the most rapidly expanding sources of wealth, namely slaves.[3]

Patterson's historical explication of slavery here facilitates a genealogy of the prison that situates its emergence as a direct derivative of the American particular and genocidal white-supremacist variation on the centuries-old practice of human slavery. Although the U.S. prison may be broadly conceptualized as a dynamic arrangement, or changing and strategic coalescence of power, political interest, and structural coher-ence, its "post-Emancipation" form has pivoted—fundamentally—on its capacity to strategically operationalize the putative "legal fiction" of (white-supremacist) dominium. This strategic mandate has become especially crucial to the reconstruction of the prison regime in its post-1970s "law-and-order" incarnation.

"The prison," as a durably reified American juridical structure and indispensable pillar in the (white) imagination of societal well-being (or "law and order"), is consistently a work in progress, in fact the geo-graphic and discursive site of a seemingly endless political-military labor that variously establishes, rearticulates, and reforms the material content and putative social meaning of state-proctored human capture. A genealogy of the prison regime is, in part, an organic history of this labor that works from the premise that the prison is neither a natural nor an inevitable feature of the social landscape: its dominion must be constantly (re)defined, defended, and justified.

Imprisonment, (mass-based) human captivity, and carceral punishment encompass a range of state and state-sanctioned practices—from the stridently ritualized to the arbitrary and informal—that inscribe a commonsense and militarized structure of "authority." A genealogy of the prison regime thus affords primacy to the essential instability—the unnaturalness—of its object of discussion, suggesting a mode of historical analysis and theorization that methodologically extends beyond (1) the particular and mystified institutionality of the prison, or its persistent reinscription as the discrete and narrowly bounded entity we know as the prison, and (2) the juridical and institutional formalities of the state's supposed "ownership" of and orderly proctorship over the prison as it is conventionally conceived.

To the contrary, I am attempting to examine the ways in which *it is the prison regime that possesses and constitutes the state.* Here, I am invoking a doubled meaning to the terms of "possession": first, in the sense of a haunting intervention—the state's "possession" by the sometimes ghostly and always haunting technologies of power and violence that emanate from the prison (echoing sociologist Avery Gordon's conception of ghosts and haunting as material social forces);[4] and second, as a reference to the furtive though undeniably massive political influence of the prison regime's designated agents and administrators on the broader architecture of the state. The mandates and desires of the prison's resident and affiliated organizational leadership (most conspicuously, correctional officers' organizations and unions, and pro-prison political action committees) have heavily shaped (and, some would argue, virtually dictated) different scales of state formation in recent decades.

A critical or radical genealogy of the prison regime, as opposed to a traditional history or sociology of the prison as a discrete institution, thus foregrounds the processes and struggles through which the coherence of this categorical arrangement—the grounding of the prison's dominion—is restored through and from varieties of historical crisis. We must, in other words, pay fundamental theoretical attention to the historical inconsistencies, structured anxieties, political contradictions, and constitutive crises that characterize the sociohistorical *production* of the prison and its accompaniments.[5] Essential to the political drama of this production is the structuring tension between two essential productions of the regime itself:

1. *The prison regime's constitutive technology of violence:* the sanctioning and exercise of dominium (absolute ownership and "inner power") over its human captives, a total power that does not require formal political approval or ethical consent from the ostensible polity.

2. *The overarching political project of portraying the prison as an (abstracted) object of state "authority":* the discursive construction of the prison as a respectable and commanding institution that securely inhabits the realm of an everyday common sense, and enjoys a popular consent around the apparatus of its rule.

The structuring tension between the regime's technology of violence (which is impervious to the vicissitudes of "consent") and self-constructing discourse (which produces and galvanizes popular consent) amplifies the centrality of the prison regime to the state's pedagogical project of rendering itself intelligible to its presumed audiences, including and beyond its formal polity. The prison regime has become an indispensable element of American statecraft, simultaneously a cornerstone of its militarized (local and global) ascendancy and spectacle of its extracted (or coerced) authority over targeted publics. *The specificity of the prison regime as a production of state power is its rigorous and extravagant marshaling of technologies of violence, domination, and subjection otherwise reserved for deployment in sites of declared (extradomestic) war or martial law.*

It is through this state mobilization that the prison (re)composes as a surface and site—a dominion—of domestic warfare. As Patterson observes:

Those who exercise power, if they are able to transform it into a "right," a norm, a usual part of the order of things, must first control (or at least be in a position to manipulate) appropriate symbolic instruments. They may do so by exploiting already existing symbols, or they may create new ones relevant to their needs.[6]

The prison regime, in the process of exerting control over the symbolic, constructs a discourse of respectability and "authority" through the mediating material of the prisoner: the abstracted/projected figure and living embodiment of the captive compose an immediately accessible terrain for state occupation and symbolic "appropriation," perhaps the most profound example of the prisoner's essential fungibility.

This reconceptualization of the prison regime resonates with Michel Foucault's seminal discussion of the displacement of unitary sovereign powers in modern and postmodern social formations. Foucault is famously concerned with the production of regimes of power through situated apparatuses and institutions (e.g., the asylum, the clinic, the prison, the military), which in turn circulate power socially through various embodiments, including symbolic orderings, "sciences," (para)military technologies, and strategically sited and situated human bodies. In his lecture of January 14, 1976, Foucault contends:

Our object is not to analyze rule-governed and legitimate forms of power which have a single center, or to look at what their general mechanisms or its overall effects might be. *Our object is, on the contrary, to understand power by looking at its extremities, at its outer limits at the points where it becomes capillary;* in other words, to understand power in its most regional forms and institutions, and especially at the points where this power transgresses the rules of right that organize and delineate it, oversteps those rules and is invested in institutions, is embodied in techniques and acquires the material means to intervene, sometimes in violent ways.[7]

Foucault's "capillary power" designates the manner in which power circulates, materializing through the form and movement of its outermost (extreme) points of expression. The prison, precisely such a capillary site for the production and movement of power, exerts a dominion that reaches significantly beyond its localized setting. This is to argue that the post-1970s emergence of a reformed and reconceived prison regime has become central to constituting the political logic as well as the material reproduction of the U.S. social formation.

It is worth addressing Foucault's conceptualization a bit further: capillaries, in the medical definition, are "the tiny blood vessels that connect the arterioles (the smallest divisions of the arteries) and the venules (the smallest divisions of the veins)." These blood vessels, like the prison, form crucial sites of passage for the transfer of the (social) body's life-sustaining nutrients as well as for the spread of (alleged social) disease, infection, and impurity. They are evidence of a functioning order, a living organism. "Although minute, the capillaries are a site where much action takes place in the circulatory system."[8] Apropos of this medical definition, an essential (warfare) technology of the prison regime is its circulation of violence *through* its legitimated practitioners—the bodies of designated agents (guards, doctors, wardens, prison educators) and guardians of the dominion—and simultaneous performance and materialization *on* the bodies of an immobilized captive population. This is to extrapolate Foucault's conception of capillary power beyond its metaphorical deployment, and to suggest its relevance as a literal designation for the materiality of the prison regime's modalities of violence on the imprisoned subject's *bodily* capillaries, that is, her or his flesh and blood.

I am thus reconceptualizing the prison as a putative "centering" and consolidation of power that, in practice, *necessarily exceeds and violates its official directives and juridical norms.* This regime functions through excesses and violations, at times uncodified or nominally "illegal," though generally occurring within generously interpreted rubrics of institutional policy and protocol. As an arrangement of power that harnesses and rearranges its logics of human domination and disintegration, this regime belies and abrogates its "rule-governed" and "legitimate" discursive-institutional inscription as the prison. Incidentally, this remapping of the state and its regime of carceral violence disrupts extant liberal and progressive "human rights" critiques of imprisonment and policing practices, which largely reify such varieties of proctored bodily punishment as *pathologies* of the state, often framed in the language of "brutality" and "torture."

To situate the prison's strategically sited technologies of violence and human subjection as a normal and "everyday" regime of punishment is to firmly locate these alleged excesses of the state within the larger sociohistorical fabric in which they are enmeshed, and of which they are constitutive. The state's contemporary modality of power and enunciation—its statecraft—works through the constant exceeding of its announced material boundaries and juridical limits. Brutality, torture, and excess should be understood as an essential element of American statecraft, not its corruption or deviation. This is to suggest that the prison, as a state articulation of rigidly centered and conservatively ordered institutional power, does not actually exist, and that it is best conceptualized as a rigorously reproduced mythology of sober and narrowly deployed state power.[9] This mythology effectively rationalizes and renarrates a domestic (or systemically internal) site of aggressively one-sided, racially gendered warfare. Within the operative political technologies of the prison regime, war is business as usual, and the myth of the prison is its resident public relations campaign.

Punitive Prototyping on the Black (Guerrilla) Body: Pursuits of the Black Liberation Army

Foucault contends in *Discipline and Punish* that the "birth of the prison" is part and parcel of a "transformation of the way in which the body itself is invested by power relations," an assertion that conceptually reshapes the comprehension of the European and American prison as a circulating (rather than strictly located and calcified) power apparatus of the "disciplinary society."[10] For all his profound insight, however, Foucault never quite examines whether and how the captive body/subject also, perhaps inevitably, attempts to dissipate, appropriate, resist, absorb, and rearticulate these power relations. Allen Feldman's theorization of violence, the body, and political agency offers an incisive engagement with the trajectory and scope of Foucault's analysis in this regard:

Foucault's analyses looked to one side of this economic formation—the application of force to the body. But even in this instance, power only attains efficacy by functioning *as an action upon the action of another*. . . . The historicized and historicizing body is a pluralized site of torsion and contestation. But it is not a passive site. Exteriority folds the body, but agency, as a self-reflexive framing of force, subjectivates exteriority and refolds the body. It is not only a matter of what history does to the body but what subjects do with what history has done to the body.[11]

If we are to address Feldman's concern with "what subjects do with what history has done to the body" in the context of this genealogy of the prison regime, it is necessary to reflect on a formative moment in the regime's genesis. While the prison has become an expansive site for mobilizations of the state's variable disciplinary capacities, its earliest prototyping as a regime of white-supremacist violence—a multiply scaled, though institutionally focused technology of gendered racial domination—occurred through the prison's veritable transformation amid a coalescence of forces that stretched across state and civil society.

The prison's contemporary reconstruction was presaged by FBI Director J. Edgar Hoover's issuance of his (now somewhat infamous) August 1967 memorandum announcing a "new counterintelligence endeavor . . . to expose, disrupt, misdirect, discredit, or otherwise neutralize the activities of black nationalist, hate-type organizations."[12] Essentially a declaration of domestic war on a racially and politically "profiled" civilian population, Hoover's directive shaped a comprehensive rearrangement, elaboration, and deployment of the state's monopoly on the legitimate use of violence. To consider the *bodies* of this targeted population—a targeting that I would argue encompasses a conception of the black body as essentially incorrigible, antiauthoritarian, or insurrectionist—is to also revise Feldman's critique of Foucault to address the specificity of the *racialized* (and here, specifically black) state-pursued body as a uniquely "pluralized site of torsion and contestation."

Hoover's description of the Counterintelligence Program's "long-range goals" in March 1968 appropriately situates the necessity of a theoretical approach that foregrounds the state's white-supremacist constitutive logic. His agenda also reflects the particularity of a mar-shaled and martial state formation *that is internal to the United States:*

> For maximum effectiveness of the Counterintelligence Program, and to prevent wasted effort, long-range goals are being set.
> 1. Prevent the *coalition* of militant black nationalist groups. In unity there is strength. . . . An effective coalition . . . might be the first step toward a real "Mau Mau" in America, the beginning of a true black revolution.
> 2. Prevent the *rise of a "messiah"* who could unify, and electrify, the mili-tant black nationalist movement.
> 3. Prevent *violence* on the part of black nationalist groups. This is of pri-mary importance. . . . Through counterintelligence it should be possi-ble to pinpoint potential troublemakers and neutralize them before they exercise their potential for violence.
> 4. Prevent militant black nationalist groups and leaders from gaining *re-spectability,* by discrediting them to three separate segments of the community[:] . . . first, the responsible Negro community. Second . . . the white community, both the responsible community and to "liber-als" who have vestiges of sympathy for militant black nationalist [*sic*] simply because they are Negroes. Third . . . Negro radicals, the follow-ers of the movement. *This last area requires entirely different tactics from the first two. Publicity about violent tendencies and radical statements merely enhances black nationalists to the last group; it adds "respectability" in a dif-ferent way.* [emphasis added]
> 5. A final goal should be to prevent the long-range *growth* of militant black nationalist organizations, especially among youth. Specific tactics to prevent these groups from converting young people must be developed.[13]

As if to follow the lead of the Hooverite FBI, a durable coalition of (para)-military, governmental, political, and popular cultural blocs has arranged and operationalized the domestically militarized state since the turn of the 1970s. In this portion of the chapter, I am especially concerned with the emergence and institutional renaissance of the prison regime as a con-stitutive logic of American social formation, materialized through the exhaustively militarized production of domestic warfare and discursively articulated through the various guises of "law and order," Homeland Security, and the valorized "wars" on "crime," "drugs," "gangs," and "terror."

This section frames and elaborates a "warfare" genealogy of the contemporary prison regime through a brief discussion of the political history and embodied praxis of the Black Liberation Army (also known as the Afro-American Liberation Army). The positionality of the BLA as both an armed underground resistance force and a guerrilla revolutionary movement renders it central to a discussion of the prototyping and material genesis of the U.S. policing, juridical, and prison apparatuses as intersecting and strategically convergent forces. This convergence of coercive state forms centrally structures the material moment and social imaginary of what I have invoked (in the introduction) as the post-1970s White Reconstruction. Specifically, the history and legacies of the BLA reveal precisely how the prison, as a discursive terrain and geographic-institutional production, is at once the emblem of an abstracted and rigorously mystified policing-juridical telos (arrest—prosecution—conviction—incarceration), an approved zone of high-intensity combat (as a place of legitimated capture, interrogation, punishment, torture), and a site of experimentation for new domestic and globalized war-waging techniques.

It was precisely at the moment that Hoover pronounced that "the Black Panther Party, without question, represents the greatest threat to the internal security of the country" that the amoebic matrix of underground guerrilla resistance known as the Black Liberation Army became a central focus of the racial martial state.[14] The BLA, while often portrayed as a derivative of the Black Panther Party (BPP), actually preexisted the BPP's formation and was composed of several geographically dispersed components. The introduction to the 1972 BLA/Afro-American Liberation Army pamphlet *Humanity, Freedom, Peace* defines its organizational modality:

> The Afro-American Liberation Army is not a regular army but a guerilla army. Consequently, it has no central headquarters that directs. It is directed by revolutionary principles and is made up of small units that are

knowledgeable of the particular area in which they operate. True to all guerilla operations, each unit is not aware of any other units' actions unless they are directly involved. The major requirements for membership are adherence to progressive, revolutionary principles and above all, action.[15]

According to one former rank-and-file Black Panther woman (who will remain anonymous in this text), as well as the intensive research of scholar Akinyele Omowale Umoja, the BLA broadly encompassed the "underground military forces of the revolutionary nationalist Black movement,"[16] and included elements of such "aboveground" organizations as the Southern Christian Leadership Conference (SCLC), Malcolm X Grassroots Movement, Revolutionary Action Movement (RAM), NAACP, All-African People's Revolutionary Party, Congress of Racial Equality (CORE), Student Nonviolent Coordinating Committee (SNCC), and Provisional Government of the Republic of New Afrika (PGRNA or, more commonly, RNA).[17] The anonymous former Panther has stated that, far from being a conventionally politically structured paramilitary group, "the Black Liberation Army was simply composed of black people that were fighting for justice, freedom and equality. They did not all consider themselves members of the Black Liberation Army, but generally, that is what they were."[18] Assata Shakur, whose praxis and legacies I will discuss in more detail later, writes in her autobiography:

> [T]he Black Liberation Army was not a centralized, organized group with a common leadership and chain of command. Instead, there were various organizations and collectives working out of different cities, and in some of the larger cities there were often several groups working independently of each other.[19]

As a decentered matrix of guerrilla resistance and revolutionary cells, the BLA was largely developed in response to the heightened (and often deadly) state and state-sanctioned repression that the "aboveground" elements of the black liberation movement—and its civil rights counterpart—confronted throughout the 1960s and early 1970s.

In the aftermath of Hoover's 1968 denunciation of the Black Panther Party, the BLA emerged as a crucial (if largely unrecognized) facet of the besieged black liberation movement. The reach and tactical intensification of COINTELPRO between 1968 and 1971 effectively disrupted and poisoned the internal political culture of the Black Panther Party, deploying a stunning variety of infiltration and propaganda techniques to foster internal dissension and conflict among BPP leaders, as well as polarizing the Panther rank and file. COINTELPRO similarly ruined or preempted solidarities and coalitions between the Panthers and other nationalist, revolutionary, and even some liberal organizations. This state espionage and psychological warfare, once combined with the tediously coordinated and militarized deployment of domestic police/militia forces unseen since the frontier conquest of indigenous peoples, effectively forced many BPP members to go underground. It was at this point, according to Umoja, that the Black Liberation Army obtained a significant infusion of member-combatants who stretched the historical continuum of the most radical elements of the Panther political lineage:

> [T]he intense repression of the BPP did replenish the ranks of the Black Liberation Army. Since the BPP was the largest revolutionary nationalist organization of the Black liberation movement of the 1960s and '70s, its membership contributed greatly to the BLA. Panther participation in the BLA represented a continuation of the radical legacy of the BPP and was a response to the counterinsurgency strategy to destroy the Party and the Black liberation movement.[20]

Political prisoner/BLA soldier Jalil Muntaqim, in the 1979 prison communiqué "On the Black Liberation Army," affirms that the BLA was initially conceived as "a politico military organization, whose primary objective is to fight for the independence and self-determination of Afrikan people in the United States."[21] He specifically marks 1971 as the moment of the BLA's acceleration into full underground insurgency, as the destruction of the BPP and proliferation of COINTELPRO made aboveground radical/revolutionary political work in its extant forms virtually untenable:

> Based upon the split and factionalism in the BPP, and heightened repression by the State, the Black underground was ordered to begin establishing the capacity to take the "defensive-offensive" in developing urban guerilla warfare. Hence, in 1971, the name BLACK LIBERATION ARMY (or Afro American Liberation Army) surfaced as the nucleus of Black guerilla fighters across the United States.[22]

Crucial to the context of this genealogy is that the originating tactical conceptualization of the BLA was that it was to serve as a paramilitary "defensive (self-defense) front that would offensively protect the interest of the aboveground political apparatus' . . . movement towards national liberation."[23] During the 1970s, however, as BLA members and affiliates were relentlessly pursued, framed, incarcerated, and assassinated by the state, this ostensibly paramilitary organization was also consolidated as the necessary *political* underground of the black liberation movement.

In fact, imprisoned BLA combatants embodied a touchstone formation of radical prison praxis during this period, as the site of state capture was reconstituted as a space of resistance, survival, and antisystemic struggle. Interviewed in Los Angeles County Jail in 1971, Black Panther political prisoner Roland Freeman provides an incisive and insistently historical analysis of this warfare trajectory, which culminates in the heightened conflict (and revolutionary possibility) of the carceral war zone:

> The way I look at it, there was the struggle in the 50's and 60's—ban the bomb, then civil rights, demonstrations, riots, and then into Revolution. And now, the prisoners have taken the vanguard role in the struggle. Many of the "soldiers" are here in the prisons and continuing the struggle. . . .

The situation facing the U.S. power structure is that they have to get rid of the revolutionaries [by putting them] in jail, but the structure can't handle it. Like cancer, the Revolution will spread.

If they continue putting revolutionaries in jail, they're going to make the revolution in jail.[24]

Written some eight years after Freeman's jailhouse interview, Muntaqim's 1979 missive recalls the decisive shift in the political geography of the BLA's confrontation with the state, outlining the new forms of praxis that the BLA conceived as it rearticulated and contested the condition of imprisonment. Muntaqim's tracing of the BLA's movements and dispersals illustrates the culmination of Hoover's declared racial warfare, and similarly resites the prison as a central, rather than marginal or incidental, location of liberationist praxis:

By 1974–75, the fighting capacity of the Black Liberation Army had been destroyed, but the BLA as a politico military organization had not been destroyed. . . . [T]hose imprisoned continued escape attempts and fought political trials, which forged ideological and political theory concerning the building of the Black Liberation Movement and revolutionary armed struggle. The trials of Black Liberation Army members sought to place the State on trial, to condemn the oppressive conditions from which Black people had to eke out an existence in racist America. . . . The captured and confined BLA members were deemed a terrorist, a criminal, a racist, but never a revolutionary, never a humanitarian, never a political activist. But the undaunted revolutionary fervor of captured BLA members continued to serve the revolution even while imprisoned. . . . The BLA trials sought to undermine the State attempts to play-off the BLA as an insignificant group of crazies, and therefore the trials of BLA members became forums to politicize the masses of what the struggle and revolution is all about. The trials served to organize people to support those being persecuted and prosecuted by the State, as a means from which the oppressed masses would be able to protect themselves from future persecution. . . .

> By late 1975, the Black Liberation Army established a Coordinating Committee, which essentially [was] comprised of imprisoned members and outside supporters gained during the years of political prosecution in the Courts.[25]

In the spirit of Muntaqim's tracing, I contend that the history of BLA combatants—an entanglement of pursuit and flight, torture and survival, repression and insurrection—profoundly demystifies and renarrates the formation of the U.S. prison regime as a crisis of the unnatural. This legacy of insurgency invokes a history of confrontation with U.S. state power at its capillary points of articulation and domination, where the technology of state violence, including its self-legitimating public and hidden rituals of production, materializes through the punishment/liquidation of black bodies and an acute aggression against a form of black political existence.

Although I am only offering a short meditation on the political biographies of three BLA soldiers and political prisoners here, I do so with the intention of situating their experiences as both an embodied diagnosis and a theoretical implication of a broadly social and historical configuration of gendered white-supremacist domination. The figurative and literal prototyping of technologies of policing and carceral violence on these targeted black (political) incorrigibles, I argue, ordained a regime of bodily punishment and immobilization that has proliferated with stunning breadth and depth onto succeeding generations of black and Third World people in the United States. Finally, although it is difficult to ascertain precisely how many former BLA combatants are in prison as of this writing (owing to the BLA's commitment to secrecy), there are at least ten who openly identify as BLA prisoners of war, and several more who are living in exile outside the United States.[26]

Longtime BLA prisoner of war Nuh Washington's poem "Pain" constructs a schematic outline for the theoretical task at hand.

Pain

Psychic pain
caused by internal pressures
compounded by external forces
Pain, pain, pain

Spiritual pain
caused by a suffering humanity
compounded by faithless men
Pain, pain, pain

Physical pain
caused by brutality
compounded by oppression
Pain, pain, pain

Sexual pain
caused by pented up desire
compounded by prison bars
Pain, pain, pain

Mental pain
caused by isolation
compounded by insensitivity
Pain, pain, pain

There is a healing for all pain[27]

Washington, Muntaqim, and Herman Bell (known as the "New York Three") were given life sentences in 1975 for the alleged shooting of two New York City policemen.[28] Washington wrote in 1992, after suffering through numerous unsuccessful legal appeals, that "the state has conceded that I committed none of the acts for which I am incarcerated. However, it is argued that, as an 'admitted' member of the BLA, I taught political education classes and that it is therefore 'appropriate' that I remain in prison under the tightest possible security."[29] In 2000, after almost three decades of imprisonment, Washington died of liver cancer. Weeks before his passing, he gave a final interview in which he reflected on the significance of his lifework, and articulated a subtle though radical theorization of his own sickness and imminent death.

Washington is, within the self-narrative of this interview, a survivor of his own disarticulation, a revolutionary subject engaged in a war of liberation that is centuries ongoing. As such, he consistently references the manner in which he defines his political existence through the existential and bodily confrontation with the very regime that is destroying his body. Washington's language alternately affects a sense of disbelief at the speed of his physical deterioration and echoes the historical persistence of precisely such a *collective historical* experience with early and unnatural mortality, resonating Ruth Gilmore's racism and "premature death."[30]

> I want us to think about something. You know, for years, I've been saying everybody with a life sentence is on death row. . . . But if you had told me a year ago that my time was short, based upon the way I took care of myself and my exercises, it would've been hard for me to believe. But, it happened. *And the longer we stay in these places, the more we're apt to succumb to the ravages of time and those diseases and illnesses that come with it.*[31]

Here, Washington locates his condition amid a historical "we" that recalls a recent lineage of assassinated and imprisoned black revolutionaries. Simultaneously, he is speaking to an ontology of black and Third World captivity, conceived and materialized through the historical formation of multiple white-supremacist hegemonies within and beyond the United States.[32] Enmeshed in his black-liberationist and internationalist commitments (the Black Liberation Army, contrary to some, did not conceive its praxis as exclusively local, nationalist, or "domestic" in scope), Washington's "we" encompasses and exceeds the categories of the self-identified radical/revolutionary political intellectual, political prisoner/POW, or imprisoned activist.[33] It is, according to Washington, precisely the prefigured destiny of the captive to "succumb"—this is her or his mode of and reason for existence as such—especially when she or he is the *derivative* of a national and global American formation that variously targets racial Others for enslavement, containment, and elimination (forms of domination that explode conventional Marxist categorizations of "exploitation" and render them fundamentally inadequate). Elsewhere in the same interview Washington quips, "to survive under those conditions makes us unique."

Washington's conception of the irrevocable connection between disease, illness, and death *"in these places"* indicts the peculiar centrality of the prison to the contemporary American social (global) formation. Structures of human captivity and bodily punishment, though perhaps most spectacularly actualized at the locality of the jail or prison, necessarily elaborate into other, at times counterintuitive, sites of targeting: the school, the workplace, and the targeted neighborhood or community. "These places" are, for Washington's black/Third World "we," encompassing, immanent, everywhere. Washington's reflections, situated by his profound awareness of impending premature death, provoke immense political and theoretical questions: What would it mean to consider his assertion that unnatural and painful death, as well as profound psychic and corporeal suffering, is an enforced condition of (non)-existence "the longer we stay in these places," if we understand "these places" as the circulating spatial-political logic of the prison regime's technologies of violence? What if Washington's conception of "succumbing"—as the telos of the "ravages" wrought by these places—inscribed a point of entry into a larger theorization of the United States of America (and, by extension, its expansive global domain) as a social formation incommensurate with the banal vernaculars of civil society, and more befitting the languages of death generated by its (dying) black/Third World captives? Echoing Washington, one need only take a passing glance at the wealth of first-person testimonials, interviews, and other primary texts generated by imprisoned people since the 1970s to see that a discourse of death and disappearance has become a common way for the currently and formerly imprisoned to describe both the social logic and the experience of incarceration.[34]

Former BLA prisoner of war Safiya Bukhari-Alston, who passed away in 2003 at age fifty-three, powerfully narrates a paradigmatic encounter with the contemporary prison regime at its moment of genesis. Targeted by local police and the FBI for her leadership in the East Coast wing of the Black Panther Party, and later for her activity as the commander of an armed BLA unit, Bukhari-Alston survived a 1975 shootout with police in Norfolk, Virginia, that killed BLA soldier Kombozi Amistad and left codefendant Masai Ehehosi with gunshot wounds to his face.[35] (Bukhari-Alston and Ehehosi were given forty-year prison sentences after a one-day trial.) Bukhari-Alston's memoir "Coming of Age: A Black Revolutionary" describes a series of confrontations with the white-supremacist state ("the powers that be"), inhabited in part through a mortifying state-sanctioned violence that liquidates and neutralizes target bodies—in this case, unrepentant and armed black revolutionaries—as a matter of course: "They pulled out the stops in their campaign to rid the streets of rebellious slaves."[36]

Shifting scene to her initiating encounter with the reinvigorated policing/punishment apparatus, Bukhari-Alston sustains an intensely embodied explication of the contemporary prison's technologies of violence. Writing in 1979 from the Virginia Correctional Center for Women in Goochland, she narrates the logic of bodily disintegration that intertwines white-supremacist and misogynist vectors of domination within the procession of the prison regime's prototype formation:

> The "medical treatment" for women prisoners here in Virginia has got to be an all-time low. . . . In December 1976 I started hemorrhaging and went to the clinic for help. No help of any consequence was given, so I escaped. Two months later I was recaptured. While on escape a doctor told me that I could either endure the situation, take painkillers, or have surgery. I decided to use the lack of medical care as my defense for the escape and by doing so do two things: (1) expose the level of medical care at the prison, and (2) put pressure on them to give me the care I needed.
>
> I finally got to the hospital in June of 1978. By that time it was too late, I was so messed up inside that everything but one ovary had to go.

Because of the negligence of the "doctor" and the lack of feeling of the prison officials, they didn't give a damn, I was forced to have a hysterectomy.[37]

Firmly situated within a radical black feminist/womanist lineage that conceptualizes "the interdependence of thought and action" as the basis of political epistemology,[38] Bukhari-Alston's theorization reassesses Foucault's periodization in *Discipline and Punish*, which asserts, in part, that "at the beginning of the nineteenth century . . . the great spectacle of physical punishment disappeared; the tortured body was avoided; the theatrical representation of pain was excluded from punishment. The age of sobriety in punishment had begun."[39] In fact, "Coming of Age" must be understood as a primary testimonial that directly addresses the prison's reconstruction around a program of direct bodily disarticulation: Bukhari-Alston's biography signifies a narrative-theoretical point of departure for considering the structured rituality—hence the institutional normality—of a reoriginated, gendered, white-supremacist violence, a technology of domination that finds affinity and discursive kinship with earlier programs of North American racist and misogynist social formations and echoes histories of the state and state-sanctioned genocide, murder, and ritualized (sexual) torture of racial/gender Others. "Coming of Age" similarly foreshadows the breathtaking institutional expansion of women's imprisonment from the 1980s onward, a momentum obtained through the criminalization of poor and working poor black women and other women of color: the number of women held captive in state and federal prisons increased about twentyfold during the two decades following Bukhari-Alston's initial incarceration, while rates of incarceration for black and brown women far exceeded those of their relatively decriminalized white counterparts.[40]

Most significant to the current study, however, is the manner in which Bukhari-Alston's memoir anticipates the normalization of preventable death, untreated illness, and other forms of state-proctored physical disintegration in the contemporary formation of American penality. San Francisco–based human rights organization Legal Services for Prisoners with Children, among the few activist groups to focus its work on currently and formerly imprisoned women, rigorously documents the regulated commonality of bodily violence in a document prepared for legislative hearings on the conditions inside California women's prisons, held before the California state assembly in October 2000. The 180-page report presents evidence and first-person testimonial regarding the structured absence or refusal of prison medical care, sexual violence against imprisoned women by staff, and high-tech torture conditions of the women's Security Housing Units.[41] Many of the stories contained in this document echo earlier accounts of radical black and Third World women, like Bukhari-Alston, upon whose bodies the prison regime had prototyped an emergent technology of punishment.

Centering the political lineage of BLA soldier and political exile Assata Shakur further illuminates the historical formation and political trajectory of this prototyping, while offering a context for my departure from Feldman's theorization of agency, history, and the body. Shakur, who escaped Clinton Correctional Facility (New Jersey) in 1979 during an audacious maneuver by a BLA guerrilla task force, currently resides as an exile in Havana, Cuba.[42] She represents a venerated (if sometimes fetishized) signification of liberatory desire and possibility for many U.S. radicals and revolutionaries, including countless imprisoned and formerly imprisoned activists.[43] Her body is literally and indelibly marked by the legacy of a historically unprecedented campaign of white-supremacist political repression, coordinated by the U.S. government and multiple local police forces, and ultimately exceeding even the mandates of the FBI's Counterintellegence Program.[44] In fact, Shakur continues to be listed among the New Jersey State Police's "12 Most Wanted" under the birth name JoAnne Chesimard.

The police description of Shakur/"Chesimard" reifies her body in time and space, borrowing from the white-supremacist identifying modalities of plantation slavery, which similarly noted the "marks and scars" on the bodies of escaped slaves for the purposes of reapprehension and (mortal) punishment: the police poster specifically indicates "bullet wounds under right arm and left shoulder," the result of the 1973 New Jersey Turnpike shootout with police that resulted in her and Sundiata

> NJSP Home | > Crime & Technology | > New Jersey's 12 Most Wanted

NJSP Quick Links   Crime & Technology

New Jersey's 12 Most Wanted

If you have a tip call our hotline (24 hours a day)
800-437-7839

JoAnne Chesimard
Wanted for Escape - Convicted of
Murder of NJ State Trooper

CONSIDER VERY DANGEROUS

AKA:
Barbara Odoms, Mary Davis, Justine Henderson,
Joanne Byron, Josephine Henderson, Assata
Shakur, Joanne Chesterman

Description:
DOB: 7/16/47

Height: 5'6"

Weight: 125-138 lbs

Hair: Black

Eyes: Brown

Complexion: Medium

Race: Black

Blood Type: B+

Marks and Scars:
- Round scar left knee
- Bullet wounds under right arm and left shoulder

Remarks:
Wanted for escape - was serving life plus 26 to 33 years
for the murder of a New Jersey State Trooper.

SS Number: 051-38-5131
SBI Number: 335640A
FBI Number: 11102J7
FPC
AA AA AA 07 11
AA AA AA 04 10

Fugitive Unit File Number: H02379193

Authority:
NJ State Police, Fugitive Unit
Hunterdon County Prosecutor's Office

contact us | privacy notice | legal statement

Assata Shakur (JoAnne Chesimard) as depicted on New Jersey State Police "12 Most
Wanted" Web site in 2004. http://www.njsp.org/want/chesimard.html.

Acoli's imprisonment, and Zayd Shakur's death.[45] In addition, efforts during the late 1990s by New Jersey Governor Christine Whitman and Bob Franks yielded a 1998 congressional resolution (H. Con. Res. 254) titled "Calling for the Extradition of Joanne Chesimard from Cuba." Overwhelmingly passed (and unanimously supported by attending members of the congressional Black Caucus), the resolution carried on the strength of Franks's glib assertion that "This escaped murderer now lives a comfortable life in Cuba and has launched a public relations campaign in which she attempts to portray herself as an innocent victim rather than a cold-blooded murderer."[46] Mediated by the (visual) figure of Assata Shakur and the power nexus of the policing and prison regimes, state discourse here composes an ahistorical "official" memory of the contemporary (escaped) slave/prisoner/terrorist, forming a vernacular that attempts to frame a popular common sense through anticipation of a peculiar "justice"—in fact, the violent and decisive force of retribution—to be exercised on the incorrigible/black/woman's body.

Assata Shakur's living political biography (including and beyond the content of her autobiographical *Assata*), however, articulates a subjectivity (and hence a body) that has been persistently reconfigured through and beyond the totalizing regimes of state capture/pursuit and their accompanying discourses. An endangered, though nonetheless insistent political agency defines her personification and revision of Feldman's theorization. For example, Shakur's opening testimony before the jury in a 1975 bank robbery trial (she and codefendant Ronald Myers were eventually acquitted) foreshadows a life praxis that works through and upon the gendered-racialized *political* materiality that history has made of her body:

> I have decided to act as co-counsel, and to make this opening statement, not because i have any illusions about my legal abilities, but, rather, because there are things that i must say to you. I have spent many days and nights behind bars thinking about this trial, this outrage. And in my own mind, only someone who has been so intimately a victim of this madness as i have can do justice to what i have to say.[47]

In the aftermath of several trials, imprisonment (Shakur and Acoli were convicted in 1977 by an all-white jury on murder charges relating to the 1973 gun battle with police on the New Jersey Turnpike), and 1979 escape, Shakur has sustained the essential political logic of this enunciation; that is, rather than posit the finality of her nominal freedom from U.S. political repression and its prison regime, or celebrating her individual "liberation," Shakur consistently identifies the structuring ambivalence of her condition. Since her escape from prison, she has articulated the creeping terror of nominal freedom for the black political exile. In 1998, some twenty years after her liberation from prison, she self-referred as such: "My name is Assata Shakur, and I am a 20th century escaped slave."

Since the 1987 publication of her celebrated autobiography *Assata*, which concludes with an extended rumination on the ecstasy of her successful flight from prison (and the United States) and long-awaited reunion with her mother, daughter, and aunt, Shakur has consistently invoked the fundamental endangerment of her status an *escaped and always fleeing* black liberationist/prisoner/slave. Referencing her country of exile, Shakur closed her 1998 open letter by naming Cuba as "One of the Largest, Most Resistant and Most Courageous *Palenques* (Maroon Camps) that has ever existed on the Face of this Planet." (Maroon societies were community formations of indigenous people and Africans that became primary zones of liberation for "escaped slaves" during the epoch of plantation chattel slavery.)[48] Shakur thus locates her life and mortality within a history of the present, resituating the iconography of vindication and freedom that surrounds her experience. Her sustained liberationist praxis constitutes a dynamic, critical postscript for her now widely read autobiographical text.

> [A]t this moment, I am not so concerned about myself. Everybody has to die sometime, and all I want is to go with dignity. I am more concerned about the growing poverty, the growing despair that is rife in Amerika. I am more concerned about our younger generations, who represent our future. I am more concerned that one-third of young black are either in

prison or under the jurisdiction of the "criminal in-justice system." I am more concerned about the rise of the prison-industrial complex that is turning our people into slaves again. I am more concerned about the repression, the police brutality, violence, the rising wave of racism that makes up the political landscape of the U.S. today. Our young people deserve a future, and I consider it the mandate of my ancestors to be part of the struggle to insure that they have one. They have the right to live free from political repression. The U.S. is becoming more and more of a police state and that fact compels us to fight against political repression.[49]

Assata Shakur's repossession of history through subjectivity, and thus her principled disarticulation of the United States of America as an imagined community and valorized liberal democratic nation-state, puts a finer point on our working conception of the prison regime. The state violence technologies that were conceived, experimented, and deployed on Shakur, Washington, Bukhari-Alston, and other BLA combatants betray the tediously organized and ad hoc harnessing and shaping of the regime's prototype form, while also revealing the repressive, violent, and disarticulating condition of agency, history, and the body under the terms of a gendered white-supremacist (domestic) warfare formation. Following the implications of the state's counter-BLA prototyping, the following section develops a language of engagement with the prison regime's core logic, with specific reference to the bodies through which its power is constituted.

"A Language of Pure Force": The Terms of Imprisonment

Consider the contemporary captive's racialized-gendered embodiment, her or his subjectivity in all its complexity, as the object of a program of immobilization and disintegration under the contemporary U.S. prison regime. The dimensions and nuances of this aggression exceed the increasingly documented apparatuses of individual physical and psychological torture that characterize the expansion of detention facilities across the United States, and encompass even more intimately coerced alienations.[50] State captivity, in its current forms, effectively elevates the destruction of affective bonds—on individual and mass scales—to the level of institutional priority and premise. There is also, in the procedure of this regime of disintegration, a persistent imputing of the perverse soul or conscience of the gendered racial *incorrigible* (frequently paired with its supposed opposite, the rescuable model or standout white/multicultural prisoner). Such captive bodies, in turn, become subjects of individualized aggression for the sake of demonstrating the prison regime's relation of direct violence with the embodied category of incorrigibility. The regime structures and ritualizes a disintegrating violence against an immobilized population, not for the sake of punishing the "individual prisoner" per se, but rather as part of a relation of dominance with the categories that such individuals embody. Inscribed on this production of power and domination, and arguably the central discursive task of the prison's self-production, is the work of constituting the sub- and nonhuman. The aforementioned relation of dominium surfaces through the state's access to and relentless assault on the captive body as a fungible material of *exercised* power that is located outside the historical framework, nominal political entitlement, and cultural geography of civil society and its coinhabiting field of recognized social subjects.

I am arguing that the post-1970s prison regime mediates the genesis of a qualitatively new "apparatus" or "institution" for the articulation of power, as well as encompassing a point of departure for the conception and conduct of power itself. Notably, Foucault's *Discipline and Punish* (1977), with its focus on the formation of the penitentiary at the cusp of Euro-American modernity, does not anticipate the emergence of the U.S. prison regime in its current form.[51] His primary concern with the emergence of "the power of normalization and the formation of knowledge in modern society,"[52] as Joy James notes, betrays an overwhelming tendency to conflate the production of post-nineteenth-century technologies of criminalization, punishment, and discipline with the universalized figure of the white, European/American male subject.[53] Anchoring Foucault's historical genealogy is a consistent reference to the material embodiment of the modernist conception of the human being, a subject whose body and "soul" become the discursive material through which the Foucauldian "disciplinary society" practices and articulates.[54] Although Foucault clearly understands this abstracted, universalized human being as a production (fabrication) of the modernist scientific-juridical apparatus (characterized by its proclivity for efficiency, classification, and rationality), his failure to explicitly examine the racialized boundaries of modernity's "human" runs the risk of reifying the term.

Disrupting Foucault's genealogy are those whose exclusion from the domain of the fully human (and thus, from assumptive possession of the modernist soul) has been the requirement of emergent "modern" techniques of correction or rehabilitation, including those of the Euro-American prison. David Theo Goldberg's exhaustive discussion of the relation between race and modernity offers useful nuance:

> The drive to exclude is not antithetical to modernity but constitutive of it. Domination and exploitation assume new forms in modernity and postmodernity, not in contrast to an increasingly expressed commitment to "liberty, equality, and fraternity" as well as to cultural preservation but as basic to the realization of such ideals for those espousing the commitment. Moreover, the self-conception of "modern man" as free, productive, acquisitive, and literate is not delimiting of racisms' expressions but a framework for them. *It forms the measure by which racialized groups are modern and deserving of incorporation, or premodern and to be excluded from the body politic.*[55]

Regimes of "rational" discipline, moral correction, and "progressive" (rehabilitative) incarceration are, in this sense, invented, institutionalized, and reproduced through the abstracted figure of the (potentially) wayward white (male) subject, *the categorical "human,"* whose body and soul require incorporation into the eminent domain of the modernist historical telos. As Goldberg observes, however, the seductions of the universal and inclusive generate their attraction through the constitution of the sub- and nonhuman, and thus the construction of regimented exclusions from regimes of progress, including (especially) those of the modern—and allegedly corrective and rehabilitative—prison.

> [The] colonizing of the moral reason of modernity by racialized cate-
> gories has been effected for the most part by constituting racial others
> *outside the scope of morality.* . . . Thus, the racializing paradox of liberal
> modernity is firmly established: Liberalism's commitment to principles of
> universality is practically sustained only by the reinvented and rational-
> ized exclusions of racial particularity.[56]

It is useful here to reconsider Foucault's conception of "the body" as an
"object of knowledge" for modernity's reconceived technology of disciplinary power:

> [T]he body is also directly involved in a political field; power relations
> have an immediate hold upon it; they invest it, mark it, train it, torture
> it, force it to carry out tasks, to perform ceremonies, to emit signs. This
> political investment of the body is bound up, in accordance with complex
> reciprocal relations, with its economic use; it is largely as a force of pro-
> duction that the body is invested with relations of power and domination;
> but, on the other hand, its constitution as labour power is possible only
> if it is caught up in a system of subjection (in which need is also a politi-
> cal instrument meticulously prepared, calculated and used); the body be-
> comes a useful force only if it is both a productive body and a subjected
> body.[57]

As the contemporary prison regime articulates with and through the
organizing logic of white supremacy, the investments of dominant power
sediment in the particularity, more specifically the hierarchized gendered racial differentiation, of captive bodies.

Such a regime hinges on the *structured impossibility* of disciplining,
correcting, or otherwise reassimilating certain pathologized, abject bodies into the graces of white civil society, or the trappings of the "free
world." Angela Y. Davis argues:

> [The] process of individualization via the panopticon assumed that the
> prisoner was at least a potentially rational being whose criminality merely

evidenced deviation from that potential. This architecture and regime also assumed that the individual to be reformed panoptically was in possession of the mental and moral faculties that could be controlled and transformed by the experience of imprisonment.[58]

Echoing Davis, the narratives of Washington, Bukhari-Alston, and Shakur focus on the prison regime's fabrication of, and violent enactment through, racialized/gendered incorrigibility as its logic of reproduction and essential technology of power. To this extent, the regime elaborates the exclusionary dictates of the larger U.S. social formation, resonating with Davis's contention that at the moment of the modern U.S. penal system's genesis, "black men and women . . . were ideologically barred from the realm of morality" and therefore conceived as outside the realm of disciplinary rehabilitation or individual reform a priori.[59] Although Davis is primarily concerned in her essay with the genealogical linkage between the post–Civil War convict lease system and the recent proliferation of "super-max" prisons, I would argue that the logic of this continuity should be theorized through a more dynamic and flexible conception of the prison regime's variable articulations rather than through the narrowed and exclusive analytical lens of a certain class of prison. Foucault's theorization of "the body" in prison is, in the shadow of these severe and durable categorizations of racialized/gendered incorrigibility, drastically constrained in its applicability to the logic of the contemporary U.S. prison regime.[60]

On reflection, Nuh Washington's final interview, Safiya Bukhari-Alston's "Coming of Age," and Assata Shakur's praxis of maroonage conceptualize a punitive order that is essentially, if not entirely corporeal in its focus, and often spectacular in its performance. For them and their radical black/Third World cohorts, a primary (rather than excessive or incidental) political articulation of the American social formation during the 1970s (and since) has entailed precisely the public production of "tortured" black/brown bodies—within and beyond the increasingly conspicuous demonstrations of the prison regime itself—that Foucault's *Discipline and Punish* fails to address. Their testimonials resonate with

Fanon's enunciation of the comprehensive and everyday oppressive violence at the locality of the colony's internal borders:

> [T]he policeman and the soldier, by their immediate presence and their frequent and direct action maintain contact with the native and advise him by means of rifle butts and napalm not to budge. *It is obvious here that the agents of government speak the language of pure force.* The intermediary does not lighten the oppression, nor seek to hide the domination; he shows them up and puts them into practice with the clear conscience of an upholder of the peace; *yet he is the bringer of violence into the home and into the mind of the native.*[61]

Washington's, Bukhari-Alston's, and Shakur's overlapping stories of bodily subjection at the hands of state agents, from police to judge (in civil society), and guard to doctor (in prison), invoke the Fanonian sociohistorical vector of "pure force." It is the vernacular and semiotics of pure force, directed against the body of the black incorrigible, that renders the fundamental intelligibility of U.S. white civil society, the reconstituted "white Atlantic" of Goldwater's dreams.

The state's neutralization and liquidation of the black radical, insurrectionist, and liberationist—who emblematizes the imminent apocalypse of white civil society in its 1970s moment of crisis—prototypes the technology of civil society's coherence more generally, especially as it has become the site of a proliferated domestic warfare that no longer exclusively (or even primarily) targets black/Third World activists and revolutionaries. These convergent narratives of terror, survival, and bodily disintegration speak to the onset of the normative spectacle of a regimented racialized-gendered state violence that is the common language of American white civil society's order, the organic requirement of its everyday social intercourse: "[t]he death of black subjects or the invisibility of blackness serves to ward off a nation's collective dread of the inevitable. Someone else bears the burden of the national id; someone else (always already) dies first."[62]

The relation of pure force, in relation to the history of the BLA, articulates centrally through the regime of the prison, as both the logical geographic destination for the policed black radical/revolutionary subject and the productive site for a technology of power/domination that prioritizes the disintegration of these captured black bodies, with profound effects on their communities of origin and (political) identification. The otherwise isolated and invisible scenes of bodily violence produced at these sites of policing and imprisonment compose a readily available material for reenacted virtual spectacle, produced as elemental weaponry for the regime's practical technology of power. Reembodying the Fanonian "native" through their testimonials, Shakur, Bukhari-Alston, and Washington invite a rendition of the state that threads the continuity of terror, suffering, and bodily disarticulation into the ontology of America's incorrigibles. The experiences of countless captive radicals, revolutionaries, and "common" or social prisoners (including children and those incarcerated under the auspices of mental illness) similarly contradict Foucault's allusion to "the disappearance of the branded, dismembered, burnt, annihilated body of the tortured criminal" under the rise of the modern Euro-American penitentiary.[63]

The racialized and gendered specificity of the aforementioned narrations of carceral violence differentiate both the severity and the regulated vulnerability of certain imprisoned subjects to the regime's spectrum of bodily-psychic violence. The repression of the BLA, in particular, illuminates the normalized proximity of black bodies to the state's most profound and disarticulating technologies of violence. This coerced intimacy with death and normative bodily disintegration reveals the prison regime's hierarchical organization of violence as a prototyping of white supremacy. As a state-mediated and state-sanctioned logic of social and carceral organization, this white supremacy thrives from its sustenance of easily populated frontiers and death zones, historically reproduced through the state's prioritized access to abject black, indigenous, and Third World bodies. As such, the U.S. prison regime must be conceptualized as something akin to a white-supremacist "mode of production" that proliferates and hierarchizes a site-specific technology of domination: the material logic of the U.S. prison regime, in its current form, coheres through the white-supremacist vectoring of a multiply scaled, though consistently mass-based, immobilization and disintegration.

How, then, are we to make sense of a regime that collapses the difference between correction and liquidation, individualization and de-humanization, or "discipline" and "punishment"? Tracing the conception and elaboration of the post-1970s U.S. prison regime allows for a critical departure from Foucault's analysis of the modern prison, while sustaining Joy James's critique of his genealogy of the body:

> If the "art of punishing, in the regime of disciplinary power" is designed not to expiate or repress but to "normalize," as Foucault argues, then one must recognize that some bodies cannot be normalized no matter how they are disciplined, unless the prevailing social and state structures that figuratively and literally rank bodies disintegrate.[64]

I am concerned with how objectified and incorrigible bodies—that is, bodies that are objects of the prison's regime of disintegration—are also *subjects that inhabit their own incorrigibility* as a form of self-conscious and ethical praxis. This is to consider a politically inhabited incorrigibility as both a critique and a disarticulation of the prison regime's constitutive logics.

Conclusion: "An Insurrection of Knowledges"

This genealogy is, from its outset, entangled in the essential incommunicability of the violence that it proposes to trace, analyze, and (re)-encounter: as countless captives and prison survivors testify, their formal and totalizing subjection to a regime of legitimated brutality is a condition that largely exceeds communicative possibility, that is, it is a condition beyond words. Still, the echoes and resonances of this lineage of radical intellectuals orchestrate a symphony of flight from the normative cultural, political, and institutional structures of the United States, decisively disrupting its self-valorizing narratives of freedom and democracy (powerful discourses that increasingly exert, by consensus and by force, a global cache). Inescapable is the *social* logic of the contemporary U.S.

prison, its integral role in organizing and disrupting the matrices and possibilities of everyday human intercourse, and, more crucially, its overwhelming presence in the production of modalities of bodily domination, state and state-sanctioned forms of violence—within and beyond the prison proper—that betray the limits of Foucault's "disciplinary society" and install rituals of spectacular punishment that illuminate the intersections and gaps between various axes of power.

The significance of contemporary radical prison praxis—the far-ranging political-discursive work embodied by imprisoned radical intellectuals that I will outline in the next chapter—is its antagonism to the punitive and disciplinary technologies enmeshing its formation. Invoking Foucault's 1976 reference to the "insurrection of subjugated knowledges" as the catalyst of new forms of locally situated critique, imprisoned radical intellectuals are uniquely situated to offer the beginnings of a material genealogy, as well as an urgent political critique, of the state's capillary extremities, where its most profound techniques of domination emerge.

The following chapters elaborate on this bloc and its praxis, the historical contents of which "have been buried or masked in functional coherences or formal systematizations." This is to attempt, in Foucault's terms, a genealogy of the prison regime that proceeds through "a whole series of knowledges that have been disqualified as nonconceptual knowledges, as insufficiently elaborated knowledges: naïve knowledges, hierarchically inferior knowledges, knowledges that are below the required level of erudition or scientificity."[65] The prison's power of domination, while exceeding the staid formalities of the state, simultaneously generates capillary spaces of radical subjectivity and knowledge production that exceed the logical structures of legitimated political-intellectual discourse. Compounding the form and substance of the discourse itself, the praxis of imprisoned radical intellectuals entails the invention of new communicative modalities and strategies, from the production of new political vernaculars to the construction of subversive pedagogical spaces and networks. A genealogy of the prison regime, in the current historical context, traces the outlines of a political crisis of meaning for extant paradigms of social change and transformation, confronting the logic of immobilization and disintegration that defines the regime's procession. "If you like, we can give the name 'genealogy' to this coupling together of scholarly erudition and local memories. . . . Genealogies are, quite specifically, antisciences. . . . They are about the insurrection of knowledges."[66]

The prison constitutes the site and moment of radical prison praxis as a crisis for the state: to the extent that imprisoned intellectuals articulate and mobilize varieties of counterhegemonic or antisystemic power (from collective insurrection and guerrilla combat to "nonviolent" resistance and formal institutional reform demands), they embody a strategic vectoring of political-intellectual insurgency and antiauthoritarian resistance that disrupts—and ultimately reconstitutes—the prison regime's production of dominion. It is the enactment, in other words, of the fundamental—*and inescapably political*—relation of the very institutionality of the prison itself as a definitive zone (dominion) of warfare.

There are subjects and populations that, through the material-discursive structures of the American social formation, exist as embodied crisis, or figures of incoherence.[67] The consistent and sometimes amplified productions of non- and subhumans (discovered most profoundly in the shifting historical categorizations of blacks and Native Americans) constitute the necessary figures of negation and productive figures of crisis for the reproduction and coherence of modern Euro-American social formations. In this sense, the birth of Foucault's nineteenth-century prison can also be understood to incubate a genealogy of human apocalypse within the formation of a putatively inclusivist, modernist disciplinary order. The genesis of this incubated technology of death, what might be considered the rebirthing of the prison as a regime of immobilization and disintegration, is precisely that which is traced by the recent lineage of imprisoned radical intellectuals.

CHAPTER 2

"You Be All the Prison Writer You Wish": The Context of Radical Prison Praxis

Apparently, they imagine we prisoners who have forever sentences are just supposed to disappear, but unfortunately, it doesn't work that way.

—Standing Deer, "Prisons, Poverty, and Power" (1992)

I am a bleak heroism of words
that refuse
to be buried alive
with the liars.

—Audre Lorde, "Learning to Write" (1986)

"A Radically New Sense of Time, Space and Movement"

Imprisoned radical intellectuals have inhabited and shaped the formation of the U.S. policing, juridical, and punishment apparatuses since the rise of the Goldwater–Nixon "law-and-order" state. This chapter attends to the unique set of historical, spatial, and bodily conditions of possibility for imprisoned radical intellectuals to engage in "praxis," or what Paulo Freire (in the Marxist tradition) famously invoked as the profound political aliveness of "reflection and action on the world" with the purpose of transforming it.[1]

Through an extraordinary mirroring and rearticulation of the dystopic structure of imprisonment—a regime founded on the symbiosis between the logics of displacement and degradation—this political-intellectual work inaugurates new vernacular forms, including the construction of new languages of agency, politics, freedom, identity, community, sovereignty, and struggle. These meanings constantly exceed and slip from the grasp of conventional modes of political, academic, and activist discourse. Thus, my use of the term "(radical) prison praxis" foregrounds the institutional and historical condition of this lineage of political work as it is constituted and delimited by a carceral structuring of totalizing and legitimated state violence. *Radical* prison praxis is fundamentally an institutional and discursive antagonism, that is, an insurgent or insurrectionist formation of critique, dissent, and rebellion that (1) elaborates a conception of political subjectivity—its context, possibilities, and historicity—specific to the formation of the prison as a particular regime of power; (2) conceptualizes praxis through the terms with which it is organically linked and historically "belongs" to, a lineage of imprisoned radical intellectuals; and (3) shifts the presumptive political geography of praxis by examining its formation at the site of imprisonment, a disjuncture from the juridical and cultural domains of civil society.

Puerto Rican *independentista* José Solís Jordan, writing as a U.S. political prisoner in 2001, speaks to this altered condition of praxis when he reflects on his initial struggles with solitary confinement: "The aloneness had washed all over me. . . . It was like a baptism, a rite of passage, a leap into a radically new sense of time, space and movement."[2] Jordan, a Chicago-based political educator, community organizer, and university professor prior to his incarceration, reconstructs his visions of pedagogy, affect, and change through the ambivalent *embrace*—rather than metaphysical transcendence or escape—of his coerced existential and ontological transformation. This self-immersion into the thickness of one's own subjection is a primary *political* practice for many imprisoned women and men, and is particularly central to constituting the (collective) identity and praxis of captive radical intellectuals.

It is the comprehensive punitive technology of imprisonment, its rigorous completion of multiple circuits and scales of suffering and immobilization—temporal, spatial, and bodily—that forms the materiality of the "theory-practice nexus" for imprisoned radical intellectuals like Jordan.[3] Speaking from an intimate and lasting entanglement with the structure of (self-)alienation operationalized by the prison regime, Jordan enlivens a philosophy of praxis for the incarcerated activist or liberationist:

> Clearly, the challenge for all of us is a pedagogical project, one whose res-
> olution requires our sincerest commitment to social justice, to caring. . . .
> [T]o really care I must return to that solitude, to the tearing-away im-
> posed by my arrest, arraignment, trial, conviction and imprisonment.[4]

Beyond Jordan's formal structural alienation from civil society, that is, in
excess of his inhabitation of the categorical negation of legitimate political existence (civic death), is the even more profound violence of a
deformed ontology.

The categorical production of the "prisoner"—as the bodily signi-
fier and living evidence of the prison's statecraft—generates the mediating object for the prison regime's materiality, exercise, and affirmation:
the prisoner represents the epiphany of state power and social order,
massive legitimated violence and civil society's coherence, as a coalition
of interest. Jordan's missive denotes recognition of his capture and captivity as a "rebirth" into estrangement, that is, the procession of imprisonment as a material practice of white-supremacist and neocolonialist
domination that actualizes at the precipice of the human and the nonhuman or antihuman. This regime is structured by alienation so profound
as to compel captives like Jordan to seek solace, agency, and identity
from within the substance of their own disintegration as social subjects:
the "solitude" of experience marked by an ongoing, mind-boggling "tear-
ing away" from that which provides coherence to one's self-recognition—
community, family, loved ones. Jordan's rhetoric of becoming a *stranger
to himself* is a language and sentiment that resonate with many who have
been or are currently imprisoned.

This condition of praxis decisively refigures Marxist political
philosopher and Italian political prisoner Antonio Gramsci's venerated
conception:

> A philosophy of praxis cannot but present itself at the outset in a polemical
> and critical guise, as superseding the existing mode of thinking and exist-
> ing concrete thought (the existing cultural world). First of all, therefore,
> it must be a criticism of "common sense," basing itself initially, however,

on common sense in order to demonstrate that "everyone" is a philosopher and that it is not a question of introducing from scratch a scientific
form of thought into everyone's individual life, but of renovating and making "critical" an already existing activity.[5]

As he wrote from his own political imprisonment during the early twentieth century, Gramsci's overarching theoretical concern was with the
construction of balance and interchange between the political forces of
coercion and consent as the guiding tension of "hegemony," the relative
equilibrium that was generated through the "coordination of the interests of a dominant group with the general interests of other groups and
the life of the state as a whole."[6] Gramsci was interested in the genesis
of a form of political rule that was specific to the emergence of capitalist
modernity, especially within those industrial societies that were characterized by a rapidly increasing complexity of relations and antagonisms
between individuals, social groups and classes, cultural and economic
institutions, and the various apparatuses of the state. The production of
common sense, which Gramsci conceived as the dynamic, fragmented
"terrain of conceptions and categories" establishing that which is "taken
for granted" in the everyday discourse of a given social formation, was
integral to the relative equilibrium of hegemony: that is, common sense
provided the accessible set of signs, truths, and assumptions that structured the generalized cohesiveness of modern civil society.[7]

Gramsci's philosophy of praxis was thus structured as a theorization of a form of political-intellectual work that critically engaged a
hegemonic common sense, an engagement that carried with it the aspira-
tion of transforming popular or "mass" political consciousness through
the rearticulation of the meaning and significance of everyday (or taken-
for-granted) activities, vernaculars, and power relations. Crucial to this
discussion is that Gramsci's praxis *was situated within the terrain of civil
society,* embodied by (presumptively white and European) subjects whose
relative mobility, nominal freedom, and bodily autonomy were in fact
the hallmarks of modernity's definitive liberal humanism. Praxis, for
Gramsci, was the work that "belonged" to blocs of critical or radical

"organic intellectuals" (in distinction from the organic intellectuals of the dominant groups and classes) whose ambition was to enable new identifications and solidarities, within and across subaltern, subordinate, and otherwise nondominant groups.

Jordan's meditation on solitude, estrangement, and political pedagogy displaces and revises Gramsci's theorization. Praxis, as a critical engagement with the formative common sense of a given social formation, takes on a wholly different context, substance, and ontology when it is generated from within the *antisocial carceral formation* of the prison regime. It is precisely because the prison has, in its contemporary inception, been variously and simultaneously structured as civil society's underside, opposition, and negation that it houses a peculiar technology of power and domination, intensively collapsing hegemony's (and civil society's) multiple levels of mediated coercion and massaged consent into the totalizing and univocal sovereignty of the prison regime. Common sense, as the primary terrain of discursive contestation in civil society, is displaced by the union of statecraft (state discourse) and bodily disintegration within the prison's technology of power. The possibility of a legitimate common sense—that is, a common sense that forms a conceptual terrain for ongoing human discourse, contestation, and social intercourse—is *preempted* by the ontological death, and disintegrating telos, constituted and enforced by the regime of imprisonment.

The production of a "carceral/prison common sense," contrary to the assertions of many criminologists and ethnographers of "prison culture," is not simply a mimesis, deformation, or appropriation of civil society's (the "free world's") structures of common sense. It is through the state's production of the categorical "prisoner" through an ontology of civil and social death—*the prisoner exists for the purpose of succumbing*—that imprisoned political intellectuals, like José Solís Jordan, must work with a different epistemological circumstance altogether.

The prison regime's internal logic is scaffolded by the superfluity of consent among its captives—the regime conceives consent as a privilege that has been decisively and permanently withdrawn from the prisoner. Imprisoned people are the regime's durable nonhumans, to the extent that they are seen as bodies that have been judicially (that is, officially and formally) emptied of their presumptive political and social subjectivity. In this sense, the imprisoned are categorically outside the "civil" domain of social formation and its terrains of common sense, due both to the fundamental denial of access to engagement with both, and to the overwhelming immanence of punitive bodily disintegration that enmeshes any furtive attempts at such political agency. Therefore, for the imprisoned intellectual, "praxis"—traditionally conceived—*is structurally impossible.*

The significance and political possibility of prison praxis is defined by its temporal, ontological, and institutional specificity. Jordan's reflection on solitude and (self-)estrangement as the condition of possibility for praxis, in this context, critically reinscribes and amplifies the condition of captivity while abrogating the social logic of incarceration. As Barbara Harlow writes in her important text *Barred: Women, Writing, and Political Detention,*

> Penal institutions, despite, if not because of, their function as part of the state's coercive apparatus of physical detention and ideological containment, provide the critical space within which, indeed from out of which, alternative social and political practices of counterhegemonic resistance movements are schooled.[8]

The failure of the prison's institutionalized violence and systemic repression to evaporate political unruliness on the "inside" testifies to more than just the intellectual intractability or genius of individual prisoners. At a glimpse, it seems that there is something deeply collective and historical about the willingness—in moments, the compulsion—to speak truth against the very juridical, technological, and institutional jaws of state power.

The remainder of this chapter elaborates a theory of and historical context for contemporary prison praxis, while distinguishing it conceptually from the politically domesticating and delimited nomenclatures of "prison writing" and "prison education." Although this attempt to reconceptualize the political work of imprisoned radical intellectuals is in its own way a domesticating gesture, in the sense that it reorders, appropriates, and selectively interprets a field of discourse that is otherwise subjected to the state's coercive disarticulation and decentering, it is worth emphasizing that the notion of prison praxis attempts to enable a problematic of political subjectivity and agency that antagonizes its condition of possibility rather than reifying it.

"You Be All the Prison Writer You Wish": The Problem of Prison Writing

Numerous authors, activists, and scholars have anthologized U.S. "prison writing" in the last few decades. H. Bruce Franklin's *The Criminal as Victim and Artist* (1978), Chinosole's *Schooling the Generations in the Politics of Prison* (1995), Bell Chevigny's *Doing Time* (1999), and Joy James's *Imprisoned Intellectuals* (2003), demonstrate how imprisoned writers, poets, and activists have come to occupy a discrete—if marginal—discursive space within academia and the literary "market" at precisely the time of the prison's transformation into a primary economic, political, and social institution of American life. The nominal intent of such compilations has varied: some, like Franklin, wish to etch out a space within the contested canon of American literature for the subaltern voices of those "members of the oppressed classes who have become artists with words through their experience of being defined by the state as criminals."[9] Chevigny's anthology, on the other hand, reflects the rehabilitation mandates of prison education and literacy training programs, culling winning entries from the PEN "annual literary competition for prisoners" (begun in 1973) for the purpose of "honoring literary excellence" while "encouraging some beginning writers."[10] *Doing Time*, according to its editor, offers "an incisive anatomy of the contemporary prison" by allowing writers to "bear witness to the secret world that has isolated and would silence them."[11]

Others, such as Chinosole, conceive the purpose of collecting the writings, interviews, and speeches of current and former U.S. black-liberationist political prisoners as contributing "to memory, analysis, and practice directed at the complete liberations of people of African descent."[12] James's collection, in a similar political vein, invokes the praxis of black liberationists, white anti-imperialists, Puerto Rican anti-imperialist *independentistas,* Native American sovereignty fighters, and other radical and revolutionary political prisoners in order to offer their writings "as gateways to avenues that bypass a pantheon in a difficult journey toward liberation movements." Distinguishing *Schooling the Generations* and *Imprisoned Intellectuals* from many contemporary anthologies of "prison writing" is the modality in which the books themselves attempt to sustain and provoke a continuum of progressive-to-revolutionary praxis. James reflects, "I see that the purpose of [compiling *Imprisoned Intellectuals*] was to foster or force an encounter between those in the so-called free world seeking personal and collective freedoms and those in captivity seeking liberation from [oppressive] economic, military, racial/sexual systems."[13]

Following Chinosole and James, this chapter attempts to disturb and displace the reification of the figurative "prisoner's" creative agency in the common aestheticization of her or his work into a "genre" of literary text. In fact, the very suggestion of "prison writing" as a literary genre begs larger questions: What are the conditions of possibility for these carceral texts? What are the contexts—emphasis on the plural—of their production in U.S. prisons, jails, and detention centers? What kind(s) of political practice(s) do these texts signify, transform, and create?

This chapter breaks from the epistemological and political confines of "prison writing" in order to foster a substantive, critical engagement with the counterhegemonic prison praxis that has especially emerged since the historic swell of U.S. prison and political prisoner activism in the late 1960s and early 1970s. In rejecting the term "prison writing," I take my cue from Paul St. John, a writer and critic imprisoned in the Eastern New York Correctional Facility, who deconstructs the phrase in his award-winning 1994 essay "Behind the Mirror's Face":

> Prison Writing. The term reverberates in my brain case like kettledrums. The anger returns. I can't recall the psycho-speak, but I know it's like a

form of Pavlov's. People are set off by certain sights, sounds, even smells, that affect them in very special ways.

. . . I will call her Mother Nature, an artist who came into the prison to "find flowers where others saw only weeds." I taped the Author's Release to the wall two weeks ago. I feed a blank sheet to the machine.

Dear Mother Nature,

. . . I think you are a unique spirit for daring to tap into the voices of this miserably dark place. However, I regret to say that you are on the wrong track if your intentions are to use this so-called Prison Writing Experience as a means for reform, simply because prisoners, although they understand what is wrong with the system better than any criminologist, judge, cop, or outsider, have the credibility of elves. In this sense prison writing's dead wood.

The only other way to look at prison writing is as a way of expression. And, frankly, who wants to hear about loneliness, hopelessness, despair, loss of autonomy, harassment, contempt, or civil death, except to feel real good that things aren't as bad out in the world? Please don't think that I will allow myself to be used as consolation for a civilian audience.

. . . I will be a writer in prison, for now. You be all the prison writer you wish. . . .

Prison writing is as free as the author. Again I engage the machine and begin to spin out a little speech I have prepared for my prison writing group, which I polish up as I go.

On the Subject of Prison Writing

Good evening, fellow writers. I would like to take a few minutes tonight to discuss prison writing and its place in the larger world of letters.

. . . Subject, genre, specialty—the writer enters it by choice. But prison writing is a matter of status. It comes with the bid and that's that. It must take as subject matter life in prison. Prison writing is literally forced upon the writer, who, incidentally, has been stripped of just about everything else. Now, that's supposed to liberate.[14]

The persistence of "prison writing" as the broad categorical designation for incarcerated cultural production, as St. John's narrative suggests, legitimizes and reproduces the discursive-material regime of imprisonment. To the extent that "the prison" becomes a homogenizing modifier, designating the institutional location of the writer's labor, the genre equilibrates state captivity with other literary moments and spatial sites in civil society, or the free world.

Yet, the political relation between imprisonment and writing—within and against this absolutist state regime—remains a troubling and rather undertheorized problematic. One anonymously written polemic, written in Soledad Prison (California) and smuggled out for publication during the early 1970s, dislodges the presumptive category of "the writer," while displacing the literary process of "writing" and resiting it in the carceral "House of the Dead." Titled "The Problems of Writing in Prison," the piece anticipates and incisively critiques the free-world reader's/voyeur's mode of consuming, interpreting, and aestheticizing such an illicitly inscribed and circulated text.

> The problems of writing in prison you ask? Did you ever lie on a steel prison bunk and listen to the insanity that rages on the concrete tiers? The gasp of a dying man, stabbed brutally to death? Ever watch a man go insane? The embers of intelligence frozen with madness. Have you lived like a hermit in the nine by five cell furnished by the tax payers? Ever been in one of the prison holes? Darkness man, ever where [sic], cold pavement, a hole in the floor to shit in. Crazed animals chained in the cells of terror, fed by the insanities of a sub-culture of humans. And you talk about the problems of writing in the prison system.
>
> Have you abided by rules of oppression that stale mate [sic] the mind? Has your mind ever reeked with firey [sic] hatred, inflamed with the help of degeneracy structured by an indolent prison structure? And you ask about the problems of writing in prison.
>
> . . . If you are an artist, have you ever been told what to paint? And what not to paint? And when you do sell, the fat cats of the prison system deducts twenty five percent. It's the same with a book or story. I see people

> coming that I can't avoid, to be rude to them would be cause for a killing, for they know nothing else. I chuckle in merriment at the writers of the free world who bemone [*sic*] their problems of writing.[15]

The academic and cultural fabrication of "prison writing" as a literary genre is, in this sense, a discursive gesture toward order and coherence where, for the writer, there is generally neither. Structuring the alleged order and coherence of imprisonment is the constant disintegration of the writer's body, psyche, and subjectivity—the fundamental logic of punitive incarceration is the institutionalized killing of the subject, a process far more complex than even the spectacle of physical extermination emblematized by the death-row execution. This logic is precisely that which is obscured—and endorsed—by the inscription and incorporation of prison writing as genre.

The writer in prison is never simply free to write. St. John's political allegory, and the anonymous Soledad writer's serial rhetorical questioning, illuminates the complexity of a cultural production that is both constituted and coerced by state captivity, a dynamic condition that preempts and punishes some forms of writing, while encouraging and even forcing others (state education, therapy, and rehabilitation programs often mandate writing exercises). Overdetermined by the institutional mandates of "rehabilitation," prison writing is sometimes domesticated through narratives of "individual transcendence," framed by notions of the imprisoned author defying physical incarceration by finding (intellectual/spiritual) freedom in the creative act. Others, however, have emphasized the material embeddedness of their writing in the condition of imprisonment, rupturing the insistent coherence of the prison-writing genre by amplifying the incoherence of captivity, an altogether different condition of possibility for literary production.

George Jackson's posthumous *Blood in My Eye*, completed days before his assassination by San Quentin prison guards, offers a departure from the traditional "prison writing" rubric. His vernacular speaks a condition of existential disarticulation, a state of living wedded to the inevitable death destiny of enslavement:

> Born to a premature death . . . that's me, the colonial victim. . . . I've lived
> with repression every moment of my life, a repression so formidable that
> any movement on my part can only bring relief, the respite of a small vic-
> tory or the release of death. In every sense of the term, in every sense that's
> real, I'm a slave to, and of, property.[16]

Speaking to the impossibility of transcendence and authentic creativity
under the threat of imminent death, Jackson's literary work is defined by
its rejection of the political and moral legitimacy of a capitalist, white-
supremacist state and an even more tangibly incorrigible opposition to
the existence of the prison itself. Rendering such insurrectionist texts
into typically conceived realms of "genre," in spite of—or perhaps because of—the critical or politically progressive intent of professional
(academic) intellectuals (and some publishing houses), is immediately an
exercise of political domestication, an immobilization of text that subjects it to a structure of enjoyment that thrives from the horror of an
imprisoned Other's suffering. To echo Saidiya Hartman, "at issue here is
the precariousness of empathy and the uncertain line between witness
and spectator."[17]

Although this chapter does not pretend to offer a convenient path
of escape from either the danger of Hartman's "uncertain line" or the
voyeuristic gratification that may be derived from the consumption of
"prison texts," it does attempt a point of departure from current structures of academic and political disciplining. I am attempting to disturb
the theoretical premises of academic as well as extra-academic "activist"
appropriations of prison praxis vis-à-vis its consumption as self-indulgent
literary enjoyment, iconic valorization, or spiritual transcendence. The
production of prison writing as a literary genre, in this sense, shares a
political logic in common with the disciplinary structure of prison philanthropy programs, to which we now turn.

"To Cultivate Better Purposes of the Heart":
The (Christian) Whiteness of Prison Philanthropy

A brief recollection of the longer history of U.S. "prison education" may
be useful for the sake of situating current prison philanthropic ventures

within a genealogy that is more than two centuries old. It is necessary, in other words, to consider the origins and continuities of prison philanthropy, from its conception in the early American penitentiary to its entanglement in the emergence of the contemporary prison industrial complex, as a way to assess the current practices of "prison educators," who are among the most important embodiments of the prison's extended technologies of surveillance, as well as its regimes of immanent and direct violence.

During the early national life of the United States of America, the Pennsylvania Prison Society played a prominent and agenda-setting role in the new state's prototyping of the penitentiary. Affirming a liberal interpretation of principles of Christian philanthropic benevolence, the Society described its mission, in 1787, as a commitment to "discover modes of punishment" that "instead of continuing habits of vice, become the means of restoring our fellow creatures to virtue and happiness."[18] Revealing the Society's practical and conceptual conflation of the missionary's benevolence with the penitentiary's repressive incarceration, the organization christened its annual publication the *Journal of Prison Discipline and Philanthropy*. The Pennsylvania Prison Society was integral to the genesis of the American criminal justice and penal systems, and was especially central to the establishment of the Quaker-inspired "Pennsylvania/Philadelphia Model" of incarceration, which disavowed the "mass treatment" of prisoners in favor of individualized regimes of discipline, correction, penance, and rehabilitation. In fact, this model of punishment is not unlike the political logic underlying much of what passes as rehabilitation and education programs in the current prison regime, which elevate the revivification of the "good subject" to the status of programmatic objective.

Near the end of the nineteenth century, and not coincidentally in the immediate aftermath of the formal abolition of racial chattel slavery, the Pennsylvania prison regime claimed to encounter a peculiar institutional crisis. The January 1892 edition of the *Journal*, by then well known as a major intellectual medium in the ongoing debates over effective penal techniques, articulated the problem of what it perceived as a qualitative shift in the demographic of the prison population:

[T]o a very considerable extent the places once occupied by low, ignorant, depraved criminals, without homes, without respectable relatives and without position in society, are being taken by criminals of a higher order, by those who are educated.[19]

The question of whether this was an empirically accurate description of changes in the prison population is, for our theoretical purposes, not particularly important. To the extent that the Society *perceived, posited, and acted upon* such a change, it instantiated a theoretical shift in the production of prison education as both a "rehabilitative" and a disciplinary technology. Prior to the alleged entry of these "criminals of a higher order," the logic of prison education was, for the Society, a utilitarian form of individual rehabilitation—prison education was, on its face, generally intended to train illiterate white males how to read and write.

The proposed problem confronting the Pennsylvania prison regime near the turn of the nineteenth century entailed the following: what purpose would prison education serve when many of its clientele/prisoners (to this point, still predominantly white and male) were *already* literate and "educated"? The resolution of this supposed crisis was found in the amplification of the ideology of Christian penitence that lurked throughout the entire structure of the Pennsylvania prison regime to begin with: the Society, for the first time, explicitly articulated the ideal of "a higher *moral* education" as its main pedagogical purpose, clearly distinguishing the notion of "moral education" from that of "mental education." The object of correction for the Society, to foreshadow Foucault's genealogy in *Discipline and Punish*, was no longer the mind or the body, but the soul; not the prisoner's gesturing or movement, but rather the presumptive *moral* intent underlying his every move and thought. Hence, the regime of education-as-correction no longer addressed the inmate's *lack* of knowledge (or his ignorance), but rather intervened upon the *corruption* of that knowledge (his sinfulness). Prior to this articulation, the Society and its allies conceptualized prisoners as people who essentially needed to be taught how to function as productive law-abiding citizens, to obey the disciplines of labor and other compulsory routines. In 1892, however, the technique of rehabilitation was shifting toward something different: there was a marked anxiety among architects of the Pennsylvania prison regime that the "new breed" of prisoner was well aware of how to function as a productive law-abiding citizen, and fully equipped, materially and mentally, to do so, but that *he simply chose not to.*

These "criminals of a higher order" represented the corruption of the American white male entitlement to bodily mobility, property, and citizenship—the very premises of coherence for the relatively new social ordering of the United States. Thus, the Society reached consensus that the point was no longer to fill the prisoner's mind with knowledge, but rather to discipline the prisoner's *soul* so that his mind and body would follow. Such emerged the ideological structure of prison education and philanthropy at the turn of the century. Again from the 1892 issue of the *Journal of Prison Discipline:*

> Do we need higher mental education? Do we not rather need a better moral education? Is it mind alone that must be educated? Are we not to cultivate the better purposes of the heart? . . . "Knowledge is power" has often been quoted and repeated, but it may be *a power for evil as well as for good.* The very powers that might be useful may be prostituted to bad uses, and thus disgrace the very name of education.[20]

I invoke this moment in the genealogy of prison education to suggest that the current prison regime has drawn from an apparatus that collapses the difference between "correction" and "punishment." At the site of the prison school (as well as other prison philanthropic ventures) is the mandate of state violence to repress, expel, or liquidate those prisoners who might use the power of knowledge as a "power for evil," those captive students who, against the liberal humanist aims of prison philanthropy, threaten to "disgrace the very name of education." Thus does the prison school become an extension of the prison regime's technologies of coercion and bodily violence. More mundanely, the prison school stretches the *epistemological and intellectual limits* of the state's capacity to surveil and proctor its captives.

The philanthropic venture of the prison school composes a liberal humanist refrain that organically accompanies the harsher tones and choruses of the prison regime. In this vein, we should inquire: In the current context, what actions, gestures, or political articulations by imprisoned people might provoke the instant evaporation of the prison's alleged "school" into the punitive violence of those armed and deadly officers who lurk just outside the classroom door? How does the prison regime (in concert with its philanthropic extensions) attempt to (re)constitute its captive subjects by ruling, dominating, disciplining, and at times encouraging them through the apparatus of the prison school?

It is worth emphasizing that the Pennsylvania Prison Society was, at the close of the nineteenth century, proctoring a prison population that remained largely white and male; that is, its pedagogical forms were committed to the successful reassimilation of convicts into the trappings of the white man's civic "free world." The current prison regime, in juxtaposition, enmeshes and immobilizes a population that falls with enormity under the category of the racialized (and gendered) unassimilables of white civil society: while poor black, brown, and Native populations are imprisoned in proportions and at rates that suggest, for some, a mass-based social liquidation, whites remain a relatively decriminalized population. Poor black women, women of color, and undocumented brown and black migrants, moreover, constitute the fastest-growing demographics within the reaches of the prison industrial complex.[21]

Under this regime, the logical structure of prison education and prison philanthropy is irrevocably altered, echoing political scientist Mark Kann's delineation of the birth of the U.S. penitentiary in the crucible of white-supremacist conceptions of "manhood":

The founders' Enlightenment optimism about deterring crime and rehabilitating criminals had racial limits. Many white leaders considered black males as inherently unmanly because they lacked individual independence and control of their families. This putative absence of manhood precluded public officials from deterring and punishing black men's crimes by threatening to confiscate their manhood. *It also eliminated any incentive for rehabilitation, because black convicts had no manly freedom to redeem. Black convicts were often considered incorrigibles.*[22]

Kann's qualification of the early penitentiary as a white-supremacist racial formation invokes the *structural incorrigibility*—or principled immunity to "correction" and "rehabilitation," conventionally conceived—that particular prisoners represent to the prison regime, including prison officials and prison educators.

This brief meditation on the paradigmatic significance of the Pennsylvania Prison Society during the eighteenth and nineteenth centuries contextualizes a sustained critique of current forms of prison education as they are embedded in this lineage of white liberal Christian prison philanthropy. The Bush administration–sponsored "faith-based" social-service initiatives, for example, have reached into the realm of prison administration and institutionalized a carceral Christian fundamentalism. The evangelical "InnerChange Freedom Initiative" in Ellsworth, Kansas, provides pastor Don Raymond full access to a 140-person wing of a medium-security prison. Journalist Samantha M. Shapiro outlines the institutional everyday of this carceral philanthropic venture in her investigative article "Jails for Jesus":

> Raymond's wing, the faith-based InnerChange Freedom Initiative, is identical to the rest of the prison but feels like an entirely different place, an excessively well-lit church basement perhaps. Prisoners have arranged their desks, stacked with Bibles and workbooks, in a tidy circle. . . . Raymond keeps a steady flow of church volunteers, mentors, and teachers circulating throughout the wing. They don't behave toxicly, because the InnerChange staff doesn't treat them like they are murderers or rapists, even though some are. . . .
>
> Later that evening, after most prison staff have left, [Raymond] leads InnerChange prisoners across grounds off-limits to them because they are outside the view of security cameras. They set up amplifiers and a drum kit for an evening revival in the mess hall. With a backup band of prisoners chanting, "You are the air I breathe," Raymond preaches until the sun sets.[23]

Funded by the politically powerful right-wing fundamentalist Prison Fellowship Ministries, similar initiatives have spread throughout the country. As a particular technology of power, this evangelical incursion into the geographic organization and political pedagogy of the prison represents more than a religious fundamentalism—it is, in fact, an *institutional* fundamentalism, in the sense that the contemporary prison is fostering a symbolic and material return to its historical roots in the "Christian penitentiary."

> In the phylum of prison staff, Raymond defies classification. He is not a tight-lipped warden, vindictive guard, or burnt-out social worker. . . . In a building that hums with hostility, Raymond is attentive, unguarded, gentle. . . . [Raymond] often puts in 14-hour days working the cellblocks of the state's prisons, recruiting men to transfer to his wing. *In prisoners' marked bodies, averted eyes, and bristling rage, Raymond sees the debts and wounds, not of poverty or addiction, but of sin alone. He believes there is only one cure—Jesus Christ—and that it is a perfect and complete cure.*[24]

Following Kann's aforementioned historical schema, we must address the underlying conception of (racialized and gendered) *incorrigibility*—here, the "marked bodies" immune to the "cure" of Jesus Christ—as a durable, though dynamic, facet of prison philanthropy. I am asking, in other words, whether and how the institutional sanction of certain forms of prison philanthropy inscribe and endorse *new disciplinary and punitive consequences* for those racially gendered "political" incorrigibles—imprisoned radical intellectuals—who occupy and rearticulate these putatively philanthropic spaces, including prison classrooms and chapels, for the sake of catalyzing counter- or antisystemic political activities.

"They Were Shockingly Normal-Looking People": The Problem of Prison Education

The current regime of imprisonment has been characterized by sustained contestation over the form and content of institutionally sanctioned "rehabilitation" and schooling programs (including vocational, degree earning, and "life-skills" training courses). Since the 1960s, state and state-sanctioned attempts to absorb and institutionalize the political-intellectual work of imprisoned intellectuals and activists have largely occurred through the negotiation of the tentative and structurally ambivalent category of "prison education," which itself is often linked (through the pedagogy of "prison teachers") to paradigms of religious intervention and twelve-step personal therapy programs. Although philanthropic ventures at the site of the jail, prison, and penitentiary are not new—in fact, the conception and historical emergence of the U.S. penitentiary can and must be understood as a philanthropic project in and of itself—the movement to harness, rank, and rationalize the *political-intellectual production* of captive radical intellectuals, artists, scholars, and organizers is a distinctly contemporary phenomenon, obtaining sweeping momentum as a post-1970s response to the rebellions, "riots," and other forms of political crisis that occurred at the site of captivity.[25] Deriving from both liberal reformist efforts to "humanize" and "rehabilitate" ostensible "criminals" and the state's evolving interest in exerting a more structured, disciplinary surveillance over the reading and writing of imprisoned "students," state-sanctioned schooling programs have sometimes become places of severe political conflict between teachers and the taught.

Activists and prisoners' rights advocates have struggled to institute and/or preserve prison education programs, which often offer the only possibility of sustained literacy training, accredited GED (high school equivalency) conferral, or collective political-intellectual interaction within the legitimated routines of the prison. Additionally, the space of such classrooms is frequently transformed, appropriated, or rearticulated by imprisoned radical and protoradical intellectuals, who may galvanize new communities of solidarity or political kinship among and between course participants (including, at times, volunteer teachers, tutors, and teaching assistants from the free world). In fact, this very study would have been severely undermined without the difficult and risky work of building lines of communication and critical engagement within—and beyond—the space of the prison classroom. Prior to focusing on these delimited maneuvers of resistance and opposition, however, I am interested in elaborating the schematic outlines of a current genealogy of prison education (and, by extension, prison philanthropy) that examines its entanglement with—rather than its supposed distinction from—the larger punitive and violent regime of the post-1970s prison. An extended critique of the political logic of schooling at the site of imprisonment—the set of activities and power relations that are euphemistically termed "prison education"—offers a useful preface for conceptualizing the context and significance of radical prison praxis. Although this meditation is limited by both its conciseness and its narrow empirical scope, its applicability to other scenarios should become clear.

The political and structural symbiosis between prison educators, prison philanthropists, prison staff, and prison administrators involves the production of new institutional spaces (the "prison classroom") and intra-institutional relationships: hence, the prison school requires a particular vectoring of power between "teacher," correctional officer, and warden. This vectoring, in turn, folds into the production of new punitive discourses and technologies: a particular technology of power lurks just beyond the stated intent of corrections officials who approve or condone prison education programs, and underwrites the material domination that provides the condition of possibility for the humanistic goodwill of "prison educators" or "prison teachers." How, then, does the "philanthropy" of prison schooling articulate and operationalize a matrix of *intellectual* as well as *bodily* violence, repression, and immobilization?[26] The following critique offers a symptomatic reading of the alternately disingenuous and naive assertions of many prison educators and other prison philanthropists who suggest that the essential function of their prison programs is to enhance the intellectual enrichment and worldliness of their imprisoned "students."

One veteran prison teacher, who acceded to the directorship of the college extension program at one of the United States' oldest prisons, effusively embraces the concept of prison schooling as a pathway to rediscovering the humanity of the wretched. Her narration of the faceless, formless "inmate" as a figure of fear, crisis, and death preludes her own involvement as a volunteer service worker for the prison's expansion into the realm of the classroom's disciplinary liberalism. Interviewed in 2002

by Martha Escobar, a PhD student in ethnic studies, this prison educator recounts:

> When I heard about [the prison's college] program. . . . I was really scared
> to go in. I had a lot of very negative expectations, mostly about how the
> inmates would behave towards me. . . . When I walked in the very first
> time, I remember as we walked through the gates the thought went
> through my mind, "OK, I'm going to die now." . . . [M]y anxiety level just
> started to totally rise, and I just thought, I'm entering this space and I'm
> going to be trapped in there and these people are going to be really scary
> and violent, and this is, like, the end of my life![27]

In fact, the ambivalent incorporation of schooling programs as a marginal function of the contemporary prison regime can be understood in
direct correspondence with the racialized-gendered bodily anxiety that
is so excitedly voiced through this white prison educator's encounter with
the imago of her civil and social Other. The fear of death that projects
the black/brown captive as the aggressive negation of white civic life
resonates through the establishment of the carceral classroom as the site
of an aggressively (de)politicized reconciliation between free and unfree.

Escobar's critical study of this college extension program provides
a primary insight into the sentiment of banal liberal humanist transcendence that overwhelms recognition of abrupt differences in social mobility, political power, and epistemo-ontological condition. Escobar notes
that, according to this prison educator, most of the "inmates" who participate in the college program are *never released from prison*. This prison
educator also acknowledges that neither she nor her supervisors (correctional officers and administrators) have made any attempts to obtain
knowledge of the whereabouts of the program's former (or "graduating")
students, and reveals that there is no evidence that participation in the
program—or even successful completion of the college degree—can
assist in facilitating or accelerating a participant's release or parole. Yet
persistently, this teacher's ruminations reflect ambitions of the wildest
philanthropic promise. Openly dreaming of one day becoming the "dean"
of a "prison college program" so institutionally secure and prestigious as

to obtain the designation of a state university satellite campus, she recalls the moment in which she transcended her intense fear of "inmates":

> When we walked into the room, and there were guys already there . . . they were friendly and smiling and *shockingly normal-looking people*. It's like being on jury duty or something, and there's this large cross section of human beings, except everyone's wearing the same thing. *That's really the only difference.* (Ibid., emphasis added)

This scene of (mis)recognition exhibits what might be called the existential structure of "white bad faith": the prison educator's blinding rhetoric of sameness and normality—the flattening of difference between herself and the imprisoned "guys" to a matter of attire, as well as her exclamation of the prisoners' "shocking" (pheno)typicality—is inaugurated through a profound denial of the institutionalized violence underwriting and surrounding the moment and site of the encounter itself. Her white bad faith amputates the scene of her alleged communion with "this large cross section of human beings" from its pivotal basis in the condition of her Other's immobilization and capture: she must forget or disavow that the classroom is in the basement of a prison, literally shadowed by death row, and physically surrounded by armed guards who possess walking orders to obliterate or immobilize the "students" for the protection of her privileged (white) bodily integrity.

This prison educator's enunciations elaborate the constitutive discourse of the prison school (and related forms of prison philanthropy), extending the form and reach of the prison regime's resident technologies of power. She, in fact, openly affirms that she is an agent of the regime's functioning, expansion, and self-presentation:

> What some people would argue is that programs like this make the prison look good. It makes it sound like this is a "humane" prison. And that is a huge problem, and that's a huge danger. So it's not that I don't worry about my being co-opted. I am being co-opted. I do make the prison look good. But the conclusion that I've drawn is that the good we're doing outweighs the bad. (Ibid.)

The moral vision of the director's accomplished "good" is worth assessing as a point of departure for a larger critique. It is a matter of routine, it seems, for the prison educator to ultimately evoke an ethic of self-indulgence that edifies the spirit of philanthropy at the site of captivity.

Philanthropy, by most definitions, is understood as the voluntary and benevolent assumption of a perceived burden of caring or providing for those deemed less fortunate or disadvantaged. Crucially, the genesis and reproduction of most philanthropic ventures relies fully on the sustenance of the power arrangements, discursive categories, and material inequalities that fabricate their realms of possibility: philanthropy *requires* a "poor," "homeless," "untouchable," or otherwise abject constituency in order to fulfill its earthly objectives. Crucial to the specific political logic of the prison school, then, is the juxtaposition between the free teacher's (philanthropic) mobility and her or his immobilized unfree students. The program director reifies this structured opposition in her mind-numbing rendition of the prison educational enterprise as an exercise in egalitarianism and banal stereotype rebuttal:

> My perspective on this whole situation is . . . that the college program is like a window, or a little door, and we're basically propping this little thing open and allowing fresh air, and information and access to flow between these different worlds. . . . Not only are we educating these inmates, but at the end of the day . . . they are educating us. By our coming in and their talking to us, and their giving us the opportunity to work with them in the classroom, our worlds are sort of rocked. . . . *So my feeling is that the main political function of the program is this sort of mutually beneficial education. . . . We're educating people, and that seems incredibly precious to me, because of the impact that it has, above all else, on the way in which we imagine inmates.* (Ibid., emphasis added)

The program director's presumed civil society audience—the asserted "we" whose vaguely posited "imagination of inmates" requires rehabilitation—necessarily excludes the millions throughout United States and global civil society, overwhelmingly poor, black, brown, and indigenous, who experience the trauma and legacies of having close family members or loved ones forcibly dislocated from familiar and familial kinship networks and incarcerated under the auspices of generalized inaccessibility. For this carceral public—beyond and perhaps against the program director's civic "we"—the "imagination of the inmate" often entails living memories of a person whose absence is defined through a history of affective bonds and personal connection, intimate if not loving, and not by the image of subhuman, homicidal monstrosity projected by this prison educator's mind's eye.

Several imprisoned students in this college extension program challenged and demystified the punitive structure of the school during the months prior to Escobar's study. Led by Eddy Zheng and Viet Mike Ngo, recognized by a small community of "free-world" activists to be incisive political educators, public intellectuals, creative writers, and antiracist organizers, they offered the program director a well-reasoned, cogently argued proposal to introduce Asian American studies and ethnic studies courses into the prison's college curriculum. According to one journalist's investigation, "the document urged the college to add an ethnic studies elective and establish an academic advisory committee representing 'various cultural, political, and social viewpoints' to determine future electives."[28] I reproduce the text of the original proposal here (sans signatories), for the sake of transparency:

3-11-02

In an effort to expand academic freedom as well as promote the free and open exchange of ideas, opinions and viewpoints which are offered in classes through the . . . College Program, we propose the following:

The formation of an academic committee representing various cultural, political and social viewpoints to meet and confer and decide what elective courses are to be taught and by whom. We specifically oppose the manner in which these decisions are made and dictated by one person.

We are concerned that only one viewpoint is now represented in determining what classes are offered through the college program and what professors and TAs are deemed suitable for participation. We are concerned that professors and TAs are denied the right to teach classes based on arbitrary and capricious reasons.

The unilateral decisions now made concerning what may be taught and who may teach violate principles of free speech and academic freedom.

The Academic Committee should consist of professors and TAs with consideration given to input from inmates who participate in the program.

We emphasize the college program is for inmates and the cooption of the program by any individual to shape according to their vision and viewpoints, excluding other viewpoints denies our freedom of speech and expression.

We wish to exercise the freedom to exchange openly ideas and opinions that are constitutionally protected.

Further, we demand that our statutory rights to freedom of speech and association with volunteers given under Title 15, Section 3020 (copy attached) not be abridged.

As inmates, we are denied certain freedoms. We strongly object to the abridgment of the freedoms we do have, namely of speech and association by a volunteer in the college program.

In addition, we are aware that [the program director] is seeking corporate sponsorship for the college program.

We, as the inmates for whom this program has been established, strongly protest our exploitation by a corporate sponsor who may engage in business practices which we deem to be harmful to our well-being and our own religious, social and political beliefs. That [the director] would undertake to find corporate sponsorship for this program without consulting or seeking input from inmates and other professors displays the paternalistic, dictatorial and colonialistic attitudes that permeate her usurpation of this program.[29]

Invoking their geographic proximity to a pair of universities with thriving Asian American studies and ethnic studies programs/departments, and invoking the periodic presence of Asian American studies and ethnic studies undergraduate and graduate students as teaching assistants, tutors, and lecturers in the college program, this proposal's authors advocated a curriculum change that would bring the prison's college program into a closer resemblance to the course offerings of its free-world analogues. Reflecting on the context of the proposal's conception and circulation, Zheng writes:

> I have made numerous requests to the current college coordinator . . . to offer an Asian or Asian American history class. [Her responses] to my requests were ambiguous. She told me that it was a great idea to teach an Asian literature or history class. However, she claimed that she did not know anyone who could teach these classes. . . .
>
> I have acquired and forwarded to her the names of several history professors . . . who are teaching Asian American studies. . . . The refusal . . . to offer any courses on Asian or Asian American literature and history is only one manifestation of her abuse of power as the college coordinator. . . . Rather than promote education in areas that will promote greater understanding between cultures, races, and political philosophies, [she] has attempted to thwart the presentation of ideas and viewpoints that are contrary to her own. That type of behavior is unacceptable in any learning environment.[30]

Retrospectively, the program director referred to the introduction of Asian American studies and ethnic studies courses as inappropriate because of their "political content," and stridently objected to the proposal's "tone" as being unduly "confrontational" (Escobar, interview transcript). Zheng, Ngo, and their cohorts were subsequently reported to prison administrators for disciplinary action, and they were almost immediately placed in solitary confinement.[31] This expected outcome illustrates the *punitive* capacities of the penal reformist venture: Zheng and Ngo allege that it was the program director herself who reported them to prison officials, and Escobar's research supports the notion that the director at least facilitated and encouraged the disciplinary procedures. This episode is significant to the extent that it illuminates the structure and possibility of liberal prison philanthropy as a civil medium—and active agent—of manifest state violence:

[A]fter word [of the proposal] got out to the correctional staff, the men's cells were searched, correspondence with likeminded TAs was confiscated, and before the close of the semester, the prison had barred the four signatories [of the proposal] from all classes and extra-curricular programming, transferred two of them to other prisons, and placed three—all Asian Americans—in solitary confinement where they remain at print time.[32]

This episode radically recontextualizes the director's effusive ambition, articulated at the very time of this incident and with no apparent sense of irony, that "If we're going to run this program it should be like a high-quality liberal arts college *that we would want to send our kids to or that we would want to go to ourselves*" (Escobar, interview transcript).

The production of the prison classroom as an extension of the regime's overdetermining technologies of immobilization and punishment is contiguous with the prison regime's recent institutional history. Such figures as Zheng, Ngo, and others simultaneously recall and amplify the institutional anxieties enmeshing the mid-twentieth-century emergence of an activist and insurrectionist California "prisoner intelligentsia," a bloc whose formation was ostensibly facilitated by the spread of rehabilitation and prison education (or "bibliotherapy") programs during the prison's 1950s "treatment era." Eric Cummins, in his theoretically flawed but useful study *The Rise and Fall of California's Radical Prison Movement*, evaluates the role of this emergent bloc in appropriating and rearticulating the scope and substance of contemporaneous prison-reform discourse:

[W]hat became most important was not the failure of the California treatment-era prison to live up to its own reform ideals, or even its failure as social control, but how it allowed inmates to manipulate and subvert this reform rhetoric, ultimately spawning a radical prison movement in the Bay Area.[33]

Cummins's rhetoric is revealing for (1) its implicit valorization of repression ("social control") as the durable tenet of the rehabilitation-oriented prison, and (2) its pathologization of the "inmates'" attempts to appropriate institutional space and exert a political agency independent of the prison's "reform ideals." His evaluation resonates with the institutional vision of the aforementioned program director, who clearly understands that the material premise of her college program is the captivity of her students. The director's captive students are, at the site of the prison classroom, objects of philanthropic intervention, displaced from the legitimated capacity and nominal freedom to make even the most piecemeal political demands, much less to enunciate reasoned political dissent from her educational agenda. Al-Jaami, a graduate of the college program, offers a sobering assessment: "When I started [the college program] in '98, we were really at liberty to discuss the topics we wanted to discuss. . . . But in the back of my mind I knew at any given time a person could be called in or taken to account for any paper they wrote."[34] At the site of the prison school, philanthropic "reform" constructs the language, affect, and juridical-military structure of a profound institutional repression.

Following Al-Jaami's assessment, the production of prison education and other forms of prison philanthropy invokes and enforces the liquidation or prevention of potentially critical or counterhegemonic forms of prison praxis, including the most banal forms of political writing. The conflicted incorporation of prison education into the functioning of the regime has actually enabled the criminalization and liquidation of more organic political education networks among imprisoned activists and radical intellectuals. The program director's pained rationalizations spill forth a creeping sense of kinship with her students' captors:

> The more that we alarm the staff or the administration or seem like we can't be trusted or relied upon to uphold the rules of the institution, the more the pressure grows within the prison to shut us down. . . . [The prison staff and administration] do trust me increasingly, in the sense that they have come to understand that I just want this program to keep running. *And I'll basically do anything to keep the program running.* So in that sense, maybe I'm not quite one of them, but they have gotten used to me. (Escobar, interview transcript; emphasis added)

While this disclosure (confession?) reveals the primary relation that the tenuous institutionality of the prison school nurtures between teachers and captors, illuminating in particular the intimacy of cause—bodily integrity vis-à-vis the militarized enforcement of institutional stability—that coalesces their personal and professional interest, it nonetheless fails to engage the logic of the prison philanthropic project: a *management* approach to the problem of mass-based, racialized civil and social death, tethered to an accommodationist political liberalism that incessantly sacrifices lives for the sake of reproducing the management enterprise itself. In 2004, the program director appropriately voiced support for the California Department of Corrections' plan to expand San Quentin State Prison's death row, a $220-million project endorsed by Republican Governor Arnold Schwarzenegger "that would turn as many as 40 acres of prime waterfront property into pod-like cellblocks and other facilities." The new "Condemned Inmate Complex" would *more than double* the capacity of the existing death row (from six hundred to more than fourteen hundred), and would not only provide a boon to the California prison industry (employing hundreds of new prison guards and up to six hundred construction workers for the erection of the facility and its accompanying lethal, electrified fence), but would also accumulate a ripe new population of condemned students for the education program.[35]

Thus, to suggest that prison education and other philanthropic programs are *only* complicit in the reproduction of the prison regime as a discursive, political, and institutional apparatus is to obscure the proliferated technology of domination that is conceived through the symbiosis between the prison's resident guards/wardens/administrators and the accommodated presence of the teacher/tutor/volunteer/missionary/philanthropist. *I'll basically do anything to keep the program running.* One anonymous imprisoned artist, writing in the early 1970s, accurately and incisively addresses the despotism of the philanthropic dream inhabited by this prison educator and her ilk, casting political retort by way of verse:

> come then you cowards,
> and spare us not one dream of other

> life in other places in other times;
> spare us from your dangling prizes
> for successfully tangling the wailing
> strings of our rebel spirits into
> knots so we too shall never sing
> one original song nor breathe one
> innocent breath. spare us from your
> conniving charity and investments
> against the certain doom of your
> systems and mechanics and machines
> which exalt cowardice and hate to
> incredible fascist thrones . . .[36]

Elaborating the facetious invitation of this poem, titled "A Sunny Sole-dad Afternoon," we might ask whether the prison school amounts to a material and discursive gesture toward order and coherence, progress and promise, where, for the captive student, there is frequently none. The student in prison is never simply free to learn.

Conclusion: Toward a Conception of Radical Prison Praxis

The final section of this chapter departs from the disciplinary and immanently punitive categories of "prison writing" and "prison education" in order to offer a theoretical elaboration of radical "prison praxis." Contesting the repressive and punitive technologies of prison education and philanthropic ventures, as well as the production of prison writing as a domesticating and contained literary genre, imprisoned radical intellectuals exert pedagogical interventions of their own, within and against these contrived material-discursive spaces. Autonomous, and usually illicit prisoner-organized political education circles have often directly spurred acts of individual and collective defiance on the "inside" (hunger strikes, work stoppages, underground prisoner publications, rebellions), at times generating substantive solidarities with activists and supporters on the "outside." Juanita Díaz-Cotto writes of such underground Latino prison collectives in the 1970s:

> While Latino prisoner leaders sought to educate their Latino peers about the need to change prison conditions, the ultimate goal of much of their political education was to contribute to the formation of political cadres who, upon release, would struggle to change disparate power relations at all levels (e.g., local, national, international) beginning with their Latina(o) communities on the outside.[37]

What distinguishes imprisoned radical intellectuals from other radical and revolutionary "organic intellectuals," however, is that they do not construct their political identifications through participation in discrete social movements or political organizations. Rather, their individual formation as imprisoned political subjects occurs in a context of systematized repression that, in turn, forces them to map out new "cognitive territories" within which ways of knowing, feeling, and living the experience of unmediated state violence create new spaces and political trajectories of dissent, radicalism, and antisystemic possibility.

This far-reaching, decentered, and counterinstitutional knowledge production initiates an epistemological break with the hegemonic common sense of both civil society and the left, illuminating Ron Eyerman and Andrew Jamison's definition of contemporary social movements and collective identities:

> A social movement is not one organization or one particular special interest group. It is more like a cognitive territory, a new conceptual space that is filled by a dynamic interaction between different groups and organizations. . . . It is precisely in the creation, articulation, formulation of new thoughts and ideas—new knowledge—that a social movement defines itself in society.[38]

This theorization offers a crucial epistemological intervention, countering the tendency of many American sociologists to objectify the knowledge production of social movements through the empiricist categorizations of "resource mobilization theory." Eyerman and Jamison suggest a more situated and dynamic conception of "social movements as cognitive praxis":

In this empirical universe populated by most American sociologists, knowledge, and for many, even identity are seen as nonempirical objects and thus largely outside of the sociologist's area of competence. . . . [T]he problem, as we see it, is that knowledge becomes disembodied; it is relegated to a largely marginal, ephemeral or superstructural level of reality, and not to the centrality of movement identity formation where we contend it belongs.[39]

In the U.S. context, where the infrastructural paradigm that guides most current progressive social-change organizations is based on bureaucratic hierarchy, access to foundation patronage, and the "professionalization" of activists themselves, a productive rupturing of the empiricist conception of social movement formation may be in order. To consider, as do Eyerman and Jamison, that social movements are dynamic "processes in formation" implies a theorization of movements that de-emphasizes (though does not dismiss) the empirical "structures" that shape their public sustenance, and instead prioritizes the effectiveness of social movements in producing "forms of activity by which individuals create new kinds of social identities." This approach hedges against the *quantification* of a social movement's significance and effectiveness through measurement of its chronological "life" or evaluation of its ability to "penetrate" and reform hegemonic social or political institutions.

Most important, this paradigm creates a theoretical space for analysis of *radical* movement formations by distinguishing the historical and political trajectory of social movements from their empirically detectable manifestations in organizations, constituencies, and other forms of institutionalized presence. As Eyerman and Jamison argue,

the distinctiveness of social movements, indeed their very historical significance, lies in their impermanence, disorganization, transience, in short their motion. A movement moves, it can be seen as a kind of transition from one historical conjuncture to another; and, as such, its cognitive praxis can only be identified in formation. Once the ideas engendering movement become formalized either within the scientific community or in the established political culture, they have for all intents and purposes left the space of the movement behind.[40]

Few recent movements fit this definition better than the decentered, eclectic, and politically dynamic intellectual renaissance among radicals and revolutionaries incarcerated in U.S. prisons since the 1970s. My engagement with the praxis of imprisoned radical intellectuals pivots on this conception of the symbiosis between knowledge production and subject formation—processes immersed in the prison's regime of disarticulation and coercive incoherence—as *the* primary fields of political practice for this lineage of activists. For these socially and civically "disappeared" political subjects—many of whom have been imprisoned or serve additional prison time on the basis of their political convictions and social movement activities—the construction of a "cognitive praxis" happens in concert with their imprisoned contemporaries, and in resonance with their predecessors. This theoretical framing is not to romanticize, simplify, or totalize the intellectual work of imprisoned liberationists, but rather to suggest that their institutional and historical location within the U.S. prison grounds an *epistemological formation* that speaks directly out of the crisis and conflict that inevitably accompanies the repressive logic of "social order."

Radical prison praxis may thus be succinctly conceived as *the embodied theoretical practices that emerge from imprisoned liberationists' sustained and historical confrontations with, insurrection against, and dis- or rearticulations of the regimes of (legitimated and illicit) state violence inscribed and signified by the regime of the prison.* What marks this as a lineage of "radical" praxis is, first, that it is materially situated at the "base" of the state's punitive white-supremacist mode of production. This is to suggest that the production of prison space is a socially constitutive technology, to the extent that the essential fulcrum of American white supremacy is the power and institutional capacity to immobilize, neutralize, or eliminate targeted populations. Insurgencies that emerge from within this fulcrum, then, are substantively radical in their potential to disrupt or destroy a primary productive element of the existing social/carceral formation. Second, radical prison praxis articulates a critique of the United States that disarticulates its presumptive legitimacy and coherence as a juridical, military, social, and moral order.

Imprisoned radical intellectuals construct a critical political practice that cannot be easily situated within the disciplinary conventions of civil society or the academy. As Harlow contends, it is the very historical

Kijana Tashiri Askari (Harrison), untitled, 2003. Reprinted from the author's archives with permission.

condition and political substance of this cognitive antagonism that renders it outside the pale of institutional classification and pedagogy:

> Indeed, political prisoners are themselves not recognized as such by the United States judicial process. Formally defiant, by definition "subversive," "extremist," or more recently "terrorist," the literature of political detention stands as categorically and generically unassimilable within the systemic paradigms that regulate and guarantee the United States polity and its manifest social and cultural order.[41]

Although the subject of Harlow's discussion here involves the literary production of U.S. women political prisoners—those incarcerated as a direct result of their radical/revolutionary political convictions and activities—her thesis could easily be extended to the countless social prisoners and unrecognized political prisoners who have assumed a radical subjectivity behind bars, including people convicted through the state's historical criminalization of poverty, noncitizenship, and white-supremacist conceptions of racial deviance. The institutional unassimilability of imprisoned radical intellectuals is the best evidence of their effectiveness in building a collective cognitive praxis.

Suggesting that the genesis of a movement's cognitive praxis necessarily occurs in moments of departure from legitimated and institutionalized forms of political activity, social movement theorist Alberto Melucci illuminates the political possibility that fills spaces of intimacy and duress:

> By drawing on forms of action that relate to daily life and individual identity, contemporary movements detach themselves from the traditional model of political organization, and they increasingly distance themselves from political systems. They move in to occupy an intermediate space of social life where individual needs and the pressures of political innovation mesh.[42]

Melucci's reference to the politicization of daily life, when read vis-à-vis the intellectual practice of imprisoned radical intellectuals, speaks to an existence that is utterly alien to people living in the "free world." Whereas the technologies of "incarceration" increasingly configuring public space, civil society, and the polity have been noted by many scholars and activists—witness the increasingly militarized policing of public schools, spread of gated communities, and heightened electronic surveillance and civilian policing of public and private places—the qualitative difference of incarceration under conditions of punitive "imprisonment" surfaces repeatedly in the writing of imprisoned radical intellectuals.[43] None are more alienated from prevailing political systems than those who have been stripped of their civic status as citizen subjects, rendered out of the formal polity, and bodily subjected to the prison's regime of immobilization and disintegration. In this location, the intersection of Melucci's "individual needs" and "the pressures of political innovation" catalyzes a qualitatively different political practice, incommensurate with those forms of praxis readily recognized in the free world.

Confronted with the dilemma of how to foster substantive political, intellectual, and personal connections to political affiliates and loved ones in civil society, imprisoned radical intellectuals appropriate their conditions of confinement to generate a body of social thought that antagonizes and potentially disrupts the structuring logic of their own civic and social death. Amplifying the theoretical significance of this political work, Melucci conceptualizes the growth of social control outward (into spaces and institutions once relatively autonomous and private) and inward (influencing and constituting the subject formation of ordinary people) as generating new terrains and trajectories of praxis:

> Dimensions that were traditionally regarded as private (the body, sexuality, affective relations), or subjective (cognitive and emotional processes, motives, desires), or even biological (the structure of the brain, the genetic code, reproductive capacity) now undergo social control and manipulation. . . . Yet, these are precisely the areas where individuals and groups lay claim to their autonomy, where they conduct their search for identity by transforming them into a space where they reappropriate, self-realize, and construct the meaning of what they are and what they do. . . .

This potential is no longer exclusively based on material resources or on forms of social organization; to an increasing extent, it is based on the ability to produce information.[44]

The production of new and institutionally antagonistic languages, ideas, and symbols constitutes a basis for the activity of "new social movements" while simultaneously forming the conditions of possibility for the construction of new political and theoretical trajectories for radical counterhegemonic praxis. In this sense, Melucci's theoretical shift away from the empiricist fetishization of the quantifiable apparatuses and bureaucracies of social movement activity to "the ability to produce information" provides a mode of engagement with imprisoned radicals and revolutionaries who largely lack an infrastructural base and have little or no access to financial resources.

Melucci's theoretical problematic further elaborates the ongoing challenge confronting contemporary social movements. Decoupling the notion of "hegemony" from more conventional Marxist articulations, he posits a mobile, slippery conceptualization of social formation and "social order." Most important, his conceptualization of the social formation's "constitutive logic" displaces the classical Marxist notion of a "mode of production." Although Melucci's theorization is constrained by its focus on the nation-state as the unit of analysis and does not attempt to engage sites of underdevelopment, warfare, or state capture (unfreedom), it is useful for its elaboration of *knowledge production* as a malleable, material social movement practice:

> *The theoretical problem is . . . whether there are forms of conflict that engage the constitutive logic of a system.* The notion of mode of production is too closely associated with economic reductionism. Production cannot be restricted solely to the economic-material sphere; it embraces the entirety of social relationships and cultural orientations. *The problem is thus whether one can still talk of antagonist conflicts, that is, conflicts that involve the social relationships that produce the constitutive resource of complex systems: information.*[45]

Critically departing from Melucci's discussion, we might consider how the prison industrial complex and its requisite regime of violence compose crucial and convergent sites for the "constitutive logic" of the existing social system; that is, they construct a nexus for the production and sustenance of varieties of racialized domestic warfare, the articulation of the neoliberal state, and massive containment of surplused and racially criminalized populations. Melucci's central theoretical problem, the question of whether and how the "constitutive logic" of a social system may be engaged across different localities and institutional sites, sheds light on the potential *centrality* of imprisoned radical intellectuals as primary critics of (and insurrectionists against) the prison regime and the state/social formation of which it is an increasingly crucial or "constitutive" component.

CHAPTER 3

Radical Lineages:
George Jackson, Angela Davis,
and the Fascism Problematic

Down here we hear relaxed, matter-of-fact conversations centering around how best to kill all the nation's niggers and in what order. It's not the fact that they consider killing me that upsets. They've been "killing all the niggers" for nearly half a millennium now, but I am still alive. I might be the most resilient dead man in the universe. The upsetting thing is that they never take into consideration the fact that I am going to resist.

—George Jackson, *Soledad Brother* (1970)

Now even the façade of democracy is beginning to fall. . . . So what we have to do is talk about placing the courts on trial. Oppressed people must demonstrate in an organized fashion to the ruling class that we are prepared to use every means at our disposal to gain freedom and justice for our people.

—Angela Y. Davis, "Prison Interviews" (1971)

Origins and Departures:
Toward a Radical Intellectual Lineage

If one were to mark a political and theoretical point of departure for the genesis of radical prison praxis in this historical moment, the subversive texts generated by two of the most widely recognized imprisoned liberationists of the twentieth century would hold particular prominence. George Jackson and Angela Y. Davis offer a study in biographical contrasts, a fact not missed by a state-mediated popular discourse that obsessively and repeatedly rendered a racist and sexist narration of Davis as a middle-class black academic gone astray, somehow corrupted and brainwashed by her poor and working-class, pathologized and precriminalized black male cohorts within the black liberation struggle.[1] (This narrative juxtaposition was most frequently invoked through archetypical representations of Davis's relation to Jackson and her codefendant Ruchell Cinque Magee.)[2] Displacing the popular/state narrative that disparaged and degraded their personal-political solidarity, however, Jackson and Davis established a vibrant political legacy on which other imprisoned radical intellectuals would thrive: the simultaneity and strategic convergence of their intellectual production obtained significant political and cultural currency in a moment of severe social crisis.

Here I am less interested in describing the ways in which Jackson and Davis became iconic "celebrities" of the U.S. left (both in its hegemonically white "New Left" and more marginalized "black," "Third World," and "people of color" left variations) and revered figures for countless imprisoned people than in elaborating the ways these two radical activist intellectuals, working from the inside of the state's essential total institution, generated a body of political work that spurred crucial points of departure within the lineage of contemporary U.S. prison praxis. A close reading and sustained (re)theorization of Jackson's and Davis's political-intellectual production demonstrates how a radical genealogy of the prison regime is simultaneously and necessarily entangled in a genealogy of the radical praxis articulated by its captives, who are perhaps the most focused and incisive "students" of the prison regime's recent historical formation.

I am thus suggesting that George Jackson and Angela Davis should be conceptualized as *paradigmatic*, rather than superficially iconic, intellectual figures: on the one hand, Jackson and Davis constitute political-intellectual *origins* to the extent that both generated a coherent and accessible set of ideas, vernaculars, and political critiques that circulated widely within and beyond the space of the prison proper. On the other hand, both provided (and continue to provide) significant conceptual, theoretical, and practical points of *departure* for imprisoned and non-imprisoned political workers, who have subsequently inhabited while appropriating the legacies of their political labor.

As paradigmatic political figures, Jackson and Davis were fundamentally shaped by the influence and intervention of their imprisoned peers: in distinction from the numerous published American "prison narratives" that canonize themes of individual enlightenment and personal transcendence, the written works of these two imprisoned liberationists consistently reference critical dialogues, personal relationships, and (illicit) organizing projects *that occurred within the prison* as seminal influences on their political and social thought. The texts of Jackson and Davis must be understood as the organic production of their partnerships with imprisoned activists, some of whom remain imprisoned as of this writing (most notably Magee and Hugo "Yogi" Pinell, who, with Jackson, was pursued and punished by the state as one of the San Quentin Six).[3]

Davis, in the midst of her 1971 political incarceration and subsequent trial on charges of being an accomplice to murder, kidnapping, and conspiracy, argues from a condition of intimacy with her subject:

> The offense of the political prisoner is political boldness, the persistent challenging—legally or extra-legally—of fundamental social wrongs fostered and reinforced by the state. The political prisoner has opposed unjust laws and exploitative, racist social conditions in general, with the ultimate aim of transforming these laws and this society into an order harmonious with the material and spiritual needs and interests of the vast majority of its members. . . .
>
> Prisoners—especially Blacks, Chicanos and Puerto Ricans—are increasingly advancing the proposition that they are *political* prisoners. They contend that they are political prisoners in the sense that they are largely the victims of an oppressive politico-economic order, swiftly becoming conscious of the causes underlying their victimization.[4]

At the moment of this passage, Davis is speaking from a particular relation to bourgeois freedom—inside Marin County Jail—as a black professional intellectual criminalized and held in state captivity for her political work against racist state terror, affiliation with the Communist Party, and public critique of varieties of institutionalized white-supremacist violence. She has, in the moment inscribed here, been decisively dis-placed from her tenuous incorporation into the nominal institutionality of bourgeois freedom (as a university professor) and *suddenly rendered its subaltern*. Writing around the same time, Jackson, a veteran California social-turned-political prisoner and proficient prison organizer, asserts:

> The purpose of the chief repressive institutions within the totalitarian capitalist state is clearly to discourage and prohibit certain activity, and the prohibitions are aimed at very distinctly defined sectors of the class- and race-sensitized society. The ultimate expression of law is not order— it's prison. . . . Bourgeois law protects property relations and not social relationships. . . . The law and everything that interlocks with it was con-structed for poor, desperate people like me.[5]

Jackson's *Blood in My Eye* (1972), from which this quotation is drawn, remains a durable, and for some a classical, text in radical political philos-ophy and revolutionary urban guerrilla warfare. Its rigorous theoretical dismantling of American liberal-democratic mythologies and extended meditation on revolutionary armed struggle foregrounds Jackson's sta-tus as a racial and political incorrigible, infamous to prison authorities for his antiauthoritarianism, effectiveness as a prison political educator, and inspiration of insurgencies across places and historical moments. For Jackson, *radical freedom* was beyond the realm of possibility in a social formation that defined and reproduced the "free world" of civil society against the violent unfreedom that was at once the bane of his existence and the core of his political intellectual identity.

Jackson and Davis are important to this study because both figures have produced an extensive, widely circulated written and published record that constitutes a discrete and accessible body of political texts. In this sense, they are exceptional and even privileged examples of radical intel-lectual formation under conditions of state captivity. Yet, both focused on theoretical, conceptual, and practical issues that defined a broader problematic, influencing their contemporaries as well as subsequent generations of radical intellectuals. Both spoke to the problematic of a "fascist" United States of America, a conception that I will examine later as a theoretical and symbolic political gesture that fosters an epistemological break from the common sense of U.S. white supremacy and the regime of state violence on which it is premised. Rather than adhere to some conventional definition of fascism as a discrete governmental or nation-state form, Jackson (particularly in *Blood in My Eye*) and Davis (first in *If They Come in the Morning*, and again in later essays) implicate the historical trajectory of the U.S. prison regime as a way of identifying the broader relations of force that beset criminalized target populations in the post-1970s "law-and-order" era. The published work of these two radical intellectuals offers a useful mode of entry into the body of praxis generated by captive political workers who have since sustained and strengthened the political intellectual insurgency embodied by Jackson and Davis.

"A Revolutionary Literature":
George Jackson and Guerrilla Warfare

The life praxis of assassinated radical intellectual George Jackson embodies much of the political possibility expressed in the work of imprisoned revolutionaries and (proto)radicals. Incarcerated in 1960 at the age of eighteen for a seventy-dollar gas-station robbery, Jackson was given an "indeterminate sentence" of one year to life. A visceral hatred of confinement spurred Jackson's political and intellectual transformation within the prison. Shortly after notoriously racist correctional officer Opie G. Miller assassinated the widely respected black prison boxing champion, mentor, legal activist, and political organizer W. L. Nolen in January 1970 (as well as black prisoners Cleveland Edwards and Alvin Miller), Jackson, John Clutchette, and Fleeta Drumgo were accused of tossing a white prison guard over a the third-tier railing of Soledad Prison in retaliation.[6] Asked by a television interviewer whether he was involved in (or "guilty of") the act, Jackson responded in a manner befitting the circumstance:

> INTERVIEWER: Was the incident for which you are charged now, was it a revolutionary act on your part?

JACKSON: You asking me to confess to something?

INTERVIEWER: No, unless you want to. Did you kill the man?

JACKSON: Look, one of the most important elements of guerrilla warfare is to maintain secrecy. I've killed nobody until, you know, it's been proven. And they'll never be able to prove anything like that.[7]

Jackson, alongside many of his peers, conceptualized and theorized the prison as a militarized focal point, or high-intensity war zone, within a larger geography and temporality of liberationist struggle against a white-supremacist (and capitalist) state. For many imprisoned black and Third World people, the vindicating narrative (and political symbolism) of the white guard's demise amplified the conception of guerrilla warfare as a primary resistance (and potentially revolutionary) strategy that was be-fitting the condition of the captive freedom fighter. At the same time, an antiracist movement was emerging in the "free world" as a collective response to the apparent upsurge of racist brutality, state terror, and state-proctored murder of imprisoned black, indigenous, and Third World people in California prisons. The case of Drumgo, Clutchette, and Jack-son—who were known as the "Soledad Brothers"—became a center of gravity for this political mobilization, and Davis's involvement in the Soledad Brothers Defense Committee crucially shaped her political per-spectives on, and participation in, the radical antiprison and black liber-ation movements. She writes in her *Autobiography:*

This was the beginning of the story of George Jackson, John Clutchette and Fleeta Drumgo. There was no evidence that they had killed the guard. But there was evidence that George, John and Fleeta were "militants"; they had been talking with their fellow captives about the theory and practice of liberation. The prison bureaucracy was going to hold them symboli-cally responsible for the spontaneous rebellion enacted by the prisoners.[8]

As Jackson's political stature and reputation grew among imprisoned people within and beyond California, in part through the celebrated publication of *Soledad Brother: The Prison Letters of George Jackson* (1970), he became a liability to state authorities because of his effectiveness as an organizer and educator of fellow prisoners—in fact, one can still encounter a significant number of imprisoned, formerly imprisoned, and "free" people who attribute either Jackson's personal mentorship or his political influence as integral to their political formation.[9] His praxis essentially guaranteed that he would never see the light of the prison's outside—a fact that Jackson repeatedly acknowledged in both *Soledad Brother* and *Blood in My Eye*—and his brutal assassination by a prison sharpshooter on the grounds of San Quentin prison made a spectacle of his repression. It is a testament to the significance of Jackson's political legacy that a wall in the San Quentin prison "museum" contains a mounted trophy case of the high-powered rifle that killed him on August 21, 1971, along with a bronze plaque enshrining the name of the guard who pulled the trigger.[10] (Truly a spoil of carceral war.)

Jackson, in important ways, personified the political telos of Frantz Fanon's paradigmatic revolutionary intellectual. In Fanon's terms, Jackson's widely read *Soledad Brother* and (not as widely read, and far less celebrated) *Blood in My Eye* emerged as "literatures of combat," serving the dual capacities of theoretical texts and mobilizing tools. Close analysis of Jackson's knowledge production reveals congruence with the third, revolutionary phase of Fanon's developmental conception of the "native intellectual":

> Finally in the third phase, which is called the fighting phase, the native, after having tried to lose himself in the people and with the people, will on the contrary shake the people. Instead of according the people's lethargy an honored place in his esteem, he turns himself into an awakener of the people; hence comes a fighting literature, a revolutionary literature, and a national literature. During this phase a great many men and women who up till then would never have thought of producing a literary work, now that they find themselves in exceptional circumstances—in prison, with the *Maquis*, or on the eve of their execution—feel the need to speak to their nation, to compose the sentence which expresses the heart of the people, and to become the mouthpiece of a new reality in action.[11]

As Jackson found political agency in abrogating the image of the depersonalized, silent, debased prisoner, he recognized his own incarceration as the logical outcome of a collective plight. The destiny of human expendables, the surplus people left to languish under the advance of white-supremacist capital, was death, addiction, unemployment, and mass warehousing or social liquidation. Jackson consistently articulated the tortured severity of his relation to the world in these terms, rearticulating the essential American historical dialectic that rendered social antagonism, coercively structured deviance, and political disobedience the most generalized mode of existence for people like himself:

> [T]hat's the principal contradiction of monopoly capital's oppressive contract. The system produces outlaws. It also breeds contempt for the oppressed. Accrual of contempt is its fundamental survival technique. This leads to the excesses and *destroys any hope of peace* eventually being worked out between the two antagonistic classes, the haves and the have-nots. Coexistence is impossible, contempt breeds resistance, and resistance breeds brutality, the whole growing in spirals that must either end in the uneconomic destruction of the oppressed or the termination of oppression.[12]

This epistemology of resistance and insurgency structured Jackson's political praxis, and his refusal to indulge banal discourses of idealized, hopeful, and (racially) reconciliatory civic "peace" or "coexistence" was amplified by his pedagogical commitment to stating the grounds of that principled refusal. Rather, Jackson believed that the structural inevitability of state repression formed a condition of resistance for imprisoned and nonimprisoned (black and Third World) people alike. *Embracing* this condition was the pretext of an existential suicide—the necessary condition for declaring war on the dominant power:

> This monster—the monster they've engendered in me will return to torment its maker, from the grave, the pit, the profoundest pit. Hurl me into the next existence, the descent into hell won't turn me. I'll crawl back to dog his trail forever. They won't defeat my revenge, never, never. I'm part of a

righteous people who anger slowly, but rage undamned. . . . I'm going to charge them reparations in blood. . . . This is one nigger who is positively displeased. I'll never forgive, I'll never forget, and if I'm guilty of anything at all it's of not leaning on them hard enough. War without terms.[13]

For Jackson, the historic possibility of forging a utopian "new reality" could only emerge from the corporeal ashes of those who dared challenge the corporate racist state's programmatic killing of oppressed people in and outside the United States. It was this imagination of a righteous political death, a glorified "descent into hell," that allowed for the creative rearticulation of the imminent, violent consequences of repression.

In a single, creative, complex gesture, Jackson resists state violence *while embracing its inevitable fate.* He advocates a form of political rupture that defies the possibility of rehabilitation, a conception of social justice that requires the extermination of the existing order and its morphology. His analysis and anticipation of imminent bodily liquidation by the state reveal a fervent belief in the regenerative potential of a politics of refusal. Jackson's contempt for contrived "peace," his rejection of "rehabilitation" as a modality of assimilation into the fabric of an essentially oppressive and white-supremacist civil society, were inseparable from his declaration of war on the "haves," the precondition for his "reparations in blood":

> As you know, I'm in a unique political position. I have a very nearly closed future, and since I have always been inclined to get disturbed over organized injustice or terrorist practice against the innocents—wherever—I can now say just about what I want (I've always done just about that), without fear of self-exposure. I can only be executed once.[14]

Jackson's work merits extended theoretical attention because of his central role in producing a contemporary radical prison praxis as the catalyst figure for countless insurgencies and insurrections since his passing, as well as for the intellectual premises that his body of work establishes for a radical critique of—and living opposition to—current formations of American (domestic) warfare and state violence. The context of his assassination, moreover, compels an extended theoretical engagement with genocide as the logical, dynamic, and constantly reproduced condition of racism and white supremacy: the killing of Jackson profoundly signified the peculiar and fatal American relation to a particular formation of insurrectionist black political subjectivity, and indicated the trajectory of the white-supremacist carceral state as an essentially homicidal endeavor. Omer Bartov's theorization of "industrialized killing" is especially useful here.

Bartov's sociohistorical analysis of the Nazi Holocaust argues that the ideological edifice that generates and is generated by the project of mass killing, containment, and repression is embedded in the reproduction of modernist social formations. Although the technologies, strategies, and human objects of industrial killing change over time, Bartov contends that "this is the crux of the matter: . . . the occurrence of industrial killing [in the Nazi Holocaust], inevitably accompanied by its representation, made its recurrence all the more likely."[15] Bartov's conception of genocide as simultaneously a political, cultural, and military project facilitates a more nuanced understanding of relations of political force—in particular, formations of unmediated state and state-sanctioned bodily violence—as they develop within those formal liberal democracies that characterize the emergence of Western modernity.

Rather than assume a convenient historical distance from the most spectacular projects of mass containment and killing conducted or condoned by the state (as if "events" such as the Nazi Holocaust, Indian extermination in the Americas, and so forth were fundamentally disconnected from the historical conditions of one's own existence), Bartov's argument suggests that genocide may be understood as both the logical culmination of racism and the coldly rational constitutive logic of science, law, and the modern state's administrative bureaucracy:

It would seem that our main difficulty in confronting the Holocaust is due not only to the immense scale of the killing, nor even to the manner in

> which it was carried out, but also to the way in which it combined the most primitive human brutality, hatred, and prejudice, with the most modern achievements in science, technology, organization, and administration. It is not the brutal SS man with his truncheon whom we cannot comprehend. . . . It is the commander of a killing squad with a Ph.D. in law from a distinguished university in charge of organizing mass shootings of naked women and children whose figure frightens us.[16]

The profoundly constructive and socially reproductive role of industrialized killing in modern Western societies during the first half of the twentieth century stands in theoretical and structural continuity with the rise of what Gilmore has called the "industrialized punishment" of the current massive U.S. policing, criminal justice, and prison apparatuses.[17] As such, the political biography and carceral praxis of Angela Davis facilitates a critical engagement with Bartov's conceptualization of the linkage between modernity and genocide.

Ambivalent Victories:
Angela Y. Davis as Imprisoned Radical Intellectual

As one of the most widely recognized (former) political prisoners of the twentieth century, Angela Y. Davis has participated in the growth of antiprison and penal abolitionist activism as a radical teacher, activist, scholar, and organizer. In contrast to Jackson, it is Davis's survival of and nominal liberation from the political prison that sustains a living memory of counterhegemonic possibility among resistance workers of different kinds. At times railing against the popular cultural reflex that encases her in a "cult of personality" amenable to (white as well as "multicultural") liberal or progressive (hence antiradical and pro-state reformist) sensibilities, Davis argues in the introduction to her 1974 *Autobiography* that no such thing as an "individual"—in the sense of an autonomous, free-willed, fully self-conscious and self-actualizing political subject—can exist under the American condition of normalized state violence. Reflecting on her political imprisonment and eventual acquittal on criminal charges, Davis echoes Jackson in her critique of dominant narratives of rehabilitation and the vindicating telos of judicial procedure and "criminal justice":

> Many people unfortunately assumed that because my name and my case were so extensively publicized, the contest that unfolded during my incarceration and trial from 1970 to 1972 was one in which a single Black woman successfully fended off the repressive might of the state. Those of us with a history of active struggle against political repression understood of course, that while one of the protagonists in this battle was indeed the state, the other was not a single individual, but rather the collective power of the thousands and thousands of people opposed to racism and political repression. As a matter of fact, the underlying reasons for the extensive publicity accorded my trial had less to do with the sensationalist coverage of the prisoner uprising at the Marin County Courthouse than with the work of untold numbers of anonymous individuals who were moved to action, not so much by my particular predicament as by the cumulative work of the progressive movements of that period. Certainly the victory we won when I was acquitted of all charges can still be claimed today as a milestone in the work of grassroots movements.[18]

Davis was fired in 1970 by Governor Ronald Reagan from her professorship at the University of California, Los Angeles and, months later, framed and ruthlessly hunted by California and federal authorities for her alleged involvement in Jonathan Jackson's armed attempt to free black prisoners William Christmas, James McClain, and Ruchell Magee from the Marin County courthouse. Facing a fabricated charge of "kidnap for ransom, murder, and conspiracy" that was overtly constructed as a criminalization of her political activities and ideological convictions, Davis went underground and became the objective of an enormous mobilization of state intelligence and paramilitary force. The third woman in history to be placed on the FBI's "Ten Most Wanted" list, she eluded Reagan's informal 1970 death warrant for two months before her apprehension and arrest later that year.

Spurred by Reagan's pretrial call for her execution, a community of resistance emerged in response to Davis's symbolic and material status as a racially gendered object of state repression as well as her public image as a political subject performing active subversion of the state's white-supremacist terror. Although many appropriations of Davis's biography and image re-create what Joy James refers to as the "'rehabilitative' reconstruction of revolutionaries as icons" that "makes them more palatable to mainstream American culture,"[19] Davis's self-narrative (in the 1974 *Autobiography*) works contrary to this form of incorporation. Remembering the celebration of her juridical vindication, she insists on the necessity of generating political continuity between mass-based struggles to free prisoners of U.S. state repression:

> Yet in the echoes of our laughter and the frenzy of our dancing there was also caution. If we saw this moment of triumph as a conclusion and not as a point of departure, we would be ignoring all the others who remained draped in chains. We knew that to save their lives, we had to preserve and build upon the movement.
>
> This was the concern of the NUCFAD [National United Committee to Free Angela Davis and All Political Prisoners] staff meeting called by Charlene [Mitchell] on Monday evening, the very day after the acquittal. Fearing that some local committees might consider their mission accomplished, we decided to send out immediately a communiqué requesting that they all keep their operations alive. To ensure that this message filtered down to the masses, we decided that I would go on a speaking tour. While expressing our gratitude to the people who had joined the movement which achieved my freedom, I would appeal to them to stay with us as long as racism or political repression kept Ruchell [Magee], Fleeta [Drumgo], the Attica brothers or any other human being behind bars.[20]

While imprisoned, Davis consistently struggled for physical proximity with fellow captive women, from whom she was repeatedly segregated in the manner of many political prisoners (in part, it was feared that Davis's Communist and insurrectionist pathogen would be contagious).

Davis repeatedly experimented with practices of radical collectivity that could facilitate a broadly pitched political critique of imprisonment as a form of mass, white-supremacist, and misogynist immobilization. Recounting an early rally outside the New York House of Detention for Women, Davis—in concert with fellow inmates—deconstructs the enforced invisibility of the prison while offering a subtle critique of the cult of personality that had already begun to manifest around her individual case:

> On a cold Sunday afternoon a massive demonstration took place down on Greenwich Avenue. It was spearheaded by the bail fund coalition and the New York Committee to Free Angela Davis. So enthusiastic was the crowd that we [the prisoners] felt compelled to organize some kind of reciprocal display of strength. We got together in our corridor, deciding on the slogans we would shout and how to make them come out in unison—even though we were going to be spread down the corridor in different cells, screaming from different windows. I had never dreamed that such powerful feelings of pride and confidence could develop among the sisters in this jail.
>
> Chants thundered on the outside. . . . After a while we decided to try out our chants. . . . While the [outside] chants of "Free Angela" filled me with excitement, I was concerned that an overabundance of such chants might set me apart from the rest of my sisters. I shouted one by one the names of all the sisters on the floor participating in the demonstration. "Free Vernell! Free Helen! Free Amy! Free Joann! Free Laura! Free Minnie!" I was hoarse for the next week.[21]

The momentary dialogue between the jail and the street, shouted and chanted across the walls and bars of this urban women's detention center, communicates the context, conditions, and possibilities for collective political agency in the face of state capture. Although neither the women inside nor the protesters outside could pretend to harbor a determining, definitive, or discrete political agency, they found in their collaboration—verbal, performative, and defiant in its simultaneous politicization of the Greenwich Avenue sidewalk and the looming jail—

a form of resistance and radicalism that occupied a new political space while *reconstructing* it through acts of occupation and disruptive speech. Most important, this scene bespeaks a formation of political convergence and solidarity that denaturalizes the physical space and momentarily displaces the institutional integrity and authority of the prison, resulting in the fleeting formation of a strategic "trench" from which both imprisoned and free can sustain a Gramscian war of position, literally, *in concert with one another.*

The paradigmatic nature of the campaign around Angela Davis grows precisely from its inscription of a practical, philosophical, and allegorical "inside-outside" political collaboration that resulted in a nominal, exceptional, and thus all the more dramatic victory against state repression. Yet, the political-intellectual production emerging from Davis's actual political imprisonment—a body of praxis that, in its production and circulation, did not presume Davis's acquittal and nominal freedom, and instead anticipated the possibility of her long-term incarceration and, at worst, execution—provides a compelling, if often ignored and frequently decontextualized, theoretical template. I turn now to an examination of George Jackson and Angela Davis as critical theorists of the United States of America as a "fascist" social formation.

Fascism and "the Logical Conclusion": The Problematic of Radical Prison Praxis

A schematic discussion of conventional academic conceptions of fascism offers contextualizing clarity here. Political-science definitions derive largely from studies of populist, party-based mobilizations in Europe during the years between World War I and World War II. The analysis of European (and some Third World) state formations, which usually reference the Mussolini regime and Hitler's ascendant National Socialism as formative examples, generally consider fascism as a populist movement that is ideologically reactionary and totalitarian, and characterized by the large-scale incarceration or physical liquidation of targeted national populations. "Authentic" fascism—that is, fascism as a historically specific ruling/state order—is, in this sense, largely conceptualized in the academic literature as an ideological and governmental relic of the intervening years between the world wars, a logical derivative of the popular disenchantment and economic disorder created by post–World War I political-economic transformations across the European nation-states:

> World War I not only produced an unexpected and deep dislocation of the bourgeois-aristocratic class and status order and the identity of political units but also, reacting to these crises, an emergent group that perceived the war and these changes in an unique way.[22]

Political scientists and other academic theorists of fascism similarly consider its precipitation in right-wing party organizations and its reactionary, antidemocratic trajectory to be the fundamental expressions of its historical conditions of existence.

It is, nonetheless, rather difficult to find academic consensus on a nuanced theoretical understanding of fascist ideology, politics, state formation, or populist movement. The term "fascism" is in some instances so loosely used and abused in academic and popular rhetoric that it has become little more than a sloppy political pejorative referencing undifferentiated forms of state or protostate "extremism." Cold War (and some post–Cold War) appropriations of the word have even constructed socialist and communist movements as essentially "fascist" regimes, inscribing an American political exceptionalism that reifies its alleged liberal democracy as both unique and unassailable (see James Gregor's *Interpretations of Fascism* for a prime example).[23] Acknowledging the variety of conflicting and diverging interpretations of fascism among political theorists, Roger Griffin has argued that

> the phenomena denoted by the term "fascism" shrink, expand, and change in their historical and geopolitical extension according to which ideal type is applied. As a result, the definitional map being used for orientation within this field of studies can never be taken for granted: it has become an intrinsic part of the understanding of fascism itself.[24]

Although corporatism, a closed economy, the totalitarian state, and the total "subordination of the individual to the state" are broadly viewed as elements of the European historical experience with fascist ruling parties, comparative discussions yield a slightly different understanding of its political substance.[25] Focusing on the mobilizing vision of fascist cadres in various sites, Linz's essay "Some Notes toward a Comparative Study of Fascism in Sociological Historical Perspective" suggests that the most useful conception of fascism across social-historical contexts may be a negative one:

> Fascism is an anti-movement; it defines itself by the things against which it stands but this antithesis in the minds of the ideologists should lead to a new synthesis integrating elements from the political creeds they so violently attack. . . . The basic anti-dimensions of fascism can be summarized as follows: it is anti-Marxist, anti-communist, anti-proletarian, but also anti-liberal, anti-parliamentarian, and in a very special sense, anti-conservative, and anti-bourgeois. . . . Anti-individualism and anti-democratic authoritarianism and elitism are combined with a strong populist appeal.[26]

Linz's working definition is flexible enough to encompass mobilizations *against* existing hegemonies as well as actual state regimes, but it obscures the ways in which these "anti" characteristics may be ideologically embodied and institutionalized—dynamically, opportunistically, and selectively—by purportedly liberal democratic nation-states. Further, to privilege discrete and "original" sites of fascist politics, hegemony, and ideology (i.e., post–World War I Italy or Germany), as do most academic discussions, is to prematurely foreclose fascism's capacity to recompose in and through already-existing, that is, hegemonic, social formations. Therein lies one of the most significant political-intellectual interventions of contemporary radical prison praxis, hallmarked by the incisive articulations of George Jackson's polemical and theoretical writings, in critical conversation with Angela Davis's early political essays, speeches, and public correspondence.

Fanon writes of the mundane violence of colonialism as a condition of existence for the subaltern "native," who in turn manifests as a collective or deindividuated "object of violence" against which the ruling forces define and consolidate the colonial relation. In Fanon's world, public and excessive violence is not simply utilized by the hegemonic powers as a last resort to maintain their place in the social hierarchy, but is instead a normalized facet of their ruling process. *Violence is at once imminent and actual, spectacular and mundane.* Most important, Fanon illustrates the ways in which a profound though stunningly normal violence finds expression in overlapping and intersecting experiential dimensions and geographic sites. He writes, in *The Wretched of the Earth*:

> In the colonial countries . . . the policeman and the soldier, by their immediate presence and their frequent and direct action maintain contact with the native and advise him by means of rifle butts and napalm not to budge. It is obvious here that the agents of government speak the language of pure force. . . .
>
> The colonial world is a Manichean world. It is not enough for the settler to delimit physically, that is to say with the help of the army and the police force, the place of the native. As if to show the totalitarian character of colonial exploitation the settler paints the native as a sort of quintessence of evil. Native society is not simply described as a society lacking in values. It is not enough for the colonist to affirm that those values have disappeared from, or still better never existed in, the colonial world. The native is declared insensible to ethics; he represents not only the absence of values, but also the negation of values. . . .
>
> Colonial domination, because it is total and tends to oversimplify, very soon manages to disrupt in spectacular fashion the cultural life of a conquered people. This cultural obliteration is made possible by the negation of national reality, by new legal relations . . . by the banishment of the natives and their customs to outlying districts . . . by expropriation, and by the systematic enslaving of men and women.[27]

Fanon is naming a historical conjuncture wherein acute and socially disintegrating state and state-sanctioned violence and the banal everyday of the colonizer's occupation become temporally and experientially simultaneous, structurally convergent, and at times indistinguishable in the eyes of the native. The blunt normalcy of colonial violence is signified by everything from the policing of geographic boundaries between settler and native communities to the eradication of the indigenous society's collective historical subjectivity. Fanon thus directs attention to the specificity of particular social and historical locations for considering violence as a *primary and productive* (rather than merely repressive) articulation of particular social formations, an insight that Jackson and Davis amplify throughout their work.

Jackson's conceptualization of American fascism rejects the static and contradictory definitions of academic political science, disrupting Griffin's "definitional map" in exchange for a conceptual privileging of Fanon's "language of pure force." As a political manifesto and blueprint of revolutionary insurrection, *Blood in My Eye* gives theoretical primacy to the historical *trajectories* of the American social formation rather than fetishizing the tedium of its coordinated policies, political institutions, and military or juridical rituals. Jackson thus offers a diagnosis of the United States of America at precisely the moment of its epochal reformation through a symbiosis of massive state violence, white-supremacist terror, and liberal political and economic "reform":

> We will never have a complete definition of fascism, because it is in constant motion, showing a new face to fit any particular set of problems that arise to threaten the predominance of the traditionalist, capitalist ruling class. But if one were forced for the sake of clarity to define it in a word simple enough for all to understand, that word would be "reform." We can make our definition more precise by adding the word "economic." "Economic reform" comes very close to a working definition of fascist motive forces.
>
> Such a definition may serve to clarify things even though it leaves a great deal unexplained. Each economic reform that perpetuates ruling-class hegemony has to be disguised as a positive gain for the upthrusting masses. Disguise enters as a third stage of the emergence and development of the fascist state. The modern industrial fascist state has found it essential to disguise the opulence of its ruling-class leisure existence by providing

the lower classes with a mass consumer's flea market of its own. Reform (the closed economy) is only a new way for capitalism to protect and develop fascism![28]

Far from reducing American fascism to the bare realm of "reformist" capitalism, Jackson considers the comprehensive scope of U.S. social development to be overdetermined by the violence of the ruling classes, manifested in and through large-scale technologies of state repression. This argument posits a theoretical move beyond the Marxist telos of historical class struggle, and suggests that the advance of capital and the hegemony of the ruling classes are inseparable from the consolidation and expansion of the state's policing and punishing powers. Rather than being the mere expression or "superstructural" tool of the dominant classes, Jackson's advanced fascist state becomes *the condition of possibility* for the emerging (nominally liberal-democratic) economic, juridical, and "racial" order.

The authoritarian state is, in this sense, a complex and sophisticated phenomenon that does not exclusively rely on brute military repression or dictatorial leadership, and does not only articulate (as in most orthodox notions of fascism) through formal one-party rule. Rather, it is precisely the violent excesses of the corporate-state formation that provide its sustenance, a notion that contradicts the common Marxist assumption that the overindulgences of the ruling classes create the basis for their own deterioration and self-destruction:

Corporative ideals have reached their logical conclusion in the U.S. The new corporate state has fought its way through crisis after crisis, established its ruling elites in every important institution, formed its partnership with labor through its elites, erected the most massive network of protective agencies replete with spies, technical and animal, to be found in any police state in the world. The violence of the ruling class of this country in the long process of its trend toward authoritarianism and its last and highest state, fascism, cannot be rivaled in its excesses by any other nation on earth today or in history.[29]

Resonating with Fanon, this conception of fascism gives primacy to state violence as a productive dimension of capitalist hegemony, especially as it fosters a common condition of "law and order," state containment, and white-supremacist repression. Jackson is, in this sense, diagnosing a new era of mass-based civic and social death, founded on the penal liquidation of the black and Third World captive (collectively, in Jackson's terms, "slaves to property").

From her own location of political incarceration, Davis poses an analysis of the United States of America that similarly emphasizes the historical trajectory of owning class and state violence:

> Fascism is a process, its growth and development are cancerous in nature. While today, the threat of fascism may be primarily restricted to the use of the law-enforcement-judicial-penal apparatus to arrest the overt and latent revolutionary trends among nationally oppressed people, tomorrow it may attack the working class en masse and eventually even moderate democrats. . . .
>
> [T]he key to fascism is its ideological victory over the entire working class. Given the eruption of a severe economic crisis, the door to such an ideological victory can be opened by the active approval or passive toleration of racism.[30]

Distinguishing Davis's use of "fascism" here is its insistence on imminence rather than actuality. It is the "threat" of complete repression, the emerging historical possibility of totalitarian authority, and popular consent to its ascendancy that Davis constructs as the formative elements of a new, right-wing social order. Grounding her analysis of this social condition is a skillful attempt to render a seemingly unique and spectacular *personal* experience as the normalized expectation of an *institutional* logic. Here, the conventional analytic distinctions between biography and history, self and society, personal and political, are intentionally blurred in order to communicate the *embodiment* of abstract relations of force.

Davis, in a key instance, links the legitimized state institutions of policing and law—commonly understood as the militarized protection and judicial architecture of white civil society—to the direct and violent occupation of black communities, subjectivities, and experiences. Police and the law are, for Davis, the primary weaponry of a localized or domestic *warfare*:

> The announced function of the police, "to protect and serve the people," becomes the grotesque caricature of protecting and preserving the interests of our oppressors and serving us nothing but injustice. They are there to intimidate Blacks, to persuade us with their violence that we are powerless to alter the conditions of our lives. . . . They encircle the community with a shield of violence, too often forcing the natural aggression of the Black community inwards. Fanon's analysis of the role of colonial police is an appropriate description of the function of the police in America's ghettos.[31]

Here, the police-as-occupation constitutes a material and allegorical figure of repression, the personification of white-supremacist state violence, and the formidable bulwark against vindicating acts of resistance, defiance, and lawlessness by people whose conditions of poverty are enforced by bourgeois, white-supremacist jurisprudence. The dialectic between policing and racially pathologized criminality acquires a socially necessary character, producing the political and institutional context for the structural elimination and strategic militarized containment of civil society's (gendered racial/class) "deviants."

It is Davis's explicit politicization of this dialectic that constructs a dynamic conception of resistance and survival, radically questioning the political assumptions of an advanced, racialized capitalist hegemony that self-narrates as a transcendent liberal democracy:

> For Blacks, Chicanos, for all nationally oppressed people, the problem of opposing unjust laws and the social conditions which nourish their growth, has always had immediate practical implications. Our very survival has frequently been a direct function of our skill in forging effective channels of resistance. In resisting, we have sometimes been compelled to

openly violate those laws which directly or indirectly buttress our oppression. But even when containing our resistance within the orbit of legality, we have been labeled criminals and have been methodically persecuted by a racist legal apparatus.[32]

Framed by broader relations of force, this passage suggests a brand of political criminality that posits repression as a logical inevitability. Open violations of the law, committed in the name of principled resistance as well as biological survival, here encompass both the pilfered loaf of bread and the slaughtered police officer: within the conditions of white-supremacist domestic warfare, insurrection and survival frequently become indistinguishable. Further, under the proctorship of a white-supremacist judiciary, the category of "criminality" itself takes on a monolithic character as the opening gambit in the mass-based immobilization, bodily disintegration, and (political) repression of the colony's designated "natives." Although Davis does not name this circumstance as a rearticulated fascism per se—in fact, she explicitly states her theoretical disagreement with Jackson on this point, instead elaborating a conception of the early 1970s United States as a pre- or protofascist social formation—her invoking of criminality as the discursive political site at which social control, latent insurgency, and relations of force converge is instructive.

Writing from the location of the political prison in *If They Come in the Morning*, Davis attempts to rearticulate the political rhetoric of the international campaign for her release. Contesting the implied insularity of the "political prisoner" label, she suggests the efficacy of constituting the emergent movement around a radically generalized conception of white-supremacist state violence:

To move to another level on which the fight around political prisoners must be waged, we must also link up the circumstances leading to the frameup of so many revolutionaries with the generalized genocidal attack on our people and thereby, relate the issue of the political prisoner to the concrete needs and interests of Black people.

... [A] major focus of the struggle around political prisoners ought to be offensive rather than defensive in character and should consist in placing the bankrupt judicial system and its appendages, the jails and prisons, on trial. *We must lay bare the whole system and concretely associate the movement to liberate political prisoners with the grassroots movements that are exploding in the dungeons all over this country.*[33]

The manner in which the struggle around political prisoners (potentially) condenses as resistance to the totality of the "system" is crucial for both Davis and Jackson, to the extent that it reveals the centrality of state violence and white-supremacist terror to the U.S. social formation. Radical and militant (antifascist) struggle materializes as a collective confrontation with the twinned logics of mass-based immobilization and bodily disintegration, focusing on the emergent nexus of the policing-prison-juridical regimes and the technologies of power that they circulate.

In critical dialogue, Jackson and Davis focus their praxis on present conditions for the construction of a radical and socially transformative (revolutionary) historical bloc, a people's movement that partly emerges from the prison's inside and irrevocably alters the everyday of the nominal free world. Harlow speaks to the transformative potential of such a political vision when she considers the theoretical and political impact exerted by women political prisoners on revolutionary/resistance movements outside the prison:

For criminals, female as well as male, whether convicted of petty theft, prostitution, murder, or simply social deviance, the experience of prison can, at given times and in particular circumstances, provide the historically necessary conjunctural premises for reframing the stories of their individual "crimes" as constituted by a sociopolitical system of exploitation and political disenfranchisement. Political prisoners in turn, when confined together with "criminals," must often reformulate their preconceived ideological constructs of "the people" and the entailed interaction between a vanguard party and its claimed popular constituencies.[34]

Davis's and Jackson's political discourse inverted the circumstances of individual state confinement (a condition of hypersurveillance) to speak eloquently to the relations of force and structural excesses of a white-supremacist hegemony in crisis, thus reversing the individualization of the prison/captive spectacle and "looking back" through and against the state's surveilling lens. In so doing, they conceived a political problematic—framed by a rigorously elaborated and dynamic debate over the presence and meaning of U.S. "fascism"—that has deeply influenced radicalism inside and across the walls of the U.S. gulag.

The "Question" of Radical Prison Praxis:
A Point of Departure

I conceptualize this theoretical departure in the form of a question: how might our political understanding of the United States be altered or dismantled if we were to conceptualize fascism as the *restoration* of a liberal hegemony, a *way out* of crisis, rather than as the *symptom* of crisis or the *breakdown* of "democracy" and "civil society"? On the one hand, this question requires a departure from the essentialist privileging of European sites as the paradigmatic examples of "authentic" fascism, totalitarian police states, and authoritarian regimes. On the other hand, it opens a mode of inquiry that facilitates a radical antagonism to the very premises of state power and "neoliberal" hegemony. This antagonism crystallizes on several different levels.

As a theoretical gesture, this question fosters a cognitive rupture from the common sense of liberal democracy by suggesting the centrality of repression, official violence, and white supremacy to the restoration and reproduction of "social order," or Goldwaterist "law and order." The common sense of the late-capitalist, white-supremacist, nominally liberal-democratic American "Homeland," sustained as it is by persistent declarations of formal equality under the law, persistently sheds the genocidal cloak of earlier eras of conquest and enslavement through convenient exercises in selective forgetting and the constant rewriting of patriotic master narratives.[35] Here, the telos of progress necessitates sanitized portrayals of genocide that render the violence of such things as Indian killing, land conquest, enslavement, and imperial invasion the tragic excess of an otherwise progressive developmental national narrative (or bildungsroman). Contemporary "multicultural" literatures (including some "prison writing") accomplish precisely this narrative form through liberal critiques of racism and historical unfairness that reach for resolution with the permanent, open-ended hope of the nation's American Dream.[36]

The question of fascism-as-liberalism ruptures this narrative by centering genocide as the condition of possibility for the nation's formation as well as its ongoing social reproduction. Ward Churchill's critique of genocide discourse provides a more precise definition for this frequently abused term: "[G]enocide means the destruction, entirely or in part, of any racial, ethnic, national, religious, cultural, linguistic, political, economic, gender or other human group, however such groups may be defined by the perpetrator."[37] Churchill explains that the three primary forms of genocide involve physical killing, direct or indirect prevention of births, and cultural destruction. Recall, in this context, that George Jackson's polemic in *Blood in My Eye* was premised less on an indictment of historical (past) genocides than it was on a fundamental critique of liberal (economic) reform as a restructuring of relations of unmediated violence between the plutocratic ruling classes and the "upthrusting masses." Angela Davis's identification of inchoate revolt with mundane black and brown disobedience to the law speaks similarly to the structural embeddedness of socialized killing within a white-supremacist capitalist formation. Such theoretical maneuvers drastically undermine hegemonic nationalist narratives: mass killing, slavery, human containment, and other forms of coercion become dynamic objects of analysis and intervention as they are understood to be the components necessary to the (past) making and (current) remaking of nationhood and civil society.

This problematic cannot recognize a narrative of "America," nor can it imagine a "national" future, apart from the reproduction and "reform" of the United States' fundamental technologies of existence:

namely, its racialized and gendered productions of genocide, (mass-based) captivity, and other strategically deployed militarizations that generate multiple scales of bodily disintegration and subjective disarticulation, premised on black chattel/penal enslavement (social death) and indigenous genocide (biological and cultural death).[38] This theoretical departure radically renarrates the United States' conditions of existence as it draws sustenance from the fatal dialectics of life/death, freedom/unfreedom, subjectivity/dehumanization that inspire and structure (rather than inhibit or derail) social reproduction and national formation.

As a symbolic political intervention, this problematic also compels a rearticulation of the very notion of a radical praxis that is specific to the historical moment: what, in other words, is "radical" within the historical circumstances of this moment? How does one distinguish between liberalism, progressivism, and radicalism at a moment when remnants of older ideologies and strategies have become elemental to the symbolic universe and institutional reproduction of hegemonic or dominant political structures and discourses (take, for example, the veritable institutionalization of popular college and university courses on the "civil rights movement" and progressive "social movements")? The reintroduction of a conception of massive state and state-sanctioned violence as a *productive* (as opposed to merely repressive or punitive) factor within the equation of a nominal liberal-democratic hegemony suggests the necessity for new forms of praxis that strategically dramatize, subvert, or stretch thin the logic and capacities of a Jackson's durable and flexible "liberal" American fascism.

Finally, by rendering "fascism" as the primary operative theoretical term, this problematic refocuses attention on the regimes of state and state-sanctioned terror and violence that inhabit different spaces, afflict different communities and bodies, and condition social relations within allegedly liberal-democratic societies. This retheorized conception of fascism illuminates and elaborates a complex of forces that do not necessarily find static, permanent, or even altogether coherent institutional centers in state "institutions" such as police, legislature, prison, or school. Instead, massive state and state-sanctioned violence—as a fundamental expression of a social rule that is hegemonic or dominant—becomes a constantly produced and reproduced practice of relationality between different social, state, and cultural regimes, which themselves constitute multiple "centers of gravity" for the articulation and expansion of fascism as a broadly operative technology of domination.

In this sense, specific civic, political, and institutional sites—for example, the "neighborhood," "classroom," "military base," or "prison"—may temporarily cohere as strategic or tactical locations for the production and exercise of coercive state force: to simply identify the sites wherein state violence inscribes, defines, and produces itself is not especially difficult, especially in the midst of proliferating forms of state violence and domestic militarization/warfare. The central challenge of the reconceived fascism problematic, however, is to elaborate and analyze, with historical specificity, how different social, political, and institutional sites of hegemonic or dominant power such as the university, legislature, police station, and corporate boardroom—hegemony's multiple centers of gravity—exert a force on those sites, such as the prison, at which state violence is repeatedly and ritualistically performed. In short, how does the production of civil society's structure of "common sense" and "consent" (the theoretical bulwark of the Gramscian conception of hegemony) affect, transform, and enhance the proliferation of domestic war, in dialogue with Fanon's "language of pure force"? Finally, how does the ideological glue of popular/national consensus create and reproduce strategic relations of direct state and state-sanctioned domination and subjection—mediated through regimes of mass-based immobilization and bodily disintegration—which in turn perform on targeted bodies, communities, and borders that are both momentarily (as in the Japanese-American internment of World War II) and permanently (as in the categorical subjection of black subjectivity under both enslavement and post-Emancipation racial regimes) constructed as *outside* the domain of Gramscian "consent"?[39] The dynamic, strategic relations of violence condensing within the American social formation at different times and in different places are neither accidental nor excessive, and the challenge of this reconceptualized fascism problematic is to comprehend the socially reproductive capacities of coercive technologies and (proto)genocidal practice within the current order.

Conclusion: "Eating Shit,"
Twenty-seven Years and Beyond

It was precisely Angela Davis and George Jackson's location within the (political) prison's ritual circuits of bodily and psychic violence that made their sustained analysis of U.S. fascism so unavoidable. In recent years, Davis has elaborated the structure "invisibility" that enmeshes the emergence of the prison regime, invoking comparisons to the practice of mass "disappearance" (desaparecido) made infamous by U.S.-sponsored state terror in Argentina, Guatemala, the Philippines, Colombia, El Salvador, and elsewhere. Evaluating the convergence of popular, juridical, and legislative discourse in the production of the new prison hegemony, Davis argues for a reevaluation of the relation between coercion and consent, or violence and common sense, suggesting that the very coherence of U.S. civil society is increasingly structured by a mass-based, racialized social liquidation:

> The dangerous and indeed fascistic trend toward progressively greater numbers of hidden, incarcerated human populations is itself rendered invisible. All that matters is the elimination of crime—and you get rid of crime by getting rid of people who, according to the prevailing racial common sense, are the most likely people to whom criminal acts will be attributed.[40]

Davis demystifies the emergence of the prison regime and its institutional abstraction, the "prison industrial complex" by tracing its historical trajectory. Articulating with the racialized and gendered "class control" of the policing, juridical, and imprisonment apparatuses, a normalized structure of low-intensity social extermination and mass-based bodily immobilization has become central to the United States of America as a white-supremacist social formation.

Some twenty-five years after Jackson's assassination and Davis's acquittal, Mumia Abu-Jamal, in *Live from Death Row*, states that "prisons are where America's jobs programs, housing programs, and social control programs merge into a dark whole; and where those already outside of the game can be exploited and utilized to keep the game going."[41] Political prisoner Laura Whitehorn (released in 1999) similarly emphasizes the function of the prison as an expansive technology of human eradication and political repression. Her theorizing resonates with Davis's statement that "prisons do not disappear problems, they disappear human beings."[42]

> Prisons are implements of genocide and counter-insurgency. . . . On the one hand, the u.s. [*sic*] imprisons vast numbers of young Third World people, so that their lives are destroyed and the lives of their communities disrupted. On the other hand, the government metes out harsh punishments to those political activists and revolutionaries who dare to build militant resistance to injustice. *Together, these strategies produce an effective program of genocide*. . . . The massive incarceration of Black, Latino, and Native American women and men is meant to unravel the fabric of those communities, while the disproportionate sentences and conditions of confinement of political prisoners and POW's is intended not only to destroy the political organizations that exist, but also to frighten others from attempting resistance.[43]

In light of the insidious evolution of what Jackson, Davis, Whitehorn, and Abu-Jamal sequentially reference as fascism, genocide, and "the game," the political logic of the prison regime's genesis and proliferation sits comfortably within the United States' profound lineage of state terror, mass killing, and programmatic social displacement and disappearance. This resonates with black political scientist Manning Marable's prophetic discussion of oncoming large-scale, state-orchestrated black/brown premature death in *How Capitalism Underdeveloped Black America* (1983). Reflecting on the significance of the spectacular wave of antiblack, homicidal violence waged by white civil society (and generally sanctioned by the state) during the early 1980s, Marable contends:

[T]he existence of random violence against Blacks and civil terrorism is no accidental phenomenon. It is a necessary element in the establishment of any future authoritarian or rightwing government. . . .

[T]he direction of America's political economy and social hierarchy is veering toward a kind of subtle apocalypse which promises to obliterate the lowest stratum of the Black and Latino poor. . . . The genocidal logic of the situation could demand, in the not too distant future, the rejection of the ghetto's right to survival in the new capitalist order. Without gas chambers or pogroms, the dark ghetto's economic and social institutions might be destroyed, and *many of its residents would simply cease to exist.*[44]

The dreadful nature of this passage is appropriate to the condition from which it speaks. At the time of Marable's writing, the crisis of white civil society and capitalist reformation was in the early stages of resolving a host of socioeconomic crises through the drastic expansion of the prison regime as a primary means through which to address, contrive, rearticulate, or eliminate figures of social crisis. By constituting the prison as a place where increasingly massive numbers of Marable's "lowest stratum" would *"simply cease to exist,"* the 1980s saw an astronomical expansion of the prison regime's operating capacities: the total prison and jail population grew by 500 percent from 1980 to 1992, and has almost tripled since.[45] Under this police–prison hegemony, mass repression and human containment become ironically and perversely linked to the accompanying logic of profit, accumulation, expansion, and strategic annihilation that guide advanced global capital. As racially pathologized and historically disfranchised communities are effectively surplused by capital's logic of exploitation and labor expropriation, they cease to be relevant as either exploited workers or consumer markets. Rather, these racially criminalized populations are incorporated into a strategic commodity relation that invokes the history of U.S. racial chattel slavery (see chapter 6). Political prisoner Linda Evans, with activist Eve Goldberg, has thus argued, "Like any industry, the prison economy needs raw materials. In this case the raw materials are prisoners."[46]

It seems that the emergence of the prison regime has rearticulated the common sense of "law and order" (now, "Homeland Security") in the United States in terms similar to those foreshadowed by Jackson and Davis at the moment of the prison's eruption into a tool for resolving social crisis.[47] As actual and socially marked prisoners-in-waiting disappear from civil society, a growing population of civically and socially dead people are funneled into a structure of absence from the normative intercourses of the "free world."[48]

The U.S. social formation constantly draws and redraws its own internal (domestic) geographies of human immobilization and (physical, biological, and cultural) genocide, at which the exercise of state and state-sanctioned violence becomes the condition of social reproduction. It is at these sites that these unmediated relations of force crystallize within the drama of popular consent. The late black liberationist and political prisoner Albert Nuh Washington, who died of liver cancer in 2000 at Coxsackie Correctional Facility (New York), speaks to the logic of this symbiosis as he reflects on three decades of incarceration:

> Assata Shakur once asked me what I would rather do, eat a nasty bowl of Nixon's shit or do twenty years in prison. My reply was twenty years. She said she would eat the shit because every day in prison you eat shit and it is better to eat it all at once. For 27 years I have eaten shit each day, which brings its own indignities, being under the physical control of another who is basically hostile to you.[49]

It would be inappropriate and trivializing to conclude this chapter with either prescriptive ruminations or utopian visions of resistance that elide the social truth of terror and survival mediated by imprisoned radical intellectuals. Instead, I look to Washington's allegory as a point of departure for the following chapters, which further elaborate a genealogy of the prison regime's entangled logics of terror and death.

CHAPTER 4

Articulating War(s):
Punitive Incarceration and State Terror
amid "No Middle Ground"

> Doing time does this thing to you. But, of course, you don't do
> time. You do without it. Or rather, time does you. Time is a
> cannibal that devours the flesh of your years day by day, bite by
> bite. And as he finishes the last morsel, with the juices of your life
> running down his bloody chin, he smiles wickedly, belches with
> satisfaction, and hisses out in ghostly tones, *"Slur the buds!"*

> —Leonard Peltier, *Prison Writings: My Life Is My Sun*
> *Dance* (1999)

The Statecraft of Punishment and Terror

The prison regime and its correspondent abstraction, the prison industrial complex, simultaneously mystify and rationalize mass-based, state-proctored human immobilization as a way of life. "It is, we shrug, simply the way of the world."[1] Echoing and resituating William Appleman Williams's meditation on the incarnations of empire within the American everyday, the genesis of a punitive carceral formation since the 1970s has similarly (re)constructed "a conception of the world and how it works, and a strategy for acting upon that outlook on a routine basis as well as in times of crisis."[2] The multiple technologies of power inaugurated and spun outward by the prison regime enable the material practice of state power, inscribing its self-narrated dominion, authority, and (moral) legitimacy to coerce: *the ascendancy and authority of the state must be enacted, ritualized, and signified through the prison regime—and massively performed on target bodies—to become "real."* Visceral violence is the core value of this statecraft, as state power enunciates dominion over (and ownership of) targeted human bodies as its baseline measure of peace, security, and social order. This chapter elaborates two of the structuring contradictions and political antagonisms that compose the (re)production of the prison regime through its variable and sometimes troubled articulations of this core value.

First, I am concerned with the production of *punitive carcerality* as both a discursive and bodily convergence between technologies of punishment (the punitive) on the one hand, and bodily capture or institutionalized immobilization on the other (the carceral). Imprisoned activist Walter James, writing from the Security Housing Unit at Tehachapi State Prison (California), offers a concise and incisive explication of punitive carcerality as a logic of spirit-killing or dehumanization:

> I won't dwell too much on the details of the cages. The essence is not in the details and distracts from the frontal assault on our humanity that this really is. California has finally abandoned any pretense that we are considered anything more than animals to put in kennels. . . . California is going to great lengths to crush our spirits.[3]

As a state and cultural formation, punitive carcerality shapes both the popular intelligibility and the self-narration of the state's otherwise abstracted or inaccessible dominion of power, legitimacy, and authority. Yet, this penal statecraft thrives from its own endemic insufficiency and structured institutional failure to evaporate or fully neutralize dissent, resistance, and incorrigibility among its captive subjects—in fact, the prison regime *requires and produces* such institutional crisis as a premise for its constant revision and reinvention of technologies of domination. James's communiqué from Tehachapi manifests the prison regime's interpellation if not production of radically politicized captive subjects, including organic critics of its modalities of rule.

Second, this chapter addresses the specificity of *state terror* as a broadly proliferated technology of domination that is organic to the prison regime's dominion. I am interested in theorizing the extension and distension of state violence through its production of a rigorously constricted space of human subjection, wherein a primary fulcrum of power becomes the regimentation of a determinant and interpellating terror, that is, an acutely coercive structure of feeling and experience. My attempt at generating a revised, working conceptualization of state terror partly responds to Annamarie Oliverio's critique of exceptionalist definitions of the term:

> Even genocide, as it has been practiced by many states, historically and comparatively, is often referred to as a "reign of terror," or "state terror," conceptually distinct from "terrorism" or defined as a subtype of terrorism. Such a definition of "state terror" obfuscates the practices of the state, emphasizing only the state's more obvious repressive actions such as in prisons and illegal "law" enforcement. Other actions in hierarchical organizations re-presenting the state's repressive practices such as armies, hospitals, schools, or the media are not included in standard definitions of state terror.[4]

My conception of "state terror," while focused on what Oliverio would consider the self-evident institutional and geographic site of the prison, departs from conventional definitions by focusing on the production of terror as part of the prison's—and state's—regimes of the "everyday," or what I invoke above as the construction of an American "way of life." Following radical attorney and legal theorist Jill Soffiyah Elijah's historical overview of the institutional genesis of contemporary "conditions of confinement," I consider state terror as an essential and formative, rather than excessive or exceptional, facet of statecraft and social formation. Soffiyah writes:

> In the early sixties, a meeting of social scientists and prison wardens was convened by the then director of the Federal Bureau of Prisons, James V. Bennett. The main speaker for the convention was Dr. Edward Schein, a social scientist. He presented his theories on brainwashing and the application of such techniques to modify behavior within the prison population. Amongst the many techniques suggested by Dr. Schein were the following:

1. physically remove the prisoner to an area sufficiently isolated in order to break or seriously weaken close emotional ties;

2. segregate all natural leaders;

3. prohibit group activities that do not fit brainwashing objectives;

4. systematic withholding of mail;

5. create a feeling amongst the isolated group of prisoners that they have been abandoned by and totally isolated from the community;

6. undermine all emotional supports;

7. preclude access to literature which does not aid in the brainwashing process.

Director Bennett urged the conveners to experiment with Dr. Schein's theories within their respective institutions.[5]

Imprisoned radical intellectuals speak with, against, and through this evolved technology of state terror in a manner that compels a thorough revision of conventional conceptions of social formation, state formation, and critical praxis. A genealogy that centers the insurgent knowledge production of imprisoned radical intellectuals illuminates the ways in which state power is imagined, invented, embodied, and realized through its regimes of power as well as the constitutive antagonism fostered by its incomplete attempts to liquidate and disarticulate captive political subjects.

"The Fear of God":
State Terror and the Figure of the "Inmate"

It is the set of relations entangled in the regime of imprisonment that foregrounds the prison as a mode of social organization. This particular embodiment of state power resonates through historically specific enactments of punitive carcerality, entangling structures of human capture with modalities of bodily violence. Importantly, it is this symbiosis between *punishment* and *incarceration*—discrete terms often conflated in popular, academic, and state discourses—that constructs and naturalizes the practice of imprisonment. Imprisoned activist and political theorist D. A. Sheldon disrupts this mystification, speaking to the embodied relations that condition and reproduce a structure of dehumanization:

> The first and main objective of prison administrators is to maintain emo-
> tional, mental and physical suppression by systematically dehumanizing
> prisoners. The intimidation factor plays a large role in the attempt to
> break the will and independent thinking of the incarcerated, by making
> that person susceptible to suggestions that she or he is less than human
> unless they conform to the prisoncrats' idea of an "inmate."[6]

Correspondent to this technology of subjection and existential evisceration is the state-contrived figure of the "inmate," a spectacle of conjec-
ture that signifies the anxious and shadowy projection of the prison
regime's productive incapacity to *actually dehumanize*. Dehumanization,
in other words, is a constitutive logic of the regime, a modality of its
domination and dominion, not its definitive or empirical outcome. Sheldon tells us that it is precisely the irreconcilable presence and persistence
of the captive abject *human* (as opposed to the "inmate" inhuman or
subhuman) that embeds crisis bodies within the self-production and
narration of the prison's institutional coherence:

> [E]very action taken by us, no matter how simple or ridiculous, is regu-
> lated under some institutional rule or policy. . . . *This is done so we will
> become pliant and submit to every whimsical command of guards, staff and
> administrators no matter how perverted or criminal-directed. . . . This puts the
> fear of God into the hearts of those prisoners out in the general population.*[7]

The production of the prison regime composes a statecraft of intimidation, invasion, and infliction, as the institutional identity of the prison
pivots on the state's rendering of captured bodies as infinitely fungible
objects, available for whimsical and gratuitous productions of bodily and
psychic violence, while presumed always already "dangerous" and crim-
inally disobedient. State captives pass into a condition beyond any normative sense of bodily or psychic integrity: their categorical status as the
unfree manifests in a normalized production and organization of (spectacles of) human suffering. Punitive carcerality, in this manner, enacts as
social allegory, communicating ideas, commitments, borders, and limits

through (sometimes stunningly public) rituals of dehumanization—*free people (the nonimprisoned) are to learn from, take pleasure in, and obsess over the spectacle of state authority in its moments of inscription.*

The brilliance of Sheldon's critique is its analytic depiction of state punishment as drab routine, invented through and situated in a coercive, multiscaled set of relationships between the designated human stand-ins for "the state" (administrators, policy makers, and guards, hence the architects and practitioners of state power) and those enfigured by the state as virtual and juridical nonpeople. "Inmate," as a philosophical construction of this embodied state power, emblematizes a structure of nonbeing: according to Sheldon, the "breaking" of the imprisoned entails the death of the human—the repression or coerced absence of will and independent thinking—and the production of a life in terror (to live under the "fear of God"). This structure of imprisonment, however, is structured by the captive's structurally inevitable disobedience—it relies on the necessarily unattainable institutional imperative that the captive *become an inmate.* Will, emotion, expression, speech, and movement constitute permanent threats to the prison's coerced order—as such, the specters of sudden mutiny, mimetic reversals in the power relations of the prison, hover beneath the formal rationality of the state's bare authority.

The regime's official figures of force and authority persistently, obsessively urge one another to remain vigilant against those prisoners who refuse to act like inmates. At times, this fraternal discourse of domination and premeditated violence takes form as off-the-cuff psychomilitary diagnosis. Correctional officer J. McGhee-King of Pleasant Valley State Prison (California), writing in *Peacekeeper* (the monthly publication of the California Correctional Peace Officers Association), contrives a hackneyed definition and clinical categorization of the captive "maladaptive manipulator." In a subtle, though nonetheless bizarre, construction of the collective figuration of the prison guard, McGhee-King's article ("The Many Moods of Manipulation") voices the veneered rationality of an otherwise exceedingly violent formation of state rule and dominion:

> Manipulation is something that most of us, as human beings, do at some point in our lives in order to get the things we want and need. The difference between us [correctional officers] and a maladaptive manipulator *is we do not use other people or harm others in order to meet those real or perceived needs.*[8]

McGhee-King renders a banal conception of state authority that pivots on a conception of legitimated bodily domination (in fact, this is the honor-bound duty of the correctional officer) *as nonviolence*—here, state-sanctioned bodily coercion and capture are conceptualized as outside the discourses and material parameters of violence or "manipulation." Constituting this narration is a fragile, though far-reaching and insistent, logic of hyperrationality. Prison guards are the accessible embodiment of the state's obligation to exert order on and extract security from the bodies of the captive unruly: they are uniformed, walking structures of *innocent force*, the picture of a unilaterally waged war of alleged domestic security that brandishes only "peacekeeping" weaponry. Within these terms of dominion, the guard can only be—in fact, must become—the vindicated conqueror and/or tragic victim of the scheming, subversive prisoner whose ultimate purpose is to obtain, exploit, or mutiny. McGhee-King continues:

> A maladaptive manipulator is often an abuser of alcohol and/or other chemical substances, which obviously includes a high population of incarcerated persons. Regardless of the consequences, these professional manipulators go to great lengths to use various techniques in order to gain control over us and become "above the rules." Some techniques are transparent. More familiar examples include, "If you don't get me some pain medication, then I'll just do a mandown," or, "If I don't get my psych medication tonight, I'll just nut up." And there's one we've all heard, "I'll just call my lawyer, or 602 [file an official complaint against] you. . . ."
>
> I would venture to say that probably most of us have been the victim of inmate manipulation at some time or another. . . . It is important to remember where we work and the kind of people we are working with. We

must be vigilant at all times. Being human means we all have weaknesses. You can believe that day after day those inmates we deal with are constantly searching for an area in our personalities that they can use to attempt some control over us.[9]

The punishment of such imminent and anticipated disobedience is the realization and material inscription of state power: here, terror itself becomes the moral of the story.[10] Prisoners/inmates *ought to* live in fear, in return for the danger they provoke as threats to a presumably civilized order, and continue to extract as they plot and scheme acts of insurrection and "violent" mutiny. The regime's resident agents of force are thus constantly engaged in a fraternal-military discourse that echoes and appropriates the vernaculars of both public and covert state "counterterrorist" operations.

Political prisoner Marilyn Buck offers an incisive rebuttal of McGhee-King's mystification, reconstructing imprisonment as a cultural, social, and political production that transforms the surface of an allegedly individualized and nonviolent regime into a sprawling province of state power and warfare:

> Prisons function as small city-states or fiefdoms; the denizens—prisoners—are subject not only to society's laws, but also to the ever-changing, arbitrary power of the overseers and keepers. *Punishment is a province of the prison system, a policy of terror. . . .*
>
> Punishment begins the moment one is incarcerated: one is stripped of possessions, clothing, family, and both civil and human rights. The legal sentence is not only a judgment of guilt but also an assessment of normality.
>
> The first step in this process is to criminalize the individual and strip her of her long-held social and personal identity. The individual enters the prison gates as an offender. The repressive apparatus seeks to forge a "delinquent—the object of the apparatus" out of the offender in order to expand capitalist industry (criminology, criminal justice programs in academia, sociology, etc.). Some few who enter may readily accept the concept that they are criminals, bad girls, or "outlaws." Most

women know they are not criminals and struggle against the dehumanization implicit in the process of criminalization. . . .

What is normal and routine in this world would be a nightmare to
one who has not had to experience such indignity: lack of control over
one's own self, censorship, punishment and even torture by the guards with
license. The only comparable environments, besides mental institutions,
are militarized, policed "ghettoes" or "barrios," state-of-siege arenas—situations that many white U.S.-born people have never experienced unless
one has been held hostage, as in abusive relationships.[11]

Buck's conception of terror as a regimented apparatus and production of
embodied power/domination defies the theoretical and political impulse
to render prison and imprisonment as discrete and insular institutions or
facilities, marginal and inessential to the social formation's fundamental
technologies of power. Buck argues that the terror of punishment composes a constitutive logic of repression, permeating the spatiality of the
prison proper and reproducing the prison regime as a socialized technology of power. The prison's "techniques of control"—for Buck, "infantilization," "hypervigilance," "racism in the name of diversity," "defilement,"
and "mortification"—literally inscribe the logic of social formation on
imprisoned women's bodies, movements, and affective relations, sustaining impact within and beyond prison space as imprisoned women re-
enter civil society accompanied and interpellated by the indelible terror
of captivity and punishment.

Similarly to Buck, Oliverio conceptualizes the production of terrorism and the "terrorist" within the state's complex rendition of itself—
and its highest forms of coercion—as both rational and mundane:

Terrorism, with its surrounding discourse . . . is more appropriately represented as a form of statecraft and state-production, wherein the state
represents itself as the legitimate sovereign, the legitimate site of social
control, rather than as a form of domination in everyday life.[12]

The prison regime thus constructs a specific apparatus of terror that is crucial to the prison's organic technologies of power and self-construction. It is the state-mediated *social* production of "security"—the structure of feeling that fabricates safety amid imminent danger, an affective construct that inverts and opposes "terror"—that provokes and proliferates preemptive and aggressive violence for the sake of civil society's fortification, usually against its tensely projected (internal and external) frontiers of lawlessness and racialized savagery.

The punishment of people imprisoned resonates beyond any isolated effect on individual bodies, reaching beyond the juridical terrain of the laws codifying this coercive production and defying the alleged containment of the prison's interiority. One former rank-and-file Panther woman (who, for reasons of personal security, must remain anonymous) offers an intimate autobiographical accounting of the lasting legacies of state terror in the ongoing genealogy of domestic (and carceral) warfare against black liberationists and communities. This woman, an early member of a prominent Black Panther Party chapter, testifies to the theoretical connection between originating scenes of state terror/torture and the outward radiation of that violence into sustained brutality among communities of intimates and loved ones. Her experience (and survival) of the extended, concentric circles of webbed and overlapping bodily violence fostered by white-supremacist state warfare illustrates the prison regime's reproduction and extension through the survivors of its realm (identifying names and places have been deleted from the following passage in order to protect several surviving members of the BPP):

> I married a brother [and fellow Panther] by the name of _____. . . . He was charged with conspiracy to murder a police officer, when in fact he had been followed by SWAT, FBI, and some more people into a cul-de-sac one day, and they shot the vehicle up, they shot him and two more brothers up [until they were] almost unrecognizable, but they survived. They were incarcerated, and later we raised over a million dollars so they could get out on bail. Instead, they jumped bail, as they should, and they went down to _____. . . .
>
> While they were in _____, they were captured and they were taken

to _____ Prison, where they were tortured. [Prison officials] put cattle prods on their genital organs, they put plastic bags over their heads until they vomited and passed out, they were made to sleep in small cabins standing up with field rats biting on them. They did this for four to five months. They were shot with tear gas canisters quite often.

When they would go to court, the judge would be crying because of the fumes coming off of their bodies. They would tell the judge what happened to them and the judge said, "I don't know what you're talking about, I don't smell anything." And he's crying while this is going on. They were down there approximately six months. They came back to _____ and they stood trial for four years before they were found not guilty.

I married _____ while he was incarcerated facing ten years to life. At our wedding, it was eighteen sheriffs, [my husband] was shackled and chained, a witness, and myself. That's torture right there.

[My husband] came home after spending four years being tortured. When he came home, I didn't understand exactly what torture was: I mean, you get your ass kicked, you get beat, whatever, get well, get over it, it was just part of the struggle. But I really didn't understand the emotional effects of being beat or being tortured.

I would be in the kitchen and I would hear sounds coming out of our bedroom. . . . He'd be in a corner balled up in a crouching position. His eyes are blank, and he's going through something. And I didn't know how to help him. . . . I didn't understand what he was going through. It was almost a year later before he was able to tell me the emotional damage that he had suffered at the hands of oppressors, at the hands of prison guards. . . .

Later I became pregnant. I was about eight months pregnant, and one day I went to the cleaners. . . . I came back to the house and he was asleep in the bedroom. I went into the closet and I took the clothes and I hung 'em up in the closet, and I snatched the plastic bag off of them. And he sprang on top of the bed like a panther. I knew right then I was going to die. There was no doubt about it, I couldn't run, I couldn't do anything, because I was just frozen in my tracks. When I woke up, I was lying in a puddle of blood and the baby's hand was hanging out of me.

You have to understand, when you've been involved in a struggle, and you see what's happening, you get a clear sense that what he did was wrong, but also that something is not right with him. Do I call the police? What do I do? I couldn't call the police. I knew without a doubt that my child was dead inside of me, and I also knew that I had a good chance of dying because it was an excessive amount of blood. . . . So I just lay there, I don't know how long, and I finally managed to crawl to the phone and I had to call someone to come get me. . . . I could not call the ambulance because I know he would have been hunted down and killed by any of these people. So I had to call some friends in _____, and I lay there in that blood until they came for me. They carried me to _____ and they took care of my child, who had died inside of me, and I just disappeared for three or four months.

As a result of what had been done to [my husband] in the _____ Prison—that's why he treated me the way he did. As a result, we had to divorce to save *my* life, because there was nothing I could do whenever he would have these incidents that would trigger his violent acts. There was nothing I could do. . . . [My husband] and I had known each other since junior high school, and [after] what was done to him . . . I call it trickle down violence: [after] what was done to him . . . there was no help for him, because he had been brutalized, he had been tortured.[13]

This woman's narrative reveals how state terror, in its materiality, affect, and effect, generates an ensemble of performances that overshadow space while reconstituting one's sense of place. Beyond reified conceptions of state repression and violence as episodic manifestations of the state's presumed monopoly on legitimate violence, state terror bespeaks the fundamental inseparability between acute forms of state coercion and the subjects, discourses, and places that they conceive and reproduce. State terror is, in this sense, uncontained and *inescapable*. The boundaries between terrorizers and the terrorized sometimes blur or dissolve, while the technology of terror structures a relation of binary violence that persistently reconstitutes the essential relation between master and slave, settler and native, guard and prisoner.

Allen Feldman's critique of Foucault's genealogy of modern disciplinarity and penality invokes the centrality of state terror in the formation of particular sites and regimes. His study of the armed resistance to the neocolonial occupation of Northern Ireland provides some useful theoretical points of departure:

> Foucault conceived of Bentham's Panopticon apparatus within an evolutionary trajectory that progressively distanced punition from the practice of visible, hands-on violence. I find little historical evidence for this sanitized application of ocular aggression either in Northern Ireland or in other neocolonial situations. Foucauldian optical rationality is not "contaminated" by "exceptional" violence in Northern Ireland; compulsory visibility is the rationality of state counterinsurgency and of neostatist paramilitary violence—this is evident in the visual staging and technological penetration of the body by cameras, high-velocity bullets, or digitized bombs, which unite both seeing and killing, surveillance and violence in a unified scopic regime.[14]

It is precisely the structured solidarity between technologies of coercive visualization—including the "virtual" rendition and projection of imprisoned people's bodies, intentions, and movements through high technologies of surveillance—and a proliferated, militaristic, and *normal* violence that crafts and reifies the prison regime as a way of life. In the context of the prison (which is at least partially compatible with Feldman's fleeting reference to "other neocolonial situations"), Feldman's "rational" regimes of state and parastate warfare/counterinsurgency are extended, distorted, and revised through expansive state and state-sanctioned techniques of human immobilization. This is to argue that within the reach of the U.S. prison regime, the precondition for Feldman's "scopic regime"— "the agendas and techniques of political visualization" that blueprint and ordain material relations of force—is the controlled movement or coerced nonmovement of bodies: these dominated-visualized bodies *must in some way be captured* in order to be "seen" and "technologically penetrated" within such zones of militarized warfare and subjection.[15]

Lewis Gordon, elaborating on Fanon's "tragic revolutionary violence" in *The Wretched of the Earth*, suggests that the violent dialectic
sustaining the relation between oppressors and oppressed is the institutionalization of a state of indeterminate war. For Gordon, this condition
is grounded in the core antagonism of opposed conditions of sociohistorical existence. The telos of conventional warfare (its culmination in
declarations of decisive victory) and the assumptive rationality of civil
political conflict fail to cohere within this ontology of dehumanization:

> For despite the chains of command, despite the various decision-makers
> at play, what eventually confronts both the torturer and the resistance-
> terrorist is the sheer anonymity of the Enemy. The enemy whom he has
> learned to hate is peculiarly absent from the shrieking flesh-and-blood
> reality in the torture chamber. . . .
>
> The tragedy faced by any one seriously engaged in struggle against
> the institutional encouragement of dehumanization is that institutional-
> ized dehumanization is fundamentally a state of war. In such a state, the
> ordinary anonymity of which we spoke earlier is saturated with a patho-
> logical consciousness that makes any feature of human beings beyond
> their typifications fall to the wayside.[16]

None can exist outside the regime of state terror because it is fundamentally the condition of a broadly social relation: in this case, we are
concerned with how the "institutionalized dehumanization" manifesting in the prison works to categorically disappear the projected "inmate's" existence as a human while producing the bodily reinscription
of state power across different scales of magnitude (between and across
localities, and from the individualized body to targeted social bodies).
State terror, as I conceptualize it here, works beyond its formalized institutional constraints and exceeds the will of its agents, deploying the
prisoner's body as a material and allegorical point of departure for the
discursive structuring of a broadly socialized state power/violence.

Within the terrain produced by the prison regime's peculiar "state
of war," politically legitimated opposition is impossible—where the

enemy's accumulated bodies are being amassed, figuratively composted, and contrived as outside the realm of subjectivity, state power wages a war without recognized (or recognizably "human") opponents. The imprisoned cannot be accorded the implicit political status of state dissidents or sovereign antagonists, because doing so would subvert the cultural-ideological edifice of the prison regime, in which "inmates" are only—and can only be—ontologically alienated and civically (hence politically) dead.

In the general absence of "legitimate" conflicts over state authority, the production of conflict between captor and captive becomes a structured fabrication. Thus, the imprisoned radical intellectual's praxis of resistance and opposition to state power must attempt decisive, creative rupture from the very relation of terror itself. Sheldon's exhortation to his fellow captives to "dig deep," to seek sources of opposition from within the heart of the punitive carceral, reflects the open-ended insurgency of this political challenge. It is, essentially, a call to arms for categorical nonsubjects to displace and violate the logic of dehumanization, *absent the guarantee* of an ultimate, or decisive "freedom"; this is to articulate a radical subjectivity from within a condition of civic and social death, in close proximity to biological and premature death.

"Alienated Is a Safer State of Mind": The Political Subject of State Terror

Radical opposition to institutionalized dehumanization implies a leap beyond assumptive rationality toward an epistemological break from institutionalized knowledge as such. Where totalizing repression is a way of life, critical intellectuality may articulate as an emergent praxis of liberation (to be distinguished from individualized notions of personal transcendence or intellectual advancement). As it works to demystify, critique, and oppose the very condition from which it emerges, the knowledge production of state terror's captive (non)subjects fosters an epistemological modality that is in irreconcilable conflict with the prison's (and, by extension, the state's) constitutive logic of containment, silence, and punishment. Gregory McMaster, writing in the *Journal of*

Prisoners on Prisons, aptly describes the context of the "prison writer's" creative production, illustrating a problematic of narration that is specific to imprisonment: "Even when prison writers attempt to expound the nuances and intricacies of their caged existence it is as if they are on the outside looking in, narrating the emotions and experiences of someone else."[17] Marilyn Buck has consistently argued the necessity of an *alienated* counter- and antisystemic politics, theoretically centering the existential paradox of the imprisoned radical's endangered political subjectivity: "*Alienated is a safer state of mind.* Being at the margins is definitely more honorable and more productive. If one yearns for the center, the center swallows all it can. This is about resistance."[18]

Against the regime of state terror, imprisoned radical intellectuals theorize, envision, and practice a freedom that searches for an alienated safety at the cutting edge of state violence. Many, like Buck, dream resistance from within the (self-)alienation of the punitive carceral, restoring a sensibility of and incorrigible desire for radical freedom that rejects absorptive and assimilating forms of state power.

In resonance with Feldman, Joy James's critique of Foucault's panoptic "carceral network" (as theorized in *Discipline and Punish*) speaks to the irreducibility of racialized state violence and terror within a social formation that reproduces as it obsessively obscures and sanitizes multiple relations of unmediated coercion. As punishment and state force materialize on the biological and discursive surfaces of prisoners' bodies, state terror constitutes a carceral condition of existence. The prison's "inside" thus becomes a place "outside" the allegedly nonviolent disciplinary carcerality of (white) civil society:

> American prisons constitute an "outside" in U.S. political life. In fact, our society displays waves of concentric outside circles with increasing distances from bourgeois self-policing. The state routinely polices the unassimilable in the literal hell of lockdown, deprivation tanks, control units, and holes for political prisoners. In *Discipline and Punish* Foucault remains mute about the incarcerated person's vulnerability to police beatings, rape, shock treatments, and death row. Penal incarceration and executions

are the state's procedures for discarding the unassimilable into an external inferno of nonexistence. Not everything, nor everyone, is saved.[19]

Those not saved become the objects of state violence and the permanently endangered subjects of state terror. Here the question immediately arises: What happens when civil society's putative unassimilables speak back? This is neither to fetishize "agency" nor to suggest that simply acting from a condition of ontological subjection constitutes a radical praxis sui generis. The task instead encompasses some interrelated epistemological and theoretical questions: What does it mean for imprisoned subjects to foster political insurrection against the regime of *their own* institutionalized dehumanization, and how do they *make (non)-sense* of this condition? How does one construct political subjectivity, or manifest political agency, within the comprehensive and invasive institutional space of the punitive carceral?

Kijana Tashiri Askari, a writer and activist detained in the Pelican Bay State Prison (California) Security Housing Unit, echoes these questions in his narrative of politicization in the teeth of state terror:

I wasn't always this way. . . . I was basically what you can consider to be state raised. I've practically been through every juvenile and/or reform facility, from group homes all the way through the California Youth Authority and the state penitentiary—you name it, I've been there. I first came to the penitentiary at the tender age of nineteen, and it was during that time that I first began to channel my energies in a more constructive manner. . . . [I]t wasn't until my first confrontation with these fascist officials that . . . my plight actually began. [Y]ou have probably put it together by now that I'm a revolutionary. . . .

I'm presently serving a life sentence within the desolate confines of the security housing unit at Pelican Bay State Prison. I've been wrongfully sentenced to an indeterminate SHU since '94. The sole basis of me being sentenced to an indeterminate SHU has nothing to do with violence, only my political beliefs and my overall position of remaining devoted and committed to the oppressed masses within. In that, I refuse to be silenced when it comes to speaking out and/or acting on outlandish matters that directly/indirectly affect the oppressed masses within.[20]

The regime of terror structuring the broader formation of punitive carcerality presumes the existence—and persistent possibility—of political subjects that transgress the projected norm of the paradigmatic "inmate." The condensed technology of terror that emerges at this capillary state dominion ultimately reconstitutes the larger institutional and spatial regime within which it occurs, conditioning the relations between Askari's "oppressed masses within" and the technology of domination that practices on their bodies and, ultimately, alters their individual and collective subjectivities. *State terror constitutes the formation of the radical political subject as the excess of structured and institutionalized unassimilability.*

Feldman reveals the fatal linkage between power and violence within such regimes of state captivity, emphasizing that the prisoner is neither emptied of the "humanity" that persists in and beneath the surface of the body nor conceptualized as a mere blank slate of flesh upon which state violence inscribes. Rather, Feldman explicates the state's creative and persistent (re)production through a *performative* terrorism, specifically manifested through the elaborate rituals of prison torture (a nomenclature I critically engage in chapter 6). State violence does not merely *evidence* authority and domination, but also *produces it* through the exercise of terror itself:

> *The performance of torture does not apply power; rather it manufactures it from the "raw" ingredient of the captive's body. The surface of the body is the stage where the state is made to appear as an effective material force. . . . The state (m)others bodies in order to engender itself. The production of bodies—political subjects—is the self-production of the state.*[21]

Feldman's implication of torture's production of bodies and subjects, along with James's elaboration of incorrigibility in the political "outside" of invisibility and civil death, yield a theoretical questioning that frames and shapes this discussion: that is, how does the "raw material" of state terror's manufacture *act back?* Why do imprisoned radical and protoradical intellectuals such as Buck, Askari, James, McMaster, and Sheldon refuse the relative penal equilibrium of self-sustained silence when the consequences of explicit political deviance are imminent and usually severe? How does a principled embrace and absorption of the logic of punishment, accompanied by an articulated rejection of the moral,

Kijana Tashiri Askari (Harrison), untitled self-portrait, 2003. Reprinted from the author's archives with permission.

historical, and political legitimacy of the regime that produces it, generate and edify the very insurrectionist and liberationist subjectivities that this state regime abhors? Finally, how does the constituted, overdetermined space of the prison shape and transform the "cognitive praxis" (as theorized in chapter 1) of imprisoned radical intellectuals? In part, these questions form an attempt to engage an epistemology that necessarily remains outside and against the common sense of civil society.

Phyllis Kornfeld's study of "prison art" in *Cellblock Visions* reveals the way in which the lived experience of imprisonment permeates the creative production of the imprisoned, forming an alternate symbolic universe in which a generalized intimacy with terror is presumed understood and shared in common, thus encompassing a primary subject of artistic visual rendering. Kornfeld's thesis addresses the political agency of an artistic creativity that reconstructs and rearticulates the context of its production:

> The prison environment often limits artistic subject matter. For example, the revelation of that which is deeply personal is generally too risky. As one man said, "I want to go deep, but I don't want to go too deep." Personal dreams and nightmares, one's own particular demons, are best kept to oneself. Prison life is unbearable enough without being labeled "weird." Horrific images of the general evils of incarceration are quite acceptable, however, because they are commonly understood.[22]

It is precisely the visible rendering of state practices so persistently shunted from public view that restores a troubled semblance of communicative possibility, within and across the borders of the prison itself. In Kornfeld's study, visual art conveys a carceral common sense, as imprisoned artists engender their intimacy with a generalized and collective "evil" as a primary medium, evoking collective (if not populist) social identifications from within an antisocial milieu.

Expressing this creative process, imprisoned radical intellectuals embody a lineage of counter- and antisystemic political critique and praxis that emanates from their entanglement with processes of intimate devastation. Within this radical intellectual genealogy, state terror—ultimately a lasting nightmare of psychic and emotional isolation, twinned with varieties of regimented bodily disintegration or torture—is as productive as it is disarticulating and repressive. Political prisoner Bill Dunne writes in correspondence that it is the struggle to *break* the repressive regime that necessitates new ways of knowing and communicating, over and against the structured social and political alienation of the imprisoned activist.[23] Crucially, he articulates no convenient step program or rote solution to this political and epistemological problem:

> Part of the problem(s) of political prisoners' marginalization is their isolation from nonprisoners by the U.S. Gulag Archipelago. The trend in the last couple decades has been toward ever greater isolation of prisoners generally and political prisoners particularly from society generally and the activist community particularly. The ruling class and its apparatus of repression, driven by *their* (as opposed to society's) purpose in maintaining an ever-expanding gulag archipelago, has recognized such isolation as essential to imprisonment being an effective tool of control. Breaking or at least undermining that isolation, however, is not as easy as it sounds.[24]

In resistance to this violent isolation, the state's constituted incorrigibles often presume—and at times desire—their biological death within the machinery of state terror. Dunne's meditation on the fatal dialectic of violence and agency rearticulates the sociohistorical and existential terrain of the prison regime: most important, he elaborates its production as a semiautonomous state formation cohered through a fundamental solidarity of political desire between an ascendant historical bloc (Dunne's "ruling class") and its component structures of rule and dominion (the "apparatus of repression"). Working within this political genealogy, *Mexicano* political prisoner Ramsey Muñiz similarly theorizes the carceral formation through its structuring excessiveness, invoking the semiotics of colonization and the essential relation of terror that forms its everyday. For Muñiz, the prison regime and its corresponding juridical apparatus enact a drama of dominion and domination, forming the institutional fulcrum for a technology of immobilization, terror, and dis-integration that conditions the political ontology (and, perhaps, bio-graphical telos) of the imprisoned radical intellectual:

> The sentences and actions by the courts of America had to be excessive. Its purpose was to once again demonstrate to the natives that they held the power of incarceration or freedom. Fear can be a sickness and the oppres-sor understands the means of submitting fear into the masses who seek lib-eration and justice. . . . I knew I had to sacrifice my life, my freedom, my family, my people.[25]

The contradiction embedded in the imprisoned radical intellectual's pol-itical incorrigibility—as her or his constituted presence *extracts* state repression while simultaneously enacting the state's failure to fully in-capacitate or "break" the captive radical subject—signifies something beyond a contained binary conflict between state authority and subver-sive agency. Instead, the thickness and depth of state terror enacts a unique gravity on the radical subject's body, which responds by absorb-ing punishment *while socializing its implications*.

The discursive production and material ordering of unassimila-bility and incorrigibility thus form the basis for the punitive carceral's self-edifying insufficiency and anticipated political failure: the force of domination, totalizing in its logic though incomplete in its capacity, fos-ters and politicizes the captive subject's (body's) power to disobey, refuse, and act back—against the regime of domination as well as through and upon other situated bodies, including those empowered and deployed by the juridical-military apparatus of the regime itself. Moreover, as Feldman observes, this technology of capture/punishment and the im-prisoned subject's concomitant *disobedience to the unilaterality of its logic* transcribe political-historical possibilities that can only be encountered through the moving moments and sites of its regimented violence:

> The very act of violence invests the body with agency. The body, altered by violence, reenacts other altered bodies dispersed in time and space; it

also reenacts political discourse and even the movement of history itself. Political violence is a mode of transcription; it circulates codes from one prescribed historiographic surface or agent to another.[26]

I am considering the imprisoned radical subject's body as, in concert, a surface of *inscription* (for the prison regime's technologies of immobilization and bodily disintegration), *transcription* (as violence alters the formation and historical movement of the body and subject), and *political agency* (rearticulating and resignifying the intimate encounter with bodily domination through a situated praxis).

My appropriation of Feldman's theorization also suggests, however, that the excessiveness of the prison regime enables imprisoned radical intellectuals' production of "historiographic surfaces"—specifically liberationist, pedagogical, epistemological, textual, communicative, and insurgent/insurrectionist surfaces—that are often "new" and, more important, conceived in direct antagonism to the unifying political logic of the regime's self-generated surfaces and technologies. The movement and transcription of the regime's organic technology of subjection, in other words, spins significantly beyond the web of its stated desire, controlled intentionality, and juridical-military form, precisely because it is structured by an intimacy of excessive force. The following section offers a further theorization of radicalism and agency through an examination of these structuring excesses.

Articulating Wars: Revisiting Gramsci's
"War of Maneuver" and "War of Position"

In the 1999 article "The Cultural Commodification of Prisons," imprisoned journalist Paul Wright (released in 2003) elaborates the logic of punitive carcerality and argues for a conception of imprisonment that implicates the state's production of death space:

> American prisons cannot be compared to Nazi extermination camps in that quick death is not their industrial purpose. . . . However, increased sentences, overcrowding, brutality, disease and inadequate medical care all

translate into death by incarceration. The increased popularity and use of sentences of life without parole, natural life, mandatory prison sentences of 30, 40 and 90 years before release, all translate into one thing: death behind bars. The majority of the American anti death penalty movement opposes active state measures which lead to a convict's death, but for the most part supports death by incarceration as a humane alternative. The end result is the same: death at the hands of the state. It just takes longer.[27]

State terror affects more than those who formally linger at the edge of carceral death. Native American (Menominee) lesbian/two-spirit poet and activist[28] Chrystos speaks to the experience of terror and risk that the prison may wreak for the nominally free person. Banal "freedom," even (perhaps especially) for those not in state bondage, loses coherence upon intimate contact with the regime that intends a comprehensive disintegration of body and disarticulation of mind and spirit.

Chrystos illustrates how the political significance of such moments of contact between the free and the unfree may be found less in the observable content of personal intercourse or the agency exercised in the forming of personal-political bonds than in the expansive respatialization and enveloping interpellation of the prison regime's technology of terror. This power of subjection sweeps over the putative free subject (in particular the self-identified radical, revolutionary, liberationist, or abolitionist activist) in a coercive, though no less pedagogical, gesture of state force:

> I've done time behind many bars. Every time I visit the prison, I'm in terror that I won't get out again. There is no experience, including gang rape, which has tortured me as much as being locked up. One is stripped of dignity, privacy, dreams, will, silence, indeed from every kind of healing which human beings need.[29]

For Chrystos and others, terror is the essential vector of the prison's affective field, and overdetermines (even overwhelms) fleeting moments of bodily and emotional contact with captive loved ones. The putative free subject's intentional and self-conscious movement into terrorized space is generally spurred by forms of affective connection with people imprisoned (family members, lovers, friends, and extended/fictive kin) and, less frequently, inspired by a desire for progressive or insurgent political relationality across and against the free/unfree binary (visiting the prison, for the nonimprisoned activist, may suggest a radically de-limited gesture of "solidarity" with captive activists, protoactivists, and political prisoners). For the critical and self-reflexive free person, to encounter and survive this structure of contact is also to rearticulate the ideological and visceral experience of the prison regime as a dimension of (anti)social formation. In the space of the prison, violence overdeter-mines discipline while surveillance articulates as coercion, forming a physical, visceral, and psychic context that funnels and focuses opposi-tional political subjects.

These relations of direct violence suggest a specificity to state ter-ror that renders the power logic of capitalism, white supremacy, and patriarchy as something beyond the coercion/consent dyad for those incorrigibles who require advanced forms of containment and annihila-tion. The materiality of incorrigible as well as insurgent or insurrec-tionist bodies manifests in their immunity to—and frequent principled, dramatic defiance of—state and state-sanctioned forms of disciplinary normalization and civil assimilation, and their logical and involuntary attraction of the state's capillary violence through normative regimes of policing/punishment/terror. The surfaces of these incorrigible bodies compose a living border that reflects and refracts the institutional bor-der of the prison. Relations of unmediated violence condense at the material and moving borders of the unassimilable/incorrigible body, con-structing a regime of coercion, immobilization, and punitive spectacle that both contradicts and articulates with Foucault's conception of mod-ernity's normalizing regimes of discipline/power/knowledge.

In a critical piece composed prior to his release in 1990, political pris-oner and Black Panther Dhoruba Bin Wahad elaborates the presence of the police state that shadows and constitutes the alleged liberal democracy, and essential white-supremacist state formation, of the United States:

> The obvious consequence of a dual standard of human expectation is a unique system of democratic fascism and a permanent condition of police or military repression aimed at the underclass and social dissidents. Limited political "democracy" is permitted while corporate control of the economy dictates the real content and direction of the state. In this context the specter of racist subjugation resolves itself in an ongoing and continuous cycle of police repression, underclass crime and social deprivation—in other words a permanent state of crisis.[30]

The constant reinscription of the borders that materialize Bin Wahad's "democratic fascism" is a necessity of social reproduction: the inside/outside is simultaneously material, physical, and existential, manifesting the manner in which civil freedom relies on carceral and punitive unfreedom to render itself intelligible. Invoking Wright: "The intimidation and deterrence factor of prison is served by keeping it distant, remote and unknown, but at the same time a nearby immediate threat of imaginable evil. On the surface, these seem to be contradictory and impossible goals."[31]

The prison, within this discursive arrangement, must be rendered an alien cultural and geographic figuring, a place that is somewhere else altogether, territorially distant and experientially incomprehensible to the ideal-typical "free" person. At the same time, because it is a crucial capillary site of social formation, the prison encompasses a regime that haunts the popular imaginary and hovers as intimate, terrible possibility. As the regime of state terror inaugurates a formation of dominance that exceeds civil society's regimes of assimilation, discipline, and normalization, it fosters a qualitatively different conception of state power, and therefore requires a retheorization of insurgency, its context, and political signification/significance.

The prison regime's twinned technologies of immobilization and bodily disintegration depart drastically from the virtual and technically disembodied disciplinary technologies of Bentham's Panopticon or Foucault's biopolitical carceral, whose Eurocentric regimes pivot on the relative absence or infrequent physical application of direct bodily coercion and punishment. The technology of the current punitive carceral entails a constant, state-structured application of physical and psychological violence, a vectoring of coercion that generally exceeds conventional notions of torture, encompassing a profoundly sophisticated form of subjection that constantly reshapes the imprisoned body's form, content, and context. Political prisoner Janet Hollaway Africa, imprisoned since 1978 as one of the MOVE Nine, elaborates how the bodily passage into this relation of direct violence melts away the juridical formality of "the prison," establishing the political premises for an abolitionist or antisystemic practice.[32]

A permanently endangered liberation discourse, Africa contends, precipitates at the collision of agency and repression, generating subversive possibilities to state power that call for elaboration into the current moment. Africa thus argues for a radical and collective epistemological break from the regime's interpellating technologies of domination and proctorship:

> there is a wave wellin up that's been wellin up for years, that is soon to be released and will support only those who can swim, when the tide seems low it ain't safe to fall asleep and assume the wave ain't coming in . . . for this problem system must be washed away swiftly, uncompromisingly in order for true freedom to be felt, don't think that freedom is determined by a building called a prison, freedom is very simply the absence of this system, the disposal of politics, the total elimination of the confinement of enslavement. When you look to this system of prison to be released from this system of prison you ain't being released you are being recycled like scrap metal in a junk yard to be processed again and again til you are retired to the grave yard.[33]

The question of viable opposition or insurgency obtains a particular urgency under the conditions articulated and embodied by Africa. Moving within a terrorized space of absolute containment, civil death, and invisibility to the "outside" of civil society, the imprisoned radical intellectual's struggle to communicate—with other imprisoned people, political allies, family members, loved ones and solidarity seekers on the out-side—butts against the hypersurveillance of imprisonment and the direct political repression that it proliferates.

Fueling the intellectual production of imprisoned radicals and rev-olutionaries is precisely this desire for total political engagement: living at the edge of state authority, immobilized within a capillary site wherein excessive violence is the premise of institutionality, coerces a lasting negotiation with fear, self-alienation, and generalized dread that accom-panies the relative absence of meaningful human intercourse. Black Pan-ther organizer and longtime political prisoner Geronimo ji Jaga (Pratt), whose eight consecutive years in solitary confinement initiated three decades of imprisonment (he won his release in 1997), recounts a defini-tive 1974 encounter with—and creative response to—the regime's cir-cumscription of his capacity to express, experience, and interact. Ji Jaga, responding to the echoing chants and meditations of fellow captives in Folsom Prison's notorious Cellblock 4-A isolation unit, recounts to biog-rapher Jack Olsen that he channeled life through conversations with spir-its of those living and dead, friends and enemies:

> Many of [ji Jaga's] fellow prisoners chanted. . . . At night they made 4-A hum and moan like a generator—*om om ommm, ummmmmmm*. . . .
>
> Geronimo tried to train himself to chant like the others, but after a while he realized that the process worked best if he let his mind run free. "I didn't even know what I was chanting—just words, sounds, grunts, hums, little snatches of songs. Things came into my mind, new experiences, new feelings."
>
> After a few sessions he began to feel more relaxed, cleansed, ele-vated. As he chanted, he saw his mother, then [assassinated Black Panther and friend] Bunchy Carter, his brothers and sisters, the murdered Red, old friends in the Panthers, Sergeant Maddox and his army buddies. "I'd smoked a little dope in my life, but this was the best high in the world. I talked to Malcolm X, Martin Luther King, Medgar Evers, Stokely [Carmichael, then-leader of the Student Nonviolent Coordinating Committee], Huey [Newton, Black Panther organizer and leader], the Cleavers [fellow Black

Panther organizers and leaders Kathleen and Eldridge Cleaver]. I had long discussions with Frederick Douglass and James Baldwin. I told off Richard Nixon. 'You sorry son of a bitch, they sent you to a mansion in San Clemente and me to a cell in San Quentin!' I talked to ants and roaches—and they talked back! I learned how to see things from other perspectives. The ants taught me that the world doesn't rotate around Geronimo Pratt."[34]

Although ji Jaga was released from prison in 1997 after a successful appeal, and he subsequently won a multimillion dollar settlement from the FBI and the city of Los Angeles for false imprisonment and multiple violations of his civil rights, his legal vindication is utterly incommensurate with the more important political legacy signified by his three decades in political imprisonment;[35] that is, ji Jaga's exercise of surviving solitary imprisonment—"living" through an alternate form of human/spiritual intercourse—overlaps the modalities of (personal or individual) survival and the situated, creative production of politically oppositional subjectivity within the conditions of captivity. Notably, as ji Jaga chanted, meditated, and channeled, communicating with living spirits in a struggle to self-preserve and resist the imposed mental disarticulation of isolation confinement, stories and renarrations of his survival of—and stalwart disobedience to—the logic of imprisonment circulated widely among his cohorts throughout the California and U.S. prison systems. Ji Jaga became one of many imprisoned liberationists and radicals whose valorization among imprisoned people signified the radical nobility of his refusal to "break," snitch, or sell out to prison authorities, perhaps the most essential and revered form of resistance to state violence and a valued collective ethic of opposition (generally shared across the political, racial, and gender identifications of the imprisoned) to the logic of the carceral regime.

Such engagements and political articulations as Africa's and ji Jaga's articulate (and productively mythologize) a unique condition of possibility for waging an antisystemic political struggle from within the punitive carceral. Here I am positing a revision of the Gramscian distinction between "wars of maneuver" and "wars of position" within modern struggles for societal hegemony. A review and critical examination of the Gramscian schematic offers insight to the altered condition of prison praxis as a form of insurrection or emergent carceral guerrilla warfare.

Gramsci described the "war of maneuver" through the analogy of classical, military front warfare in which decisive battles occurred over determinable territories. Enemies faced off in discrete, winner-take-all struggles; thus, "in military war, when the strategic aim—destruction of the enemy's army and occupation of his territory—is achieved, peace comes."[36] There is an immediate way in which imprisoned liberationists can be involved in precisely such a war with the state, to the extent that the prison is itself the primary strategic front of struggle for those seeking to obtain their freedom against the legitimated civic and social death of state captivity.

Writing in the early twentieth century, Gramsci (himself a political prisoner in Italy) was more concerned with the passage of modern Western societies into complex, indecisive, and protracted struggles over the shaping and reshaping of hegemony—perhaps most importantly, through contestations over the form, substance, and trajectory of what he called the popular common sense. Although the war of maneuver remained relevant to Gramsci's understanding of his historical moment, it was his conception of the "war of position," encompassed in the complex, multilayered, and overlapping political struggles of emergent modern civil societies, that was the hallmark of his paradigmatic intervention: "a war of position is not, in reality, constituted simply by the actual trenches, but by the whole organizational and industrial system of the territory which lies to the rear of the army in the field."[37] Black cultural theorist Stuart Hall clarifies that this mode of warfare focuses on "the whole structure of society, including the structures and institutions of civil society."[38]

The trajectory and circumstance of the imprisoned activist's or liberationist's engagement with civil society's wars of position (that is, if there is any engagement at all) is incompatible with the Gramscian schematic: first, captive anti-imperialists, radicals, and revolutionaries inhabit a space that is structurally beyond direct access to the complex of institutions, structures, and discourses that compose the "whole organizational and industrial system" of civil society. Second, to the extent that the constitutive logic of imprisonment is immobilization and disintegration, the prison regime entirely evaporates the Gramscian coercion/consent dyad.

The regime's juridical and cultural inscription (and formalized enforcement) of civil death generally preempts the imprisoned activist's capacity to participate in the praxis of civil society's alleged social-change processes. Although imprisoned intellectuals may sometimes contribute, in fundamentally delimited form, to the discourse of emergent and ongoing social movements—circulating written text and communiqué, organizing (underground) political circles among imprisoned peers in solidarity with outside movements and organizations, and innovating creative philosophical and strategic interventions that sometimes influence the trajectory of extant or budding movements—none are allowed access to the institutional or social terrain of civil society in a manner that is remotely commensurate with their free-world persons.

The historical condition of production for radical prison praxis, in other words, positions it as a direct antagonism to the systemic functioning and formal institutionality of the prison regime's (and thus the state's) dominion, authority, and power. To generate a critical or radical political discourse from this condition is to formulate methods of bypassing, deceiving, or undermining the prison regime's technologies of domination and immobilization—particularly when that discourse aims at reaching and influencing political audiences and other nonimprisoned publics in the free world of civil society. It is, in other words, to channel a delimited gesture of political life from a site of political death.

Substantive engagement in the form of protracted, widespread, transformative struggle posited by the prototypical Gramscian "war of position" is largely impossible within the prison regime's structure of subjection: thus, while the struggle for communication with people in civil society suggests an attempt to engage with a broader war of position—

entailing a political exchange that often suggests substantive transformations in the principles, strategies, and tactics of civil society's political struggles—imprisoned radical intellectuals simultaneously envision and fantasize decisive and direct frontal conflicts with state terror's regime. The logic of political struggle articulated by this fantasy is, in fact, more compatible with Gramsci's classical "war of maneuver," wherein the terrain of confrontation is structured such that the "strategic aim" is not protracted political contestation and struggle, but rather the "destruction of the enemy's army and occupation of his territory." Foregrounding the praxis of imprisoned radical intellectuals within the political architecture of the current moment, then, requires a reckoning with white anti-imperialist political prisoner Susan Rosenberg's (granted presidential clemency in 2001) conception of the warfare landscape:

> We know that their knowledge of us is a weapon against us. We have no real options except to say either, "I will communicate despite them. I will not be silenced," knowing the psychological profile will grow. Or, we can opt to withdraw completely. There is no middle ground.[39]

The multiplicity, mobility, and complexity of contemporary regimes of domination belie as they facilitate the apparent transformation of state power and social formation into more formally liberal-democratic means. Imprisoned radicals remind us that this nominally liberal hegemony is structurally overdetermined by shifting technologies of violence that wage undeclared or low-intensity warfare on particular bodies, subjects, and sites. Thus, the terms "police-state democracy" and Bin Wahad's "democratic fascism" are neither oxymoronic nor hyperbolic: they are simply (and richly) matter-of-fact. We must acknowledge, then, the historical significance of this overdetermination within the American social formation: the condition of possibility for generating the hegemonic consent of (local and global) civil society is the persistent production and reproduction of regimes of gendered white-supremacist immobilization and bodily disarticulation. At the same time, this overdetermination forms the political possibility for creative and insurgent articulations between wars of (carceral) maneuver and wars of (civil) position.

Although the programmatic particularities of such insurgencies may vary significantly, imprisoned radical intellectuals visualize the essential relation between these two categories of struggle in rather consistent ways. Black-liberationist political prisoner Mutulu Shakur, for example, invokes a conception of radical praxis that furnishes the overriding political desire of the carceral war of maneuver—the decisive repulsion of state terror's agents—as the catalyst of potential solidarity with those in civil society waging protracted wars of position, whose political work is premised on a delicate combination of accommodation to, reasoned and rationalized dissent from, and strategic political mobilizations challenging the white-supremacist state. Shakur's rhetorical juxtaposition of the condition of (political and bodily) immobilization ("paralysis") with political desire ("passion") illustrates the possibility (and ethical necessity) of rendering an affective-epistemological break from the logic of negotiation with this state regime. Shakur asserts that any legitimate political solidarity between imprisoned and nonimprisoned liberationists requires that his captors be *expelled from the political landscape altogether:*

> I think "prison intellectuals" . . . must convince folks that without the outside forces [demanding] direct involvement at every level that is now available, within the system . . . the direct repression will escalate. The masses, on the other hand, must be able to meet prisoners who don't fit the stereotypical agenda image of the state. This task calls for contact both ways, from inside out and outside in. The overall agenda of the government and its industrial prison complex will be exposed from this position. The next question: Will fear paralyze us or will the passion for human rights drive these pigs into the sea?[40]

Articulating the war of maneuver with the war of position forms a historically and spatially specific mode of opposition to the apparatus and context of state terror. Shakur's schema is compelling because it invests agency in the notion of contact at and across the juridical and institutional borders of the prison, a political meeting ground premised on the liquidation of his captivity and neutralization of his captors. Shakur's notion of a political and physical "contact both ways" suggests a collective defiance of state authority, and, most important, a disappearance (inversion?) of the conventional relation of power between civil society's nonimprisoned activists and their imprisoned analogues, who are frequently reduced to the free activist world's reified constituency, clientele, or iconography.

Shakur's vision posits a form of radical political communion (the activity of making or building political "community") in the process of opposing a dense technology of repression and overthrowing its regime of actualization. For him and many of his imprisoned peers, the process of contact and possibility of political transgression that politically communes "from inside out and outside in" raises the immediate and urgent challenge of displacing and destroying the regime of state terror, an abolitionist desire that refuses to defer its attainability and urgency to an unnamed political hereafter. Native American (Anishinabe and Lakota) political prisoner Leonard Peltier's poem "the knife of my mind" marks the grounds of refusal for such a political deference, signifying the ontological violence of a present lost, a space emptied—his life, time, and identity are the price of negotiation for civil society's wars of position, which take the prisoner's disappearance for granted:

> I have no present.
> I have only a past.
> and, perhaps, a future.
> The present has been taken from me.
>
> I'm left in an empty space whose darkness
> I carve at with the knife of my mind.
> I must carve myself anew
> out of the razor-wire nothingness.
>
> I will know the ecstasy
> and the pain
> of freedom.

> I will be ordinary again.
> Yes, ordinary,
> that terrifying condition,
> where all is possibility,
> where the present exists and must be faced.[41]

Inhabiting the edge of hegemony's underside, a particular way of *knowing power* surfaces in Peltier's desire to "be ordinary again," that is, to reoccupy a "present": this epistemological tension both reflects and partially deforms the ontology of the "inmate" or prisoner, positing an insurgence of subjectivity and self-coherence within a regime of totalizing subjection. This is to say that, while many have facilely interpreted the political formulations of imprisoned radical intellectuals as self-evident polemics and/or nihilistic meanderings, there is in fact a profound and sometimes prophetic vision of a historical future embedded in this lineage of praxis: to stipulate and enact the *illegitimacy* of one's subjection (imprisonment) is also to dramatize state power's failure to totalize social intercourse. Referencing conditions of accelerated militarized conflict and heightened state violence, Feldman writes:

> The growing autonomy of violence as a self-legitimating sphere of social discourse and transaction points to the inability of any sphere of social practice to totalize society. Violence itself both reflects and accelerates the experience of society as an incomplete project, as something to be made.[42]

This thought partly schematizes the intellectual context of a radical prison epistemology: the violence inscribed on the prisoner's body resurfaces as evidence of historical possibility in resistance, subversion, and opposition to the apparatus and constitutive logic of (state) violence's genesis; knowledge production thus becomes a sphere of political praxis for the imprisoned person in intimate possession of this evidence, and it is precisely this praxis that sustains the articulation between the prisoner's own (individual and collective) fight for survival/freedom and the lurking counterhegemonic struggle—or imminent total insurgency—

that seeks radical social transformation. I am suggesting, in light of Feldman's linking of violence to the incomplete project of social totality, that the necessary incompleteness of social formation in the United States specifically and centrally manifests in the interpretive, symbolic, and processual gaps surfacing in the intersections of state terror/violence, insurrection, and the multiple zones of (carceral) warfare constructed therein.

Conclusion: The Challenge of Engagement

When I initiated contact with a number of imprisoned radical intellectuals during the late 1990s, it was on the basis of my acute dissatisfaction with the structure of political assumptions that appeared to cohere the organizing discourses of civil society–based activists (myself included). Yet, the correspondences and political-intellectual exchanges in which I have participated reek of the prison's coercive relations, implicating my ongoing exchanges with imprisoned insurrectionists, liberationists, and revolutionaries in a state mediation that disrupts the premises of political discourse (as a putative dialogue among civil or social "subjects") and forces a communicative modality that speaks through and around a vernacular of terror. My imprisoned correspondents, while constantly asserting a desire for "solidarity" (with nonimprisoned activists and intellectuals) and seeking a unity of purpose, often illustrate (at times unwittingly) the central paradox of our attempt to forge a meaningful (if structurally individualized) "inside-outside" relation: How can one communicate a condition that is necessarily *incomprehensible*, that is, a condition in excess of the symbolic and vernacular structures of civil society? Marilyn Buck asserts a failure of the senses, the utter impotence of rationality in negotiating and surviving prison terror as one of the encaged:

> In truth, prisoners reflect the overall social conditions—a distillation or concentration of the worst effects of capitalism on human beings, as well as the strengths we humans have to endure injustice and cruelty.
>
> So, *we are you*. Except that we have—and do—live in a world that is incomprehensible at the subjective level to anyone who has not experienced imprisonment and almost absolute loss of control over one's self. . . . There

are days when, even after more than eighteen years of prison, I still find the arbitrary viciousness of the system mind-boggling and incomprehensible.[43]

Lacking the tangible alternatives necessary for formulating typical vindicating narratives, imprisoned radical intellectuals consistently refuse to dispense with the terror that accompanies a defiant optimism of the will. Aligned with Buck, Peltier similarly narrates the limits of his own coherence as a political subject in the dominion of the prison regime's logic of death and invisibility:

> You never get used to prison life. In my sleep I hear people's voices, some of them long dead, like my father. Such voices are torture. To wonder every day, every hour, whether or not you will *ever* be free again is a very special form of torture. It takes its daily, hourly toll on your heart and in your soul, particularly when you have to explain to your grandson why they won't let you out to attend his soccer game. It eats you up inside to hear his little boy's voice ask, "Grandpa, why don't you just *finish* your sentence?" He thought my sentence was just a whole lot of words I had to write, like copying a sentence over and over for a punishment assignment at his grade school. He couldn't understand that my sentences continue for twice my natural life.[44]

It seems that the sensation and sensibility of incomprehension is an existential linchpin of—rather than an epistemological gap within—this subaltern knowledge production. *The fear of not being able to know*, the sense that one's own psychic/bodily experience is somehow outside the realm of communicability, precisely marks the point at which state terror collides with that slippery and stubborn thing we name as political agency. The necessary incompleteness of domination thus mirrors the simultaneous failure of epistemology and "discourse," commonly understood, to fully comprehend the regimentation and alien control of the terrorized punitive carceral condition. A passage from anti-imperialist political prisoner Ray Luc Levasseur's 1999 correspondence illustrates this structuring antagonism of the prison regime. Profound is the manner in which Levasseur dramatizes the failure of state punishment and re-pression to destroy or erase political identities and identifications, while simultaneously elaborating the technologies through which torture and terror relentlessly interpellate his subjectivity. Levasseur's multiple pas-sages between states of confinement mark the limits of the aforemen-tioned articulation between forms of political struggle that take place within and outside the prison proper. State terror, as it inscribes a self-contained regime on imprisoned bodies and subjectivities, coerces a form of departure from the presumed "social" of social formation. I quote his letter extensively as a conclusion for this chapter:

> Salut Dylan—Your Aug 30 missive w/enclosure just caught up with me last week. Fortunately it just caught the tail end of a ten-day mail forwarding. Everything after ten days was returned to sender—letters, periodicals, papers, etc.—which I'm still not even close to straightening out. I was in a deep, dark news vacuum for several weeks, conditions for me have dete-riorated, and I'm treading the gulag waters simply trying to get from one week to next.
>
> Things started well enough approx six weeks ago and then got worse in a hurry. I must keep check on the length of this missive—writing supplies being very restricted—but let me give you a brief update and respond to a couple of points in your letter. I finally left Administrative Maximum (ADX) on 8/20. Hell of a thing—all those years of seeing noth-ing but walls and small patch of overhead blue—and then in a moment's notice I'm barreling down the road in a vehicle with barred windows, try-ing to take in all the sights. Colors, especially. I don't recognize the makes/models of most vehicles any more. Mountains in the distance. At close range—homes, trailers, fast food joints, stores, billboards, signs, open range, lots of fences—but not many trees. I wanted trees. I never felt like I was *part* of what I saw. Too many years of isolation/exile. Chains too tight. Altitude—that area of So. Colorado is saturated with prisons. Approx twenty miles to Pueblo, CO—then by air to Federal Transfer Center—Oklahoma City, OK.

FTC looks like a slave market—shackled prisoners standing on elevated platform having the inside of their mouths examined by rent-a-cops. I got yanked from line, brought to the front, perfunctorily processed and placed directly in SHU (segregation/the hole). I'm classified "max custody"—that's not good. I'm always blackboxed ("security" device clamped over the cuffs—makes it feel like your wrists be in the jaws of a canine), and I'm put in seg wherever I'm held over. Ten days in OK City seg. Left there on 8/30—arriving at U.S. penitentiary/Atlanta on same day (former political prisoners held in Atlanta—Socialist Party Leader Eugene V. Debs; the anarchist Alexander Berkman; the great Puerto Rican Independence leader Pedro Albizu Campos).

. . . I was taken immediately to SHU (seg/hole) upon arrival—where I remain to this day, with no prospects of being let into general population any time soon. I was given a "review" on 8/31. I was told they don't like what I am nor what I represent. They don't like my political beliefs and political associations (conveniently labeled "terrorist"). They don't like that I was underground so long. They don't like the alleged "special capabilities" I'm supposed to have (what—exercising First Amendment rights!). And they don't like that I was locked-down at Marion and ADX for so many years (apparently they don't believe in their own propaganda re: the effectiveness of ADX's step-program to make prisoners more manageable, more controllable, and more fit for a less restrictive prison. No, *that* propaganda they put out for media/public consumption). So they buried me in seg—indefinitely. Go lay down for four months, they said, then they'll take another look at me. They said "if" they ever decide to let me in gen. pop. I'll have so many restrictions placed upon me I won't be able to piss without them knowing about it. Jeez—I don't feel very welcome here.

The result is I'm deeply buried in seg—with no definite end in sight. If that weren't bad enough, the conditions in seg are deplorable. There's terrible overcrowding. Two bunk/two man cells are often tripled up with third man sleeping on the floor (for weeks at a time). I'm told there's a court order prohibiting this practice—but the administration ignores it. Eighteen months ago the front page of the Atlanta Constitution proclaimed that torture was routine in USP-Atlanta's seg unit—in the form of four-point restraints being used as *punishment* (rather than to control extremely violent/suicidal prisoners). There's presently a class action suit on that. Like other seg units there's been too many assaults by guards on handcuffed prisoners. There's constant outages/shortages of hygiene supplies, cleaning supplies, clothing, bedding, writing supplies. The phone is more out-of-order than in order (when it's operational—supposed to get one fifteen-minute call per month). Anyway—bad situation.[45]

CHAPTER 5

"My Role Is to Dig or Be Dug Out": Prison Standoffs and the Logic of Death

People in here, they're dying, man. People are dying, and I don't know how to begin to make people understand what's happening to them. . . . That's what this whole thing is about. They're killing us.

> —Viet Mike Ngo, interview, San Quentin State Prison (2001)

The first year I was down, fun died. The second year, laughter; the third year, tenderness; the fourth, love. By the time I get out, there will be nothing left but echoes.

> —Christy Marie Camp, *North Coast Xpress*, Valley State Prison for Women (California) (2001)

It's not cruel and unusual [punishment]. . . . They do have contact with the staff members, so it's not like they're locked away and forgotten about.

> —Pamela Bane, "Supermax Prisons" (The Learning Channel), Correctional Officer, Westville Prison (Indiana) (2001)

Spectacles of Disappearance

The sweeping presence of the prison regime as a juridical, political, and narrative structure begets silences, absences, and disappearances over space and time. It is the negation of human beings—categorized by types, crimes, locations—that provides the lifeblood of this prison hegemony, the massive institutionalization of a *state of paralysis* (immobilization) and *condition of death* (bodily and subjective disintegration) that generates its corporeal reality. Foucault once claimed:

Our society is one not of spectacle, but of surveillance; under the surface of images, one invests bodies in depth; behind the great abstraction of exchange, there continues the meticulous, concrete training of useful forces. . . . it is not that the beautiful totality of the individual is amputated, repressed, and altered by our social order, it is rather that the individual is carefully fabricated in it, according to a whole technique of forces and bodies.[1]

Although technologies of "surveillance" have undoubtedly become a central facet in the production (or "fabrication") of subjects assimilable to civil society's alleged "social order," one must also recognize that the composition of what Foucault famously alleged to be the obsolete "spectacle of punishment" has irrevocably changed.[2] There need not be an audience present at the physical and temporal site of the spectacle for it to be rebroadcast, re-created, or otherwise reenacted for its spectatorship. Silence, absence, paralysis, and death come to permeate—and reproduce— the everyday of civil society through the production of its carceral underside/outside. The spectacle—here of the socially and civilly disappeared punished/tortured body—persists in its transmutation through the contemporary regime of the prison.[3]

Pelican Bay State Prison is a sprawling 275-acre monolith of pavement, cement, dirt, and steel at the edge of northern California, situated on the outskirts of a small waterfront town named Crescent City. Housing more than three thousand imprisoned people of varying security designations, Pelican Bay is as much a technological and military marvel as it is an architectural and environmental eyesore. Striking at first glance is the huge swath of dead ground created by the razing of old-growth forest to clear space in 1989 for the prison's construction. Among the first to incorporate the instantly lethal electric "death fence" as the manifest border of its authority, the prison has gained notoriety for devoting an entire section of buildings to the newest breed of high-tech, "low-intensity torture" incarceration strategies: the Pelican Bay Security Housing Unit (SHU) represents a carceral architecture, philosophy, and routine that are alternately referenced as the High Security Unit or "supermax" prison. It is the renovation and refurbishing of Bentham's (and, by extension, Foucault's) "Panopticon," accompanied by a theoretical reconstitution and structural amplification of the state's active, punitive capacities. The Pelican Bay SHU is no longer the panoptic carceral site wherein (presumptively white male European) "inmates" are "caught up in a power situation of which they are themselves the bearers."[4] Rather, it is the focal point of the state's merged technologies of white-supremacist bodily and psychic punishment, a legitimated zone for the synergy of "old" and "new," "low-" and "high-"intensity torture forms. The Pelican Bay SHU remains one of the world's most recognized carceral prototypes, both infamous and valorized for its use of solitary confinement and permanent "lockdown": imprisoned people are kept in their cells twenty-three to twenty-four hours a day, are virtually disallowed phone calls or personal items, and generally allowed to shower once a week. Most important, the SHU deprives its captives of any tactile contact with human beings other than guards (exercise yards are single-person kennels, and visitors can only speak with them across double-layered plexiglass).[5]

Correspondence and published testimonials from imprisoned activists and survivors of the prison regime—including the particular regime form of the SHU or supermax prison—situate and revisit one of the central theoretical concerns of this book: What is the *political logic and ontology* of the prison, and how is it inscribed through the particular and peculiar arrangement of "new" punitive technologies? I am concerned with excavating what lies beneath the veneer of pure or sterilized state control that is so profoundly symbolized and materialized in the contemporary prison, especially in (though not limited to) the formation of the supermax prison (a designation that encompasses state and federal "Control Units," "Security Housing Units," "High Security Units," and the like). Something insidious lurks beneath such clean, confident assertions of carceral efficiency as those circulated in both corporate media and official state depictions.

Technologies of Torture and Regulation:
The Emergence of the Supermax

Pelican Bay captive John H. Morris III, writing in the *Journal of Prisoners on Prisons*, counternarrates the SHU by taking his reader on a painstaking and meticulous textual "tour" of the facility, describing how the most mundane and ritual elements of his incarceration accumulate into a punitive whole: "These things taken separately mean little or nothing but when placed together they take on an altogether sinister form." Morris describes the Pelican Bay SHU as a "world unto itself"—in fact, a carceral war zone. At this point his narrative "tour" breaks down, and rearticulates as a communiqué from a captive of war or a counterstate combatant:

> The whole set-up is designed to cause mental, physical and emotional stress. First off, the prison is located in a remote corner of the state near the Oregon border. Most of the prisoners are from the southern section of California, like Los Angeles and San Diego. This means that visitors must travel more than a thousand miles to get to the prison. Most prisoners and their families are poor. Travel costs present a hardship for these families. That is why visitors are rare. . . .
>
> *It is a physical and psychological form of warfare being carried out against you.* No one could honestly say it is by accident that all these things "just happened" at once. This is done to break you, to punish you, to ruin you. After spending years in here, what comes out will not be quite "right."[6]

We, the readers and alleged beneficiaries, are invited as virtual participants and state-mediated voyeurs in this paradigmatic technology of domination, an institutionalized security that rests on the particularized nonpresence of the policed: within the state narrative, and lodged even within Morris's counterinscription, is the anticipated disappearance of any "human" behavior at all, its evaporation or dissipation into the "secure operation of the complex." In fact, the SHU's very purpose is to preempt, repress, and (upon/anticipating detection) vigorously attack the detectable physicality of the contained. The disembodiment of physical danger enacted by reactive and anticipatory state violence—as if threats to life and limb are borne solely by the armed keepers—lies at the heart of the California Department of Corrections' (CDC's) prison prophylaxis. There is no "violence" within the state's dominion other than that illegitimately wrought by the ruled, or, in this case, the imprisoned. A brief reflection on one prominent institutional ancestor of the SHU provides further insight.

Chronicling the incarceration of three women political prisoners in a "high-security underground isolation unit" (HSU) in 1986, the documentary film *Through the Wire* foreshadows the accelerated evolution of long-term torture as a central feature of state punishment technologies. The special circumstances prescribed by the federal government for the prison terms of Alejandrina Torres (granted presidential clemency in 1999), Silvia Baraldini (repatriated to Italy in 1999), and Susan Rosenberg (sentence commuted by presidential order in 2001) are noteworthy for having constituted an experiment in the gradual "breaking" of human beings through sensory deprivation and long-term isolation from human contact.[7] Using the bodies of these radical women as the raw material for a punitive laboratory in the literal underground of the Lexington federal prison in Kentucky, the state formulated a prototype incarceration of three people who had been categorized as the most dangerous and disruptive of imprisoned women. Although the Federal Bureau of Prisons steadfastly denied doing so—and despite the fact that none of these women had ever been disciplined for a "violent act" while in prison—it was clear that these women signified a discrete "political" danger within the prison's dominion. The Lexington HSU was closed in 1988 after a highly publicized lawsuit by the American Civil Liberties Union (supported by Amnesty International), but the state had already succeeded in exporting the HSU blueprint as a model for new carceral architectures, geographies, and technologies.[8]

The production of this high-technology torture in and through the bodies of two white women (Baraldini and Rosenberg) and one brown woman (Torres) fortified a white-supremacist continuum of carceral punishment: the profound forms of violence visited on these women were

structured through protocols of normality and veneers of sterility, in contradistinction to the spontaneous and ad hoc physical brutality (which
is equally regular, if not officially regulated) visited most often on
black and brown, "nonpolitical" (or, more accurately, politically unrecognized) women and men. These three political prisoners suggest in a
1987 group interview that their incarceration was tantamount to an
experimental form of *subjective disarticulation*—a sterilized, whitewashed,
and state-proctored condition that magnifies the coerced rupture of the
human from the social—reflecting Lorna A. Rhodes's contention that
"the 'box' of the prison presents a smooth surface to the outside world,
which is of course how it works as a place of disappearance."[9]

> SUSAN ROSENBERG: It's a prison within a prison. . . . There's no human
> interaction, there's no contact with anybody who is not affiliated with
> the Bureau of Prisons.
>
> ALEJANDRINA TORRES: To me, it's mind-boggling. It is an attack on the
> senses. I cannot imagine anyone putting people—human beings—in
> a basement, which was rehabilitated at the expense of about $1 million,
> for any other reason than to conduct some type of an experiment.
>
> SILVIA BARALDINI: I believe it's the first political prison in the United
> States. . . . The essential aspect of this unit is that we're totally iso-
> lated, and so amongst us we have taken to calling this place a living
> tomb. Before they painted the walls, we used to call it the "white sep-
> ulcher" because everything was white.
>
> ROSENBERG: It's what is called sensory deprivation. Everything is white.
> The walls are white, the floor is white, the cells are white, and it's lit
> twenty-four hours a day so that you are living in a totally artificial
> environment. There is no natural light. It's in the basement of a build-
> ing that was already constructed, and they built a series of cells to
> function in this space.[10]

The testimonies of Torres, Baraldini, and Rosenberg foreshadowed the
proliferation of the HSU prototype into a new and increasingly common carceral form. There was one control unit prison[11] in the United

States in 1985 (occupying a wing of the federal prison in Marion, Illinois); ten years later there were more than forty.[12] It seems clear, in retrospect, that the experimental low-intensity/high-technology torture of these three women constituted an originating procedure in the proliferation of control unit (or similarly conceived) cells as essential institutional features of the prison apparatus. The outcome has in fact been worse than Baraldini predicted—this mode of captivity is no longer the unique province of U.S. political prisoners, but has become the punitive carceral of last resort for *whomever* the leading intellectuals and administrators of the prison regime designate as their resident incorrigibles, or "worst of the worst." Further, the conventional modalities of open physical brutality and high-intensity torture have become normative facets of the supermax, symbiotic with its "high-tech" penal technologies, as its accumulated captives have been overwhelmingly black and brown (most often designated as "prison gang"–affiliated).

Pelican Bay State Prison captive Kijana Tashiri Askari (Tashiri Harrison) has been serving an indeterminate SHU sentence since 1994, among the earliest to be sentenced as such. He offers a counternarrative from within this ultramodern prison, contesting the state's portrayal of such aggressive containment and surveillance as the necessary and logical response to the presumptive—though generally undefined—"misbehaviors" of individual prisoners.

> The majority of the prisoners that are warehoused in the SHU are not in the SHU for disciplinary reasons, but for their *political views*, or allegedly belonging to a *prison gang*. The evidence used to stipulate those fabricated allegations . . . is totally absurd. . . .
>
> As the years passed on, these fascists realized the economic potential in keeping bodies warehoused in the SHU, so a substantial justification had to be created. And what better way to do it, than by magnifying the simple, isolated acts of violence (that they provoke) to the media? Because it's the same people, who by design, not only create/instigate these same acts of violence, but have also denied the public (the media) access to the inside of these prisons. . . . It should also be kept in mind that anybody

who works that hard to void access to us so-called savages, brutes, and criminals could only be working to keep the truth hidden. With the truth being, we prisoners are held in the most inhumane conditions possible.[13]

I'm a revolutionary . . . if you can catch my drift. It is this noted dedication that has caused the administration here to fabricate allegations that I belong to a prison gang of the disruptive type, and [sentence] me to an indeterminate SHU. . . . It's long overdue for [people in civil society] to be awakened with a much needed objective view, instead of the typical stereotype that . . . those of us within are nothing but predators, mass-manipulators, and above all that we are sub-human beings (criminals) who deserve whatever punishment that state officials choose to impose on us, as they please.[14]

Askari's reflection rearticulates his condition as a space-time of totalizing, preemptive repression that rests on a profoundly comprehensive and focused production of the inhuman (in this case, the black insurgency and the alleged "prison gang" affiliate).

Most important in Askari's text, however, is his absorption and refraction of the state's organizing technologies of dispersal, isolation, and deprivation: a radical political subjectivity coagulates within this structure of disarticulation, in part because the prison regime requires and contrives varieties of insurrection in order to sustain its logic of repression. Askari's radical revision of the causes, intentions, and manifest outcomes of the SHU regime—including his refiguration and embodiment of the insurrectionist captive subject—catalyzes a situated rereading of the CDC's sober self-descriptions and tautologies. Askari elaborates on his theorization in the unpublished essay "The Legalization of Genocide: Genocide as a Common Practice":

By design, the SHU in Pelican Bay State Prison in Kalifornia has been formulated to take on the role of the executioner. . . . This sensory-deprived oppressive dungeon of captivity is solely aimed at annihilating all forms of humanity. . . . At the onset of the SHU . . . its sole purpose was to *neutralize* the violence that was being perpetuated in the general [prison] population. . . . This objective was unsuccessful, as these racist government agents of these modernized koncentration kamp(s) was solely responsible for instigating the majority of the violent acts that took place. As years passed on, this objective was negated in order to satisfy these racist government agents' real objective: neo-genocide![15]

Serial oppositions inscribe on the surface of Askari's critique. For him, political repression, social containment, and economic expediency constitute the SHU's authentic function as a site of fascistic or "neo-genocidal" state practice. The bodies warehoused within are rendered *subjects in absentia:* juridical designation and the state's doubled discourse of security/endangerment generate a thick political grammar in which knowing "inmates" as (human) subjects is impossible. The imprisoned are overdetermined by a state-proctored discourse and codification that are saturated with notions of the subhuman and nonhuman, constituting their existence as one of essential repugnance to the presumptively well-ordered humanity of (white) civil society.

Askari's testimony illuminates the astounding political, ideological, and cultural expenditures that have foregrounded the control unit or SHU prison as a glimmer of a broader societal design, a historical trajectory that remakes the world in the image of the SHU. At the heart of his narrative is a war of social truths, waged between official/state moral and political hegemony and the grasping political agency of "disappeared" subjects. The conflict that emerges hangs precipitously on the uncontested literality of state mythmaking: the imprisoned subhuman/inhuman incorrigibles become the composite characters of a totalizing punitive discourse, logically yielding an exaggerated common sense of the extreme measures that the state must take to reinstate peace, justice, and stability.

Such insurgent texts as Askari's—along with many others penned and circulated by publicly unrecognized though radically politicized SHU and control unit prisoner activists—potentially displace the unilaterality of prison statecraft: Askari (re)introduces an acute sense of the irreconcilable antagonisms that lurk beneath the contrived placidity of such structures of power and domination. Here, it is the politicized, revolutionary imprisoned activist-intellectual who confronts and displaces the specter of the apolitical, criminal-incorrigible inmate. Crashing against the SHU's regime of comprehensive repression is the daily struggle to "think for oneself," while desperate attempts to circulate counternarrative and alternate history suddenly render bare the unchallenged "deceitfulness" of state truths.

Askari's political geography of Pelican Bay vividly renders imprisonment as the ritualized emptying of the prisoner's subjectivity, reflected in the state's rigorous and persistent attempts to evaporate environment and neutralize the senses. This is precisely the logical production of the nonhuman/inhuman that forms the basis of the prison regime's (re)production. Disrupting the state's static, placid, ahistorical geography of the Pelican Bay SHU, Askari's visceral narrative unveils the living spacetime of the prison's death logic:

> I'm of the *sensory deprived* type. Basically buried alive, within this concrete tomb, that affords me no view of the outside world, except for a patch of sky on the yard, that consists of four twenty-foot-high concrete walls. Not to mention that the yard is no bigger than a monkey's cage, with nothing out there but your sense of creativity.[16]

Such descriptions are virtually universal among people held captive in supermax prisons, many of whom strive for evidence of nature and life (e.g., sunlight, birds, trees) that might provide stimulation and mental sustenance. Tyrone Love (U.S. Penitentiary Administrative Maximum, Florence, Colorado) and Jay Thompson (Westville Maximum Control Complex, Indiana) echo Askari in their depictions of the supermax:

> The yard is so little . . . the place is so isolated you can only see the sky. The way this place was built, it was built for sensory deprivation. As far as grass, or anything, you hardly see birds or insects or anything.[17]

> Initially, I think it was meant to be a type of psychological reconditioning—make the place so terrible that you would never want to come back. Essentially, this place is just a warehousing facility, in my opinion. In ten years, they're gonna look back and say, we have 2 million people in prison and nothing's changed.[18]

The consistency of the vernacular—isolation, sensory deprivation, nonmovement—reveals a persistence of subjectivity beneath and beyond these routines of nonbeing.

Christy Marie Camp, imprisoned at Valley State Prison for Women (California), amplifies on this often androcentric critical discourse by speaking to the deprivations of women's prisons and control units/SHUs. Contrary to prevailing assumptions, Camp clarifies that such regimes of state violence are not exclusively inflicted on criminalized men and men of color. State narratives such as those of the California Department of Corrections focus almost exclusively on the justified harshness of punishment of incorrigible men, but the death logic of imprisonment consistently applies across gendered distinctions:

> The assault on our sense of self does not end when we leave the Reception tank. Prison life is a continuous process of mortification. First, there is the extreme sensory deprivation of prison life, the oppressive grayness of the prison environment, the unrelieved harshness of metallic surfaces which amplify every sound. The absence of flowers, plants, trees, indeed any direct contact with nature or the outside world.[19]

Whereas the common sense of the punitive carceral tends to center the male, black (and brown) body as its primary object of punishment—enforcing rituals that "emasculate" while generating a hierarchical culture of hypermasculinity—the technology of the prison regime compounds as an institutionalized and normative misogyny in the female/feminized carceral.[20] Here, the comprehensive attack on the senses incorporates a particular gendered degradation of female bodies that escalates over time and is ritually expressed through profound, discrete acts of violent male authority. Camp's analysis of self-inflicted starvation as the *preference* of imprisoned women resisting and surviving gendered state violence illuminates the flexible dominion of the prison regime:

> [T]here is a profound humiliation in being able bodied yet lacking authority to do the simplest things for oneself. We must beg for even small necessities such as sanitary supplies or toilet paper. At show time, we must line up in our hall, must wear state-issued clothing, must tuck in our shirt, must walk in a single file to the dining room, must show photo identification, must sit at the table of four in the order we came in, must eat what is provided in the time provided, must not get up from the table until our row is excused, and finally be subject to search by, in most cases, a male guard upon exiting the dining room. *Many women opt not to eat to avoid the psychological stress.*[21]

Camp's rhetoric of humiliation and subjection to state authority—male, uniformed, and armed—echoes Daniel Burton-Rose's investigative account of sexual assaults in one privately run Arizona women's prison.

Christina Foos's encounters speak to the logical outcome of state misogyny as expressed through this regime of punishment and immobilization. The prison's logic of death inscribes on individuals and institutions, producing dramas of the spectacular as well as the mundane, while simultaneously manifesting as episode and ritual. Perhaps the existential complexity and sophistication of the state's slow killing of subjects and institutionalization of living death is crystallized in the very excess of its willingness and capacity to dominate:

> No one can imagine. What it's like. Not unless you've gone through it. Christina Foos has.
>
> While incarcerated in a for-profit prison in Arizona, Christina says she was accosted by a guard, Ernesto Rivas, as she stepped out of the shower in March of 1997. Christina told *Prison Legal News* that she was startled by the sight of him, standing there with his exposed erection in hand.

Before she could think of what to do, she says, Rivas ordered her to bend over the bed in her cell and proceeded to rape her. She says he returned less than two hours later to repeat the act.[22]

The testimonial, analytic, and sometimes subversive utterings of imprisoned survivors such as Askari, Love, Thompson, Camp, and Foos in these passages suggest a generalized state of confrontation with the contingency of one's own psychological health and sensory functioning, as well as an incipient, irreconcilable antagonism to the prison regime itself.

"Every Time . . . I Lost":
Prison Standoffs and the Logic of Death

It is the struggle to survive these rituals of subjection and living death, that is, to resist the regime's logical production of the "broken" captive, that obtains fundamental political significance for many imprisoned people, in and beyond the supermax. As Askari observes, the punitive carceral produces an altered state of "the political," demanding an incipient radical practice that addresses the permanency of an immobilized condition of emergency. Forced into a posture of surrender, Askari formulates a radicalism that refuses assimilation into the two primary (and overlapping) punitive trajectories structured by this structure of low-intensity carceral torture: snitching and mental breakdown:

Recognizing that there is little that I can do from my compromised position, from a physical perspective, I employ my days exercising and studying vigorously. [I do this in order] to avoid the pious vices that remain lying in the trenches by design, to succumb us prisoners to that lifestyle of insignificance, in losing focus as to what's really going on, in putting the bigger picture into perspective. . . . This is indeed very challenging. For the human psyche wasn't designed to endure such suppressive tactics, in the vast magnitude that is being distributed in here, daily.

Many men, some of the bravest, most courageous, and considered to be of the most dedicated/committed of men, had at one point in their lives made the same vow to themselves! . . . Yet and still they became victims of the fascist doctrine, that has led them to eventually abandon that initial commitment of principle, either becoming stool pigeons for this fascist regime, or back-tracking by concentrating their energies into matters of chaos, idleness, and allowing their spirits to be broken! Their fire tamed! . . . And then they become content with trying to escape the essence of their reality, by no longer studying, no longer exercising, now spending their days hollering, and screaming . . . kicking on their doors, or anything that will help them to escape the pressures of reality. I define them as "broken-men," and I refuse to be counted amongst the broken-men.[23]

Such communiqués elaborate the subsurface of the prison regime's constitution of massively disappeared bodies and subjects as the subhuman/nonhuman medium of transaction within an economy of disintegration. This is to emphasize that the spectacle of the supermax prison—and by extension the technology of the prison regime—does not *only* operationalize the permanent modification or liquidation of human bodies as desubjectified physical and biological entities. The complexity, nuance, and raw expenditure (physical, economic, technological, and otherwise) crystallized in the statecraft of the prison, and thus the significance of imprisonment as a central, revered practice of the state, relies on the slow killing of subjects, hence the materiality of an embedded logic of death. "A sense of exposure and shame—the threat of being 'broken'— also becomes a pervasive pattern of feeling, apart from any particular incident of overt humiliation. *The prison environment could not be better designed to activate a sense of threat to the coherence of the self.*"[24]

"Death," commonly understood, is a convention of finality, ending, the absence of life and bodily movement. Death as *logic* implies something else, a necessary contradiction and impossibility that simultaneously revises our conception of death by inscribing it onto *living* bodies/subjects (here the imprisoned), while constituting a different kind of absence, a ritualized finality that articulates through the statecraft of imprisonment.

The prison regime's logic of death permeates and hovers over a

contrived standoff. Imprisonment, as statecraft, self-narrates as the fortification of state authority and civil society against the imminent and retro-
active eruption of particular varieties of pathos, disorder, and violence.
Prisoners, the allegedly duly convicted and civically dead embodiment
of antisociality, are constituted by the discursive and material axes of
white supremacy, heteronormative patriarchy, and capital as they *converge* at strategic points of bodily and institutional contact. The precise,
calculated rendering of mass-circulated conceptions of crime (as discrete acts) and criminality (as gendered and racially formed social pathology) draw comprehensively from the epistemological arsenal of the
regime's structures of domination while forming new composite characters that effectively convey the rhyme and reason of a broadly actuated
technology of domination. The state's pedantic political drama of imprisonment thus thrives on the contrivance of an essential standoff
between the designated enforcers of law and order and their categorically incorrigible antagonists: although the prison regime constitutes an
overdetermined and power-laden everyday that orbits steadily outward
from the formal boundaries of the prison, the regime is always already
the site of the "abnormal," more precisely, the fabrication of a warfare
terrain against which the violent peace and order of civil society is
defined, and through which it is constantly attained.

Robin Wagner-Pacifici's explication of the structural contingency
of the militarized standoff scenario is usefully applied to the circumstance of the prison:

> The standoff may be viewed as a frozen moment, where the mechanisms
> and processes of social interaction have ceased to function in their usual
> predictable and elastic way. They are neither the normal "structure" nor
> the periodic, but necessary "antistructure" in Victor Turner's terms. They
> are a heightened form of structure, frozen in the way that histological sec-
> tions placed on a slide are, and, simultaneously, in the manner of live cell
> samples, engaging in their own forms of movement, threatening to slide
> off the social microscope.[25]

Michael Dorrough, writing from the Security Housing Unit in the anthology *Extracts from Pelican Bay*, situates the frozen hyperstructure of the prison as a kind of regulated incoherence. The confrontation between captive and state transforms into a conditional permanence, wherein the "frozen moment" of the standoff continuously and repeatedly resonates through the prison's absolutist "heightened form of structure." In fact, it is this hyperstructuring—refining, harnessing, and unleashing technologies of violence that both formulate and proliferate varieties of incoherence through the prison's capillary sites and subjects—that becomes a necessary feature of social formation and the intelligibility of the state:

> The conditions here in the SHU are deplorable. The purpose of this place is to strip us of our humanity/manhood/capacity to be productive. In all honesty I don't see this condition changing anytime soon. Especially in light of the recent court ruling in the *Madrid* case.
>
> I was a little amazed at how on the one hand, the Judge found the conditions in the SHU—the isolation, lack of human/social contact, the lack of any meaningful programs, etc.—to be indecent, but at the same time, found justification in the continued existence of this madness, and by hiding behind the institutional security, justified the continued subjecting of certain prisoners to long term confinement ("indeterminate terms") by essentially taking the position that "some people can handle it, while others can't!" A ruling like this has nothing to do with right, wrong, or principle.[26]

Such is a regime formed on the obverse of already fragile conventions of juridical justice or (popular and state-mandated) morality, tucked on the underside of a hegemony of reason and common rationality. Dorrough's terms are precise, weaving the regime's production of dehumanization and indecency into the amoral expediencies of a punitive state. His reading of the 1995 *Madrid* case implies an incisive analysis of the political relation that bonds jurisprudence to corrections, an institutional solidarity that pivots on the state's capacity to define and instantly revise its own conception of "cruel and unusual punishment."

Dorrough's reflections haunt the jurisprudential diagnosis of legal scholar Sally Mann Romano in the *Emory Law Journal* essay "If the SHU Fits: Cruel and Unusual Punishment at California's Pelican Bay State Prison." Citing a series of psychological studies on the long- and short-term impact of the SHU on prisoners' mental health, Romano asserts the excessiveness and unnecessary brutality of such a punitive practice within the legal and ethical domains covered by the U.S. Constitution. Her critique rests on a particular projection of civil society's supposed moral sensibilities:

> These studies indicate that, at the very least, the healthiest SHU inmate runs a substantial risk of experiencing complex, formed hallucinations, developing hyper-responsivity and vivid fantasies, and suffering massive free-floating anxiety. In *Madrid*, Judge Henderson ruled that these responses were not "extreme" enough to warrant a finding that the SHU is per se unconstitutional because of the significant level of sensory deprivation. In other words, for Judge Henderson, these risks are ones that society chooses to tolerate. That conclusion is suspect. . . . If Judge Henderson is correct, our society tolerates prison conditions that are so severe that they may cause inmates to hear voices when there are no voices to be heard, to believe that they are losing their vision, to experience "frightening, visual hallucinations," or to develop a preoccupation with "entities" or "demons." *This cannot be the case in a society that calls itself "civilized."*[27]

Although the scope and logical articulation of Romano's critique are constrained by the formal and rhetorical conventions of legal argument, her essay nonetheless disavows and obscures the social possibility resonating throughout the work of imprisoned intellectuals inside and outside the SHU. For captive radical critics of the prison regime and state, the very conception of a "responsible," "civilized" society—invoked by Romano as the moral "good sense" of the extant social formation—drowns in the absurdity of the condition in which they live.

Civic death overlapping with social death is the grim reaping of "civilization's" underside, a relation of necessary irreconcilability that organizes the matrices of the well-functioning white-multicultural civil society: as it has become the focused site of massive black/brown disappearance and disintegration, the prison cannot be brought into a functional social harmony with (white or putatively "multicultural") civilization, unlike previous moments wherein imprisoned white male subjects were prepared for reentry into the entitlements of white civic freedom. This is why prison "reform" alternatives are, in the current historical period, premised on an insistent denial of the immovable logic of irreconcilability or unassimilability: the reformist perspective cannot accept (and willfully ignores) that the contemporary U.S. prison regime is a militarized and juridically (over)codified white-supremacist production of massive human banishment and liquidation.

The prison standoff is a mundane ritual, a banal element of the everyday that mocks the endangered humanity of the imprisoned by radically repressing their capacity to express and experience. Psychiatrist Terry Kupers, who has testified as an expert witness in more than a dozen class-action lawsuits addressing the conditions of incarceration in U.S. jails, prisons, and "mental health facilities," illustrates the telos of the prison regime's resident production of mental disorder, the "SHU syndrome":

> Every prisoner placed in an environment as stressful as a supermax unit, whether especially prone to mental breakdown or seemingly very sane, eventually begins to lose touch with reality and exhibit some signs and symptoms of psychiatric decompensation, even if the symptoms do not qualify for a diagnoses of psychosis. . . .
>
> Even inmates who do not become frankly psychotic report a number of psychosis-like symptoms, including massive free-floating anxiety, hyper-responsiveness to external stimuli, perceptual distortions and hallucinations, a feeling of unreality, difficulty with concentration and memory, acute confusional states, the emergence of primitive aggressive fantasies, persecutory ideation, motor excitement, violent destructive or self-mutilatory outbursts, and rapid subsidence of symptoms upon termination of isolation.[28]

Kupers's explanation guides a contextualized rereading of Wagner-Pacifici's "standoff spaces." The spatial oppositions and antagonisms of the prison regime, I would argue, facilitate a radical extrapolation of Kupers's diagnosis into a broader theorization of mental disorder, incoherence, and psychosis as a central organizing logic of the prison regime, rather than a dysfunction of the regime's residual excessiveness or brutality. According to Wagner-Pacifici:

> At any given point in time, the binary calculus of standoff spaces includes the following oppositional pairs: inside and outside, near and far, open and closed, permeable boundary and impermeable boundary, ingress and egress, offense and defense, wild and civilized, safety and danger, public and private. These binaries provide a static, frozen sense of the opposing forces of this archetypically static situation. As well, they are all culturally and morally inflected as various protagonists will view one or another member of each pair as the positive or negative position.[29]

A deeply embodied and individualized structure of domination shoots through the "binary calculus" of the prison's standoff space, constituting the given oppositionalities and antagonisms—guard/prisoner, state/criminal, free/unfree—as necessary premises for the rote resolution of the confrontation at hand. Whatever contingency appears at the scene of this standoff pivots on the capacity of domination to spontaneously exhaust its formidable capacities—and to instantly recoup those capacities in anticipation of the next opportunity to deploy them.

The binary logic of confrontation is akin to a military exercise or "war game," in which the powers of the "enemy" are utterly imagined and projected in their absence: here, a fiction of battlefield "danger" is displaced onto immobilized scarecrow targets of deadly activity. Beyond being an "unfair fight" occurring in a zone of one-sided warfare, the prison standoff reproduces as an internal state of crisis: this is the condition of possibility for the sustenance and evolution of the regime's accumulated and intersecting technologies of violence. The prison standoff disrupts the narrative progression of the conventional confrontation with the state; this standoff has no coherent ending (neither a definitive compromise nor a final armed conflict) but instead spins into an endless fracturing of temporary cease-fires between militarized soldier-guards and generally unarmed, underarmed, or disarmed inmates. As one confrontation ends, another takes its place, in infinite repetition.

Essential to the prison regime's aggressive attack on the subjectivity of the imprisoned is the violent, humiliating repression and denial of the most rudimentary forms of human agency. Central to the reproduction of the prison standoff are coercive *productions and invasions* of (bodily and psychic) space, incorporating violent assaults on the prisoner's sense of corporeality into a dynamic of permanent *displacement* that renders the shifting terrains of confrontation into new opportunities for generating the power of domination:

> The perceptual world of a control unit—and to some extent of any prison unit—includes flat, steady, artificial light, a built environment of harsh angles and flat planes, sudden noise and echoing voices that can't quite be made out, constant surveillance, and utter dependence on others for basic physical needs. This world is similar to that described by people experiencing certain extreme states of mind.[30]

A fulcrum of the prison's necessary internal crisis exists precisely at this intersection between the contrived binary calculus of confrontation and seemingly countless, endless processes of invasion and displacement. Many imprisoned people consider the forced probing and coerced movements of their bodies as fundamental ingredients of the prison's grating abusiveness. Keith R. Lansdowne's short essay "Choosing Sanity" recounts his passage into the bowels of Walla Walla prison (Washington) and the demoralization of his own stunning though routine subjection:

> During the course of a routine shakedown by the guards, my shank was discovered. As a consequence, I was sent to the Intensive Management Unit (IMU), which is a fancy-sounding title for solitary confinement, otherwise known as "the hole."

Prison policy dictated that any convict entering the IMU be sub-jected to a body cavity search . . . to put it in street vernacular, anyone going to the IMU was subject to having a finger shoved up his ass.

Naturally, I objected to this policy. As a result, when the guards came to transport me to IMU, they came in force. Five guards physically overwhelmed me, while one guard videotaped the anal assault. Following the digital rape, I was taken to the IMU and placed in a cell. . . .

The day after my arrival in IMU, I was served with a notice that I was being charged with violation of a major rule. Specifically, I was charged with assault on a staff member. This arose from my refusal to sub-mit to anal rape peacefully. . . .

While I was in IMU, I was required to submit to a strip search prior to leaving my cell for any reason. This was degrading. And the act of dress-ing and undressing gave the guards numerous opportunities to make fun of my pink-tinged IMU overalls, to tell me how alluring I looked. The guards rarely missed an opportunity to taunt me or any other IMU resi-dent. It didn't require much courage on their part: whenever we left our cells, we were handcuffed with our hands behind our backs. In addition, we were escorted by a minimum of two guards, and sometimes by more than two.

I must admit . . . I allowed myself to be goaded by the taunting; I succumbed to the rage that it triggered. On too many occasions I tried my best to cause one or more of the guards enough pain to think twice before tormenting me again. Every time I did this, I lost. Every time I did this, I was beaten. And every time I wound up with yet more sanctions, more time in IMU.[31]

Lansdowne's writing is instructive for its illustration of the excesses that constitute official routine—the numbing degradation, infantilization, sexual violence, and physical beatings that he absorbed (and resisted) appear here as inscriptions of an institutionalized conflict whose out-come is as predetermined as it is repetitive.

Lansdowne's initial violation—possession of a crude weapon—doubtlessly derived from a desire for self-preservation against potential aggressors. He suggests, however, that the pervasive violence *of the state* generates the most serious physical and psychic harm to the imprisoned. The premise of the guards' "routine shakedown" was their capacity to immobilize, their positionality as the legitimate agents of bodily violence, as well as the institution's overwhelming concentration on the production and discovery of disobedience. It is the prisoner's inevitable failure to comply that constructs the space of the standoff, the implication of his or her insidious will to subjectivity that renders these repetitive rituals of living death. After resisting and surviving the state's "videotaped anal assault," Lansdowne recounts the scene as a rather horrific pleasure fest of brutality that culminates in the physical and symbolic possession of his body by the designated representatives of the state's desires. The postrape routine of the IMU signifies the thoroughness with which the inmate's forced removals provoke new spaces of subjection, as the homoerotic "dressing and undressing" of the prisoner spurs an aggressively sexualized punitive investment in his body, the simultaneously homophobic and homoerotic play and "flirting" of the guards occurring at the scene of yet another coercive invasion of the captive male body. Suggesting that bodily domination and retributive punishment correspond with a discomforting intimacy between inspectors and the inspected, Lansdowne's story testifies to the reflexive relation between invasion-displacement, penetration-movement, as the prison instantly and persistently constitutes different sites and moments of confrontation.

The common denominator in these shifting carceral spaces is the anticipation or outright projection of a dangerous response from the object of grating degradation, as if the pounding of the captive into a state somewhere beneath and beyond simple physical submission (evidence of "obedience" thus wrought) were only meant to reconstitute and proliferate individualized sites of institutional crisis. Standoff spaces, in this context, accomplish even more than the opportunity for indulgent exercises of state power. Imprisoned insurrectionist Al Cruz, interviewed by a radio journalist in the midst of the Attica rebellion of 1971, makes an incisive analysis of the regime's (communicative) conventions of force while centering antiblack violence as the template and common vernacular of punitive carceral technologies:

> The [correctional] officers . . . don't talk to you. They use what is called the "nigger stick." They don't talk to you. The club is used as a form of communication. The guard doesn't speak to you. All he'll say is, "Line up," and when you hear a tap on the floor or on the wall—"bang!" you know—that means to walk; when you hear it again that means to stop. Everything is done by the nigger stick.[32]

There is a compulsion beating throughout the spaces of the prison regime, an almost rhythmic pulsing of desire to test the limits of power's necessarily unfulfilled capacity to exterminate subjects while simultaneously, consistently resuscitating them as the necessary antagonists of a pedantic, endless political drama. It is in this sense that *punishment is not enough*. There is no moral outcome to validate the alleged story, an utter absence of vindication (good over evil, justice over wrongdoing). The prison punishes disobedience in order to make more disobedience.

Lansdowne's humanity repeatedly shows through his outrage, physical resistance, and the very act of recounting. Yet, the rewards for his effort were torment, beating, and further punitive sanctions. It is, he asserts, a spiraling without end, a brand of suffering that is utterly comprehensive and constantly changing. Contrary to typical prison narratives (private as well as popular), the pain does not simply end: "Every time . . . I lost. Every time . . . I was beaten."

Contradicting the progressivist mythology of what John Edgar Wideman has referred to as the "neoslave narrative," such truth telling subverts a particular American nationalist telos. Distinguishing Mumia Abu-Jamal's *Live from Death Row* from the spate of popular biographical and autobiographical books about African American celebrities ("from Oprah to O. J. to Maya Angelou"), Wideman schematizes the narrative and entrepreneurial structure that Abu-Jamal—along with other imprisoned writers—critiques and ruptures:

The formula for the neoslave narrative sells because it is simple; because it accepts and maintains categories (black/white, for instance) of the status quo; because it is about individuals, not groups, crossing boundaries; because it comforts and consoles those in power and offers a ray of hope to the powerless. Although the existing social arrangements may allow the horrors of plantations, ghettos, and prisons to exist, the narratives tell us, these arrangements also allow room for some to escape. Thus the arrangements are not absolutely evil. No one is absolutely guilty, nor are the oppressed (slave, prisoner, ghetto inhabitant) absolutely guiltless. If some overcome, why don't the others?[33]

Imprisoned radical intellectuals, writers, and activists frequently dislodge the structure of the neoslave narrative, speaking into an iconic void in which their names, bodies, and biographies lack popular recognition. The impossibility of the reader's "living vicariously" through the text reflects in the imprisoned, isolated narrator's stunning loss of self-identification, her or his proximity to psychic and spiritual death, and the insufficiency of language in communicating whatever it is that the narrator is experiencing.

Activist-scholar Cassandra Shaylor's close contact with women SHU inmates such as Helen Roberts (a pseudonym) reveals this narrative departure from the neoslave telos into a condition of living death, while further unveiling the sexualized state violence that is fundamental to the carceral standoff. She quotes Roberts:

In the SHU, I felt like they were trying to take away part of my identity. . . . Your sense of creativity gets lost, your sense of identity gets lost. All I could do was just try to hold on to those fundamental things. I was fighting so hard just to hang on to a sense of self.[34]

Roberts's account speaks to a violence that is historical and ongoing, precisely because it spurs the reproduction of institutional practice in the women's SHU. Such a narrative voice defies the sentimental humanist identification of the reader, *because there is no one there to identify with.*

The alias of "Helen Roberts" signifies the necessary anonymity of the counter state truth teller, rendering her presence in the text semifictional—we must not know who she "really" is, in order that she not become further exposed to punishment beyond the current routine. More important, Roberts testifies to a coercive fracturing of self, the loss of subjective coherence and agency-in-the-world that forms the discursive center of more conventional first-person narratives. Akin to Lansdowne's terrifying passage into a state of normalized degradation, Roberts's living death is fundamentally outside the realm of comprehension: she can describe what is happening to her without claiming to understand it, existentially or intellectually; she can speak to a condition of alienation from her own body and identity without asserting confidence in the inevitability of her own reconstitution as a "whole" person. "I feel like I have been shattered into a million little pieces. . . . The threats of violence, the constant sexual abuse, the complete powerlessness that I experienced in an abusive relationship were still in my life, only in the SHU, it's the state that is doing it."[35]

The spatial logic of the prison standoff relies on the production of multiple confrontations, subsumed and generally obscured by the binary calculus of the formal opposition between prisoner and state. It is the violence occurring in the margins of official state portrayals of the prison—and betraying its discursive and architectural veneer of cold rationality, spatial sterility, total efficiency—that remakes the apparent excesses (the cruel and unusual) of institutional practice into the primary articulations of its power. These articulations hinge on the capacity of normalized degradation, bodily aggression, and dislocation to aggressively attack the prisoner's corporeality and undermine her or his ability simply to self-identify.

Violence and Myopia: Arrested Languages

Sketching the relation between power, hierarchy, and institutional practice in "everyday life," Arthur Kleinman argues for a theory of civil society that recognizes the centrality of violence to the order of things:

Wheresoever power orients practices—and that is everywhere—there is violence. That is to say, social power is responsible for (and responds to) relevance and exigency. Hierarchy and inequality, which are so fundamental to social structures, normalize violence. Violence is what lends to culture its authoritativeness. Violence creates (and reemerges from) fear, anger, and loss—what might be called the infrapolitical emotions. Violence, in this perspective, is the vector of cultural processes that work through the salient images, structures, and engagements of everyday life to shape local worlds. Violence, thus, is crucial to cultural processes of routinization, legitimation, essentialism, normalization, and simplification through which the social world orders the flow of experience within and between body-selves.[36]

Kleinman's notion of the *generative* necessity of violence to social relations implies that violence is not the cumulative sum of isolated, individual episodes of behavioral deviance from some mystified "peaceful" societal norm. Violence *is*. Violence creates order, produces as it reinforces structures of domination and hierarchy, constituting the cultures of everyday life that melt into common assumption. Kleinman's problematic resonates in the construction of prison space, especially its production of multiple locations of confrontation between state and inmate. State violence constructs the place and provokes the drama of the prison standoff, whether it occurs in the cell, yard, SHU, or strip-search chamber. Precisely because these scenes occur *outside* the scope of white civil society, producing an alternate, parallel, and forcefully disappeared institution of "everyday life," the structure of violence therein is permanently altered by the prison's normalized antinormality.

As the structured violence of the standoff flows unequally within the larger binary calculus of the prison (the state's ominous forecasting of inmate rebellions notwithstanding), the uniforms of the state often become the focused objects of the prisoner's will to subjectivity. As one imprisoned activist asserts, "The enemies *are* the badges and guns. There may be a system and hierarchy behind those people, but *I can't see beyond them.*"[37] Radical praxis within the confines of the prison's everyday standoff, within this coerced myopia, frequently manifests as unprogrammatic opposition, a seemingly ad hoc or spontaneous resistance to domination that does not—cannot—conclude in decisive vindication. In fact, such forms of insurgency are elemental to the prison regime's structuring standoff, a drama within its larger technology of power.

A central theoretical contribution of this critical discourse is its refiguring of the condition, philosophy, and historical trajectory of the counter- and antisystemic politics that imprisoned activists invent and (re)articulate. The possibility of a broader reception of imprisoned intellectuals' creative works is generally preempted by a desire (on behalf of those consuming) to read, see, and hear a discourse of transcendence, hope, and ultimate transformation (whether personal, structural, or both). Far more difficult is the political and theoretical challenge of *recognition:* in this case, that the rhetoric of nihilism and death is a seminal truth telling, a form of radical testimonial that binds an individual's condition to a broader confrontation with a death-generating institution. In dialogue, political prisoners Marilyn Buck and Susan Rosenberg illustrate the linkages between death and agency, individual experience and the structuring of state violence:

> MARILYN BUCK: Being locked up is physically and psychically invasive. All body parts are subject to physical surveillance and possible "inspection." Never-ending strip searches . . . one must dissociate oneself psychically, step outside that naked body under scrutiny by some guard who really knows nothing about us, but who fears us because we are prisoners, and therefore dangerous. . . . The guard stands there before the prisoner, violating the privacy of her body, observing with dispassionate contempt. It affects each of us. There is a profound sense of violation, humiliation, anger. . . . I do not think I will ever get used to it.
>
> SUSAN ROSENBERG: One of the things that happens is that many prisoners stop wanting to see visitors. Such invasion of our private lives leads many to isolate themselves further from their families, their children, and their communities. They do not want loved ones subjected to the

humiliation and degradation heaped upon them for being related, for visiting. The dissociation is profound.[38]

The prison regime creates new forms of subjective disarticulation—forms of living death—in its production of novel carceral spaces and an accompanying multiplication of standoff circumstances. For Buck and Rosenberg, the permanent defensiveness of the imprisoned woman, her constant absorption of banal bodily violation and violence, and her resultant political commitment to psychic and visceral self-preservation suggest a radically individualized confrontation with the logic and embodiment of state power. It is this necessary individuation of political resistance/opposition that undermines the possibility of generating resistance and subversion on a larger scale. This problematic exposes the political and theoretical questions at the core of the aforementioned challenge of recognition: What would be the *political* consequence of translating this radical truth telling—*prison as subjective disarticulation, or death space*—through other forms of praxis, including and especially the variety of antiprison, prison abolition, prison moratorium, antideath penalty, prisoner support, and human rights activisms? How would such an effort transform current political languages (vernacular and conceptual) while rendering some elements obsolete or useless?

"Dying Is Too Easy":
Talking to/through the Dead and Distant

Spatial confrontations between state and captive produce alternate—and warring—conceptions of history, biography, and temporality. The prison's logic of death exterminates time as we know it. Bodies fill up spaces that have been conceived and constructed within an ahistorical temporality—a time passage alienated from history. The prison is a place—a facility, in the clinical and experimental sense—in which experiences prior to and outside of the prison's proper domain disappear from both the official record and the institutional landscape.

Visiting rooms and plexiglass booths reunite friends, lovers, families, and acquaintances in rituals of mutual deception, as contrivances of the "private" (marked by the literally guarded exchange of conversations, emotions, and affect) belie the presence of uniformed keepers who track and enforce the temporal boundaries of these sentimental encounters. Interaction between visitors and captives frequently takes on the form of a prolonged mourning, a sudden and fleeting respite from the unspeakable pain of absence with the looming awareness that the end of visiting time is fast approaching. This symbolic purgatory, filled with pained charades of private life and meaningful human intercourse, marks the onset of a sanitized, hyperrationalized time that matches and orders the place in which it occurs. There is a choking temporality to the visit—time effectively begins in the state's threshold, freezing historical possibility at the point of entry.

Wagner-Pacifici's theory of the standoff brings attention to the death time of the prison, suggesting that the effective stoppage of conventional temporality within the standoff marks another dimension of normalized antinormality:

> By their very nature, standoffs stop time in its tracks. A certain tension, an expectancy, marks their existence in and through time. Standoffs may reflect entrenched, long-term, serious disagreements of individuals, groups, communities, or nations. Yet the kind of crisis that precipitates itself into a standoff draws attention to itself as a temporal anomaly, something outside of the normal parameters of time.[39]

The terror of the prison regime is its mundane rendering of the anomalous into the everyday. State power, according to Ray Luc Levasseur, works within the temporal logic of endless sameness—a grinding repetition of motion, sound, and vision that convinces the imprisoned that their very subjectivity is in question. "It seems endless. Each morning I look at the same gray door and hear the same rumbles followed by long silences. It is endless."[40] Levasseur deftly observes that there is often no discernible (or meaningful) distinction between the *illusion* of time frozen into a mind-boggling warp of repetition ("It *seems* endless") and the *actuality* of this time warp experienced as such (emphatically, "It *is* endless"). The institutionalized standoff of the prison appears as more than the simple reification of places and positions in a strategic gridlock; it is the necessary contingency of crisis that compels the state to enforce death time, a juridical and literal exit from the rhythms and temporal passages of civil society. Outside normal time, prison time implies a qualitatively different conception of historical possibility and political agency.

Centering the emergence of "action" within the standoff, Wagner-Pacifici speaks to the necessity for a more organic conception of the relation between space and time:

> A standoff makes the existential claim that it can actually halt action in its tracks. While the standoff continues, action is precisely that which should *not* occur. Nevertheless, a series of action chains secrete themselves into the interstices, literal and figurative, of the times and spaces of the standoff. . . . The effort taken to act during a standoff involves not just the necessary carrying out of typifications and strategizations, but requires a constant recognition that any action launches itself directly in the face of the situation-defining stasis of mutual threat and the hovering spectre of violence.[41]

Sterility, security, control, and rationality may only exist where there is the threat of disruption, infection, incoherence, and danger. Prison time manifests as an overbearing, preemptive force on the bodily and psychic energies of the imprisoned—that is, the state professes its power as the halting of any and all activity that it has not dictated as useful (labor), acceptable (limited sociability), tolerable (exercise), or necessary (biological functioning).

Tremendous human and technological energies pour into the apparatus for the express purpose of *making time happen*—the ideal type of the prison's "everyday" foregrounds the valorous expenditure of state labor against the very possibility of the captives' misbehaviors, practicing domination in the face of its spectacular and imminent reversal. However, it is precisely when the moment of counter- and antistate activity—

insurrection and rebellion of the ideologically framed and unprogrammatic varieties alike—displaces and disturbs prison time, sustaining beyond the fleeting moment or contained episode, that the temporal and spatial "interstices" of the prison actually become determinant.

The paradigmatic collective antagonism to prison time and state authority may be the Attica rebellion of 1971, when more than thirteen hundred prisoners seized control of the prison in an attempt to rupture routine and dramatically expose the hidden social truth of state violence in the punitive carceral. It was within this abrupt and daunting violation of state authority that the rebels' declarations of political incorrigibility liberated time and history from the grip of official narratives. Moreover, the call for solidarity between the imprisoned and the free converged in the expression of an incipient penal abolitionist social vision. The Attica declaration's currency as a public, counterstate knowledge production further demonstrated the power of action in the face of a violent stasis:

> There seems to be a little misunderstanding about why this incident developed here at Attica. . . . The entire incident that has erupted here at Attica . . . [is a result of] the unmitigated oppression wrought by the racist administrative network of this prison throughout the years.
>
> We are men! We are not beasts, and we do not intend to be beaten or driven as such!
>
> The entire prison populace—that means each and every one of us here—have set forth to change forever the ruthless brutalization and disregard for the lives of the prisoners here and throughout the United States. What has happened here is but the sound before the fury of those who are oppressed. We will not compromise on any terms except those terms that are agreeable to us. We call upon all the conscientious citizens of America to assist us in putting an end to this situation that threatens the lives of not only us, but each and every one of you as well. We have set forth demands that will bring us closer to the reality of the demise of these prison institutions that serve no useful purpose to the people of America but to those that would enslave and exploit the people of America.[42]

It may very well be in the realm of *displaced time*, through the intersection between agency and temporality, that radical political praxis—in this case, articulating through an insurrectionist (and homosocial) captive black/brown masculinity (*"We are men! We are not beasts."*)—can fracture the death logic of the prison regime. For the Attica rebels, led by black and Puerto Rican insurgents, the political memory of slavery, displacement, and colonization—and the histories of domination borne on their bodies as that which transmogrified them into captive "beasts" of burden—logically enacted a public demand for recognition as "men." The demand, in and of itself, was the displacement of a historical nonaccess to actualized subjectivity. Whereas the condition of death suggests time's closure for the biological body, the struggle to *make time live (or to relive time)*—discovering and reinventing history, constructing myth as social truth, short-circuiting state domination in the process of breaking protocol in the prison standoff—suggests the subversion of the prison's condition of reproduction.

In the aftermath of the Attica uprising, the prison regime and its structural accompaniments (police, elected officials, jurisprudence) persistently galvanize against the possibility of another Attica—thus the overbearing commitment to a normalized antinormality, an institutionalized time that is essentially outside historical temporality. It is in the nexus of this repression that new and urgent forms of opposition may emerge: a state of emergency within the stronghold of the state:

> The action driving the parties of a standoff to the standoff state and out through the other side of it is primarily a project of interpretation. Standoffs must be set off categorically from other situations. Participants must find themselves or declare themselves to be in an emergency. Such an existentially diacritical moment foregrounds the difference between *normal* time and space and *emergency* time and space.[43]

It is difficult to speculate and impossible to theorize what might happen within such a state of emergency. As action forces the folding of time *into* space—scattering a radical sensibility of history (living time) through the interior geography of the prison—the logic of death can only reproduce its anticipated failure: the provocation of resistance, subversion, opposition, and revolt through the embodied contradiction of trying to make *nonsubjects*, including and especially the incomplete production of captive subjects who are, in fact, not outside of—and incompletely isolated from—history. The ongoing self-narrative of Hugo "Yogi" Pinell, one of the longest-held political prisoners in the United States, is illustrative.

Pinell has been in some variety of solitary confinement for about three decades, and has not had a contact visit, seen natural sunlight, or made a phone call since the 1970s. Originally imprisoned in 1965, he became a close friend of W. L. Nolen in Soledad State Prison during the early years of his incarceration. After Nolen's assassination and George Jackson's transfer to San Quentin State Prison (with fellow "Soledad Brothers" Fleeta Drumgo and John Clutchette), Pinell ambivalently embraced political leadership among his cohorts:

> When W. L. got shot down and George got locked up right there in Soledad, I got a chance to talk to him. He said, "I'm going to San Quentin, man, so you keep everybody together here." So when he gave me that responsibility the other guys said, "Hey Yogi, that's beautiful man, shit, we'll listen to you."[44]

Engaged in heightened confrontation and periodic guerrilla combat with Soledad's famously white-supremacist bloc of guards and administrators, Pinell (of African-Nicaraguan descent) quickly became one of the focal points—a conspicuously targeted black body—for the prison regime's self-production. His history of coerced bodily transfer among different carceral sites bespeaks shifting temporalities of bodily emergency. During a 2001 interview in the Pelican Bay SHU, Pinell articulated a philosophy of subjection that tangles the violence of state torture within a legacy of black-liberationist sacrifice.

Pinell provides a situated and incisive history of the California prison as a carceral war zone: he and five others—the "San Quentin Six"—were prosecuted and tortured by the state for the alleged murder of three guards and the assault of three others, casualties resulting from the prison insurrection catalyzed by the cold-blooded killing of the widely respected Jackson in August 1971. Recalling his survival of this period, Pinell articulates and revises the context and meaning of radical political practice once overdetermined by a material logic of death:

> When I got to San Quentin . . . that's when I decided I didn't like the spot I was in . . . [One of the San Quentin guards] told me, "Yogi, you're through, man, we got your father, we got all your daddies [a reference to Nolen and Jackson, Pinell's mentors], they're gone now. You're it, man, but I'll tell you what I'm going to do with you: we're not going to kill you tonight, we're not going to kill you tomorrow. But we're going to put it on you, we're going to make an example out of you to all the so-called revolutionary fools and punks; *we're going to break their spirit through you.*"
>
> So they started bringing me out and beating me up all the time. [Other prisoners would ask me,] "Why you want to come out [of your cell to get beat up]?" I said, "'cause if I don't come out they said they're going to go down the line [and beat everyone]. . . ." *I couldn't let nobody touch [anybody else] . . . so I had to take the beatings.*[45]

There is a clear sense in which Pinell historicizes as he rearticulates his own tortured body, conceptualizing his survival and suffering as both a protective practice (shielding fellow captives by taking the beatings himself) and a vessel of political education. In the context of this zone of warfare, Pinell fronts himself as fodder for the regime's violence, having been exposed and targeted by the state as a known guerrilla soldier. Whereas his codefendants in the San Quentin Six trial were eventually released from prison (three were acquitted in the trial, and two were convicted but later granted parole), Pinell is the state's chosen holdover, an object lesson for other latent or incipient combatants fighting the essential structure of the prison standoff.

As such, Pinell rethinks the meaning of survival and warfare, life and death, lineage and legacy for one whose condition of existence is to live intimately with ghosts. He reconceptualizes the terms and possibilities of struggle and liberation as he shares his physical isolation with living spirits:

> I can't protect the physical; none of us can protect the physical, we all got to go, but you got other things going: that energy when people love you for real and they keep giving it to you, then when they go . . . all the things that they gave you, the love, the care, the memories, all the time that you spent together [stays with you].
>
> So I always felt like W. L. was alive, that George was alive, [William] Christmas is here . . . they're all here.

Pinell's cohabitation with his comrades' ghostly presence/present distends and distorts the prison regime's logic of death by reembodying the terms of (bodily and ghostly) possession. Within the actively altered terrain of warfare, there is a saturation of spirits, a persistent returning of liberationist combatants killed in action. Sociologist Avery Gordon has contended that the spirits of the dead and disappeared play an integral role in the shaping of the social world, visiting the living and exerting agency on them through the undeniably historical and political work of haunting:

> There is no question that when a ghost haunts, that haunting is real. The ghost has an agency on the people it is haunting and we can call that agency desire, motivation, or standpoint. And so its desires must be broached and we have to talk to it. *The ghost's desire*, even if it is nothing more than a potent and conjectural fiction, must be recognized. . . . [T]he modus operandi of a ghost is haunting, and haunting makes its only social meaning in contact with the living's time of the now.[46]

Yet, even as Pinell is haunted, his living disappearance and social/civil death *haunts us back:*

> I was glad to see a lot of other people that had been railroaded, convicted, that they got all their cases overturned and they got out. It made me happy. Some people say, "Damn, Yogi, everybody getting out, what about you?"

I say it's alright, at least somebody's getting out. Let me be the guinea pig. It's alright. I started taking the attitude [that if it hadn't] been me it would have been somebody else, and maybe that somebody else after twenty-five, thirty years, maybe he wouldn't have held up as well as me. Or maybe he would have done better—but why chance it, you know, let it be me. Somebody got to fill a role somewhere in life. Everybody plays different roles.[47]

Gordon's meditation must be extended, in this sense, to address and encompass the forms of living death invented and massively proliferated by the contemporary social formation, to the extent that the everyday is irreconcilably shadowed, followed, and overdetermined by unacknowledged casualties of war:

In haunting, organized forces and systemic structures that appear removed from us make their impact felt in everyday life in a way that confounds our analytic separations and confounds the social separations themselves. . . . Could it be that analyzing hauntings might lead to a more complex understanding of the generative structures and moving parts of historically embedded social formations in a way that avoids the twin pitfalls of subjectivism and positivism?[48]

Gordon's insightful questioning situates the analytic and political premises of engagement with the living lineage of imprisoned radical intellectuals in the context of contemporary domestic warfare.

Near the end of our 2001 interview at Pelican Bay, Pinell rearticulates the substance and circulation of lives lost—and recirculated—within this liberationist lineage. After I acknowledge the essential and radical truth of his testimonial, Pinell observes that we are intimately linked by a tacit mandate or obligation, confronting and displacing my rhetorical gestures of valorization (and othering) by calling me closer, perhaps, encouraging my embrace of his living, haunting presence:

RODRÍGUEZ: I think everyone will be happy to know that W. L., George, Jonathan [Jackson], all those guys are still alive.

PINELL: They're going to live forever. That doesn't die. If we ever get real close and you happen to leave this world before me, which I hope doesn't happen, you're still going to live. I'm going to carry you with me. I'm going to need your energy to keep me going anyway. If I happen to go, I hope that you can feel my energy because I'm going to be there. I'm going to wake you up at night and say, Hey, have you forgotten about me or what? I'm there. Don't let me go. Don't let me die. It's not that easy. Dying is too easy. Living is what's happening.[49]

The regime "breaks" some, physically exterminates others. An uncounted many, only a few of whom are mentioned here, awaken a new and incorrigible political fantasy, which continuously haunts civil society and its resident nonimprisoned activists and intellectuals. The defeat of institutionalized terror, regimented living death, may very well lie in the radically historicized future visions of imprisoned activist-intellectuals such as Pinell and Viet Mike Ngo, whose short piece "Grave Digger" demands political praxis of a kind yet unseen, one that finds historical emergency in place of pragmatism's patience, principled hostility where typically lies the capacity for compromise with the power of domination:

Grave Digger

We all have roles to play. Some are grave diggers, others fill them. Some decide what shovels to use, others decide who goes where. We all have roles to play and it saddens me to know my role has nothing to do with what I like or what I want.

I don't want war. I want a hammock and a guitar, a beach and some shade. I want to feel the ocean lapping at my ankles and see children smiling. I want the sweetness of coconut milk and the spiciness of a kiss under the waves. I want love and peace.

But dreams don't live in graveyards. Fillers of graves don't have that luxury. My role is to dig or be dug out. Some may say this kind of change is unproductive. I say these "some" don't live in grave yards. Or if they do, they forgot the smell of wholeness; they forgot because the stink has commensurated with the marrow of their souls, and now this smell seems natural; and they forgot that to purge this stink, we need graves and diggers.

So while some preach reform inside classrooms and churches, I'll sharpen my shovel. For revolutions need grave diggers. Revolutions need role players to fill them. You fill the desks and pews. I'll fill the graves. We all have roles to play.[50]

Viet Mike Ngo pictured with godson Viet Taer Rodríguez Shigematsu, Correctional Training Facility at Soledad, California, 2004. Photograph courtesy of the author.

CHAPTER 6

Forced Passages: The Routes and Precedents of (Prison) Slavery

The colored people of America are coming to face the fact quite calmly that most white Americans do not like them, and are planning neither for their survival, nor for their definite future.

—W. E. B. Du Bois, "A Negro Nation within the Nation" (1935)

After a while, people just think oppression is the normal state of things. But to become free, you have to be acutely aware of being a slave.

—Assata Shakur, *Assata: An Autobiography* (1987)

Kinships of Immobilization

The prison regime organizes and constitutes a dynamic site of human immobilization and liquidation, extending its technologies beyond periodic rituals of state-conducted executions and into the realm of a fatal biopoliticality. As a technology of violence, it has become centrally focused on containing, controlling, and punishing the bodies of white civil society's unassimilables and incorrigibles. A durable material structure of normalized social liquidation, intimately linked to a cultural production that conveys its necessity and inevitability, has organized the growth and massive proliferation of the prison into a form of permanent crisis response; that is, the state articulates its methodology of peace, law, and order through the institutionality of the prison, a putatively stable and coherent holding point for civil society's embodied disorder.

This final chapter considers the prison as a necessary site of antisociality and mass-based civic and social death. I am concerned with the prison regime as a mode of social (re)production, a conceptualization that (1) centers the technology of imprisonment as the construction of a particular political-geographic dominion and (2) extrapolates the genealogy of mass-based violence that is essential to the structuring of the United States of America as a dynamic white-supremacist locality. I make two arguments through this conceptualization, followed by a meditation on some immediate political and intellectual points of departure evoked by the overarching theorizations of this book.

First, I contend that the epoch of white-supremacist chattel slavery and its transatlantic articulation—the Middle Passage—engender and enliven the social and political logic of the current carceral formation. There is a material and historical kinship between the prison as a contemporary regime of violence and the structures of racialized mass incarceration and disintegration prototyped in the chattel transfer of enslaved Africans. A radical genealogy of these multiple, trans-epochal forced passages from continent to plantation, or civil society to imprisonment, must focus on the logic of the *passages themselves* rather than on the putative "origin" and "destination" points of those coerced movements. Second, I argue that a foregrounding of the current and living lineage of radical intellectuals imprisoned in the United States articulates a *theoretical vernacular of death*, one that productively disrupts hegemonic and progressive counterhegemonic public-policy, academic, and activist discourses and their alleged critiques of prisons, policing, and the prison industrial complex. It is at the carceral site of antisociality writ large, where the state's biopolitical power is unmediated—qualitatively violating and violent—that imprisoned radical intellectuals are crucial interlocutors, theorists, and guerrilla combatants. Beyond simply "bearing witness" to the degradation of bodies and subjects, these captive activists and scholars generate a theoretical corpus that articulates with a trajectory of radical resistance and opposition to state violence and the social formation with which that violence melds. Departing from these two contentions, the chapter's closing section looks to the work of Frantz Fanon to suggest a historically and politically situated modality for the critical interdisciplinary study of—and lasting political engagement with—this living lineage of imprisoned radical intellectuals.

I suggest Fanon's conception of "social truth" as a working philosophy of praxis through which to conceptualize the central political antagonism that enmeshes, constrains, and potentially transforms the ongoing critical scholarship and activism that address the problem of the prison regime.

Forced Passages: The Routes and Precedents of (Prison) Slavery

Angela Y. Davis, Alex Lichtenstein, David Oshinsky, and others have closely examined the material continuities between U.S. racial chattel plantation slavery and the emergence of the modern American penal system. These studies bring crucial attention to the centrality of white-supremacist juridical, policing, and paramilitary regimes in the production of a carceral apparatus during the late nineteenth century that essentially replicated—and arguably exacerbated—the constitutive logic of the supposedly defunct slave plantation. Lichtenstein, for example, argues convincingly that the transition from chattel slave to black prison labor in the post–Civil War South exemplified the "continual correspondence between the forces of modernization and the perpetuation of bound labor":

> In the postbellum South, at each stage of the region's development, convict labor was concentrated in some of the most significant and rapidly growing sectors of the economy. . . . [The] decisive shift from private to public exploitation of forced black labor marked the triumph of the modern state's version of the social and economic benefits to be reaped from bound labor, in the name of developing a more . . . "progressive" economy. Thus, from Reconstruction through the Progressive Era the various uses of convict labor coincided with changes in the political economy of southern capitalism.[1]

By way of contrast, Davis, in an examination of Frederick Douglass's historical understanding of the post-Emancipation criminalization of black communities, offers a theorization of how "the prison system established its authority as a major institution of discipline and control for black communities during the last two decades of the nineteenth century," yielding a lineage of "carceral regulation" that arrived at "crisis proportions" a century later. Most important is Davis's foregrounding of the seamless linkage between the formal abolition of extant forms of racial chattel slavery in 1865 and the somewhat unheralded (albeit simultaneous) recodification and moral legitimization of a revised apparatus of enslavement, which materialized under the auspices of criminal conviction and imprisonment:

> When the Thirteenth Amendment was passed in 1865, thus legally abolishing the slave economy, it also contained a provision that was universally celebrated as a declaration of the unconstitutionality of peonage. "Neither slavery nor involuntary servitude, *except as a punishment for crime*, whereof the party shall have been duly convicted, shall exist within the United States, or anyplace subject to their jurisdiction" (emphasis added). That exception would render penal servitude constitutional—from 1865 to the present day.[2]

Tracing the contemporary prison regime's points of origin to the juridical and material developments of the post–Civil War South, in particular to its twinned and mutually constituting crises of economic modernization and managing/controlling a suddenly nominally "free" black population, is essential for a radical genealogy of the U.S. prison. To the extent that "the post–Civil War southern system of convict lease . . . transferred symbolically significant numbers of black people from the prison of slavery to the slavery of prison," the formation of the U.S. prison must be seen as inseparable from the relation of white freedom/black unfreedom, white ownership/black fungibility, that produced the nation's foundational property relation as well an essential component (with Native American displacement and genocide) of its racial ordering.[3] In fact, the prison can be understood through this genealogy as one of the primary productive components of the U.S. nation-state's internal coherence—via the production of white-supremacist hegemony through black bodily immobilization and punishment (and modernist expansiveness) as the prison replaced the "irrational" horrors of chattel slavery with the juridical "rationality" of the prison.

I am interested in stretching both the historical reach and the conceptual boundaries of this genealogical tracing. There are always and necessarily movements and passages between the (linked) temporalities and geographies of death, such as those of the slave plantation and post-Emancipation prison, but the contemporary case of the prison regime constitutes a site and condition of death *that is itself a form of passage.* This is to say that the prison is less a "destination" point for "the duly convicted" than a point of *massive human departure*—from civil society, the free world, and the mesh of affective social bonds and relations that produce varieties of "human" family and community. Hence labor exploitation, the construction of unfree labor (what some have loosely called a "new slavery"), and the mass confinement of a reserve labor pool are *not* the constitutive logics of the new prison regime, although these are certainly factors that shape the prison's institutional structure.[4] Whereas forced labor (formal prison slavery) was at one time conceived as the primary institutional tool for rehabilitating imprisoned white men, the proliferation of mass incarceration in the current era has complexly reinscribed a logic of extermination, invoking the rhetoric of "genocide" of imprisoned black-liberationist Tashiri Askari and formerly imprisoned community organizer Dorsey Nunn (among others)."[5]

Sharon Patricia Holland's meditations on the entanglement—in fact, the veritable inseparability—of death and black subjectivity indicts the very formation of a white Americana and its accompanying social imaginary vis-à-vis the never-ending presence (and imminence) of racial chattel slavery:

> It is possible to make at least two broad contentions here: a) that the (white) culture's dependence on the nonhuman status of its black subjects was never measured by the ability of whites to produce a "social heritage"; instead, it rested on the status of the black as a nonentity; and b) that the transmutation from enslaved to freed subject never quite occurred at the level of the imagination.[6]

I would add that, indeed, what *has* occurred is an inscription of the black nonhuman "nonentity" through the category of the imprisoned—hence illegal/extralegal/convict—subject: although the white social imagination has been unable to assimilate the notion of a "freed (black) subject" in its midst beyond cynical or piecemeal gestures of "inclusion" (which is to say, ultimately, that it cannot assimilate blackness at all), the actual "transmutation" has been from the white social imagination of the slave to that of the (black) prisoner, or what Frank Wilderson III theorizes as the new black "prison slave."[7]

The status of the enslaved/imprisoned black subject forms the template through which white Americana constructs a communion of historical interest, mobilizations of political force, and, more specifically, the production and proliferation of a regime of mass-based human immobilization. My theoretical centering of black unfreedom here is not intended to minimize or understate the empirical presence of "nonblack" Third World, indigenous, or even white bodies in these current sites of state captivity, but rather to argue that the technology of the prison regime—and the varieties of violence it wages against those it holds captive—is premised on a particular white-supremacist module or prototype that is, in fact, rooted in the history of slavery and the social/racial crisis that it has forwarded into the present.

The contemporary regime of the prison encompasses the weaponry of an institutionalized dehumanization. It also, and necessarily, generates a material rendition of the nonhuman and subhuman that structurally antagonizes and decenters the immediate capacity of the imprisoned subject to simply *self-identify*. Under the anonymous byline "A Federal Prisoner," one imprisoned writer offers a schematic view of this complex process, which is guided by the logic of a totalizing disempowerment and social disaffection:

> The first thing a convict feels when he receives an inconceivably long sentence is shock. The shock usually wears off after about two years, when all his appeals have been denied. He then enters a period of self-hatred because of what he's done to himself and his family.

If he survives that emotion—and some don't—he begins to swim the rapids of rage, frustration and alienation. When he passes through the rapids, he finds himself in the calm waters of impotence, futility and resignation. It's not a life one can look forward to living. The future is totally devoid of hope.[8]

The structured violence of self-alienation, which drastically compounds the effect of formal social alienation, is at the heart of the regime's punitive logic. Yet, it is precisely because the reproduction of the regime relies on its own incapacity to decisively "dehumanize" its captives en masse (hence the persistence of institutional measures that pivot on the presumption and projection of the "inmate's" embodiment of disobedience, resistance, and insurrection) that it generates a philosophy of the captive body that reinscribes and amplifies the (racial) logic of enslavement. This is why the regime's logic of power must reach into the arsenal of a historical apparatus that was an essential element of the global formation of racial chattel slavery while simultaneously structuring its own particular technology of violence and bodily domination. What, then, is the materiality of the archetypal imprisoned body (and subject) through which the contemporary prison regime has proliferated its diverse and hierarchically organized technologies of immobilization and bodily disintegration?

A radical genealogy of the prison regime must engage in a conversation with the massive human departure of the transatlantic Middle Passage, an apparatus and regime of bodily capture and forced mass movement that (1) outlined its own epochal conception of the nonhuman and subhuman, (2) prototyped other technologies of normative black punishment in the white New World, and (3) blueprinted the abject—and durably captive—black presence under the rule of Euro-American modernity. The Middle Passage foreshadows the prison as it routes and enacts chattel slavery, constituting both a passage into the temporality and geography of enslavement (crystallized by Orlando Patterson's conception of slavery as "natal alienation" and "social death") and a condition of existence unto itself—in particular, a spatially specified pedagogical production of black slave ontology.[9]

I am especially concerned with the capacity of white-supremacist regimes to experiment with novel technologies of violence and domination on black bodies, articulating in this instance with what Eric Williams considers to be the overarching "economic" logic of a transcontinental trafficking in enslaved Africans.[10] These experiments in violence yield modalities of power and bodily domination that become available to, and constitutive of, larger social and carceral formations even centuries later. Thus, although the contemporary prison regime captures and immobilizes the descendants of slaves and nonslaves alike, I consider its technology of violence to be inseparable from a genealogy of transatlantic black/African captivity and punishment. A reflection on the historical scope and theoretical significance of this chattel technology offers further context here.

Although the human volume of the Middle Passage has been a subject of empirical and methodological debate since the publication of Philip Curtin's *The Atlantic Slave Trade: A Census* (1969), a loose consensus among historians has been attained since the 1999 release of the Cambridge University Press Trans-Atlantic Slave Trade database. David Eltis, drawing from a rigorous review of previous literature and elaborating from the Cambridge University dataset, suggests a figure of about 11 million "exports of slaves from Africa" between the years 1519 and 1867.[11] Eltis, Curtin, Klein, Lovejoy, Richardson, Inikori, Engerman, and others have estimated that 12–20 percent of the enslaved died during the transatlantic transfer, with 10–15 million captive Africans surviving the passage to the Americas. It is important to note, for the purposes of the genealogical relation I am examining here, that the vast majority of the deaths at sea were the result of conditions endemic to the abhorrent living conditions of the slave vessels (the effects of disease and malnutrition, for example, were exacerbated by the conditions of mass incarceration). Many others committed suicide and infanticide in an attempt to defeat the logic of their biological expropriation and bodily commodification, while unknown numbers were killed in the process of attempting to overthrow their captors. The scale of biological death during the Middle Passage was astronomical and genocidal.

Further, this process underwrote the innovation of a distinctive maritime architecture, literally a seaborne and shipbound geography, devoted to the accumulation, storage, and biological preservation of an enslaved human "cargo." This technology of incarceration, famously portrayed by late-eighteenth-century British abolitionists in their lithograph "Stowage of the British Slave Ship *Brookes*" (see illustration), rendered a profoundly graphic conception of the racialized subhuman and nonhuman as the spatial and existential underside of an expansive European New World millennium. Yet, this mass-scale, transcontinental kidnapping must be examined in the context of the coerced transition that it induced by fiat.[12]

The Middle Passage marked a carceral condition that overlapped—and was irreversibly entangled with—various states and sites of oppression, human disarticulation, and programmatic death. At the height of the transatlantic trafficking of enslaved Africans (from the 1600s through the late 1800s, peaking during the eighteenth century), peoples in Africa were waging a desperate defense of land, ecology, and community against the military slaughter of colonial conquest and the deadly diseases introduced by the Europeans. While continental Africans were being forcibly dispersed and disorganized onto new imperial and colonial geographies, displaced Africans in North America (preceding and including the "United States of America" proper) were experiencing a historically unique condition of mass-based white-supremacist plantation slavery.

In this context the Middle Passage was, at its spatial core, a site of profound subjective and communal disruption for captive Africans: manifesting an epochal rupture from familiar networks of kinship, livelihood, and social reproduction, the voyage was the threshold of geographic, subjective, and bodily displacement for the transatlantic imprisoned. Hortense Spillers suggests that the coercive reconstruction and bodily expropriation of Africans as chattel—in resonance with the contemporary prison—both reifies and blurs the putative gendering of captives: "Under these conditions, one is neither female, nor male, as both subjects are taken into account as *quantities*."[13] This African "New World" diaspora, fundamentally constituted and mobilized through conquest, genocide, and enslavement, was and is defined by a structure of immanent alienation from the material and psychic contexts that operationalized indigenous African sociocultural forms and made their unique renditions of human community intelligible and consistent. The manner in which the Middle Passage allegorized and materialized this unique destruction of human community, particularly its displacement and interruption of indigenous African tribal and communal subjectivities, illuminates how

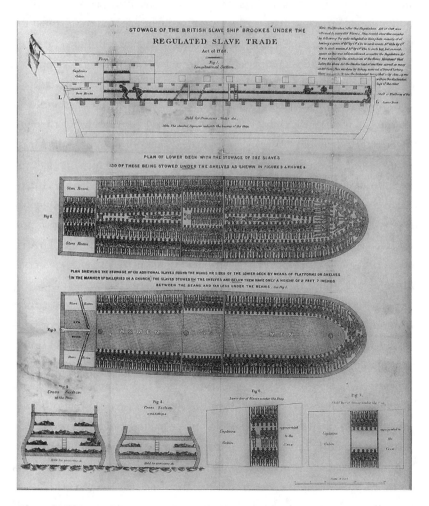

"Stowage of the British Slave Ship *Brookes*," c. 1788. U.S. Library of Congress, Broadside Portfolio 282, no. 43, Prints and Photographs Division (LC-USZ62-44000).

the construction of this seaborne mass incarceration entailed a production of power and domination that pivoted on significantly more than the logistical or economic pragmatics of a live commodity transport. Although the human cargo certainly held a lucrative potential profit for slavers incumbent on their ability to physically bring their stock to market, far more was at stake in the three centuries long institutionalization of this itinerant transatlantic "prison."

The Middle Passage was simultaneously a *pedagogical and punitive* practice that deployed strategies of unprecedented violence in order to "teach" and coerce captive Africans into the methods of an incipient global ordering. Evidentiary fragments of this complex practice are reflected in the historical data, which reveal that rates of survival for the enslaved during the era of the Middle Passage generally equaled or surpassed the survival rates of the European slave-ship crews. This perhaps unexpected phenomenon, on deeper reflection, actually speaks to the pedagogical-punitive logic of the seafaring slave carceral. A brief meditation at the body of literature examining slave-ship mortality rates is useful for the sake of contextualizing the larger trajectory of this argument.

Johannes Postma's careful and thorough text *The Atlantic Slave Trade*, culling from the most recent collections of historical evidence, projects as follows:

> Because slaves were valuable investment property, ship captains kept careful records in logbooks and mortality lists of the dates and causes of death. . . . They show that on average 12 percent of the enslaved did not survive the ocean crossing, though there was considerable variation from one transport to another.[14]

While the mortality rate of enslaved Africans during the transatlantic voyage remains a contested figure, Stephen Behrendt contends that because "the primary aim of merchants was to minimize slave deaths in the middle passage to ensure a profitable voyage," the mortality rates for the European crew were consistently *higher* than for the captives, at times doubling or tripling that of the enslaved. For the merchant slave traders, "minimizing crew mortality was a secondary consideration" to that of "preserving" their human chattel.[15] Philip Curtin's focus on the mid- to late eighteenth century similarly reveals that "the death rate per voyage among the crew was uniformly higher than the death rate among slaves in transit at the same period." In regard to this discrepancy in mortality rates, he argues that "the data are so consistent and regular . . . that this can be taken as a normal circumstance of the eighteenth-century slave trade."[16] Postma, attempting to further explain this discrepancy in mortality, adds that the high death rates among crew members were caused by the fact that "they were onboard much longer than the slaves," a contention supported by Richard Steckel and Richard Jensen's study of the journals of slave-ship surgeons during the late eighteenth century, which reveals that "the trade was extraordinarily hazardous . . . for the crew during loading" of slaves on the West African coast.[17]

Although this body of historical scholarship provides a useful overview of this era, something remains to be said theoretically about the physical labor and intellectual energy that invested in preserving the biological existence of the densely packed, and ostensibly subhuman, captive chattel over and against the lives of the white crew. Rather than assume some self-evident significance to this historical data, it is more useful to consider how these apparently (relatively) lower mortality rates for the imprisoned, even when taken at face value, invite a discussion of the complexity, multidimensionality, and rigorous protraction of the sociohistorical production that the Middle Passage encompassed.

The planned survival of the enslaved was symbiotic to—rather than a logical contradiction of—their mass incarceration in vessel cargo holds. This structure of planned survival and mass bodily immobilization animates the peculiar technology of domination and violence that conceived and persistently refigured the Middle Passage as a primary, long-term *political labor* for the emergent transatlantic European and Euro-American civilization. Establishing a blueprint for the carceral technologies of the landlocked U.S. prison, the Middle Passage simultaneously (1) remapped enslaved black bodies, (2) prototyped a conception of the imprisoned/slave as the categorical embodiment of the subhuman or nonhuman, and (3) reconfigured multiple scales of geography, constituting new conceptions of the continental (Europe/Africa/"New World") and (transatlantic) oceanic, while inventing new localities in the slave ship and plantation. Thus, the apparent commitment to preserving slave life on board the ships was more than an economic decision. Rather, keeping enslaved captives alive was integral to the production of the Middle Passage as a productive and socially constitutive modality of mass-based imprisonment that collapsed a pedagogy of ontological violence into a regime of profound bodily punishment.

A British abolitionist tract from 1839, protesting this state of incarceration, typically speaks the language of the period's liberal white humanist outrage:

> The wretched victims . . . were then fastened hand and foot to a slave ship, a vessel which has been forcibly described as condensing a greater quantity of human suffering and misery than can any where else be found in so small a space. Imagine then, five or six hundred persons linked together, but trying to get rid of each others, and crammed in a close vessel, in which, by mere pressure, they were reduced to a state of suffocation.[18]

Although it is not my purpose to contest or minimize the historical truthfulness of the scene of mass bodily violence so described, I am more interested in examining the production of power that underwrites this devastating condition of "suffering," "misery," and "suffocation." This is to suggest that the (white) humanist outcry actually misses on the fundamental labor of the conquest, capture, and maritime imprisonment: the Middle Passage situated the enactment of the subhuman and nonhuman as a site of productive rather than destructive embodiment, that is, it assumed the practical and theoretical challenge of constituting a category of subhumanity/nonhumanity that would permanently remain (rather than deteriorate or vanish) as the embedded ontological counterpoint to a globalizing, colonial, and imperial European "humanity."

Writing in 1787, Ottobah Cugoano, a London-based "freedman" and leading black abolitionist, described his survival of the transatlantic voyage and the subjugation of enslavement: "Brought from a state of innocence and freedom, and, in a barbarous and cruel manner, conveyed to a state of horror and slavery: *This abandoned situation may be easier conceived than described.*[19] Cugoano's preference for the conceptual over the descriptive explicitly attempts to flee the voyeuristic lens of the white humanist abolitionist, while refusing to entrap a narrative of slavery's terror within the discursive confines of the empirical. He continues:

> From the time that I was kidnapped and conducted to a factory, and from then in the brutish, base, but fashionable way of traffic, consigned to Grenada, the grievous thoughts which I then felt, still pant in my heart; though my fears and tears have long since subsided. And yet it is still grievous to think that thousands more have suffered in similar and greater distress, under the hands of barbarous robbers, and merciless taskmasters; and that many even now are suffering in all the extreme bitterness of grief and woe, that no language can describe. . . . [T]he deep sounding groans of thousands, and the great sadness of their misery and woe, under the heavy load of oppressions and calamities inflicted upon them, are such as can only be distinctly known to the ears of Jehovah Sabaoth.[20]

Cugoano's narration diverges from that of his white abolitionist counterparts, in that he does not choose to communicate with his readership through an endless repetition of the empirical particularities of slavery's violence; more specifically, he does not care to share in the moral outrage induced by renditions of slavery that occur through particular spectacles of bodily violence (the slave-ship cargo hold, the whipping, the auction block, etc.). The logic of Cugoano's polemic amplifies cultural theorist Saidiya Hartman's contention that

> the most invasive forms of slavery's violence lie not in these exhibitions of "extreme" suffering or in what we see but in what we don't see. Shocking displays too easily obfuscate the more mundane and socially endurable forms of terror. . . .
>
> Rather than glance at the most striking spectacle with revulsion or

through tear-filled eyes, we do better to cast our glance at the more mundane displays of power at the border.[21]

Elaborating the slave ship as precisely such a banal capillary site of power, historian Vincent Harding's incisive analysis of the Middle Passage addresses the symbiosis between the incipient white-supremacist racial formation of the transatlantic conquest and settlement and the ontological relation that characterized the capture, enslavement, and transfer of Africans:

> [T]he ships were even more than prisons. Ultimately they provided black people with an introduction to the Euro-American state, for they were mini-states with their own polity, their own laws and government; the common sailors were the ships' own indigenous oppressed class. . . . At the core of the mini-states, prisons, and kennels it was always possible to discover the social, economic, and political scourges arising out of Europe: racism, capitalism, and the deep human fears they engender. The tie of the ships to European capitalism was evident in the decision to call them "slavers," and in their relationship to the slave "factories," and to the industrial factories at home which made the goods that they brought to trade for humans. To maximize profits, the ships had to herd as many Africans aboard as possible, and to exploit their own white crews.[22]

Harding brings attention to the technologies of human containment that were invented and refined at the site of the slave vessel. This portable and moving confinement was invested with an intensive and sophisticated—and profoundly brutal—technology of incarceration. Olaudah Equiano, prefacing Harding's analogy of the ship as white nation-state, reconstructs his first impression of the slave vessel in his 1789 memoir *Equiano's Travels: The Interesting Narrative of the Life of Olaudah Equiano:* "I could not help expressing my fears and apprehensions to some of my countrymen: I asked them if these people had no country but lived in this hollow place (the ship)."[23] It was within the logic of this power relation— one that significantly exceeds the contained binary relation of torture as a structure of personalized violence and extracted suffering—that bodies were respatialized, and space was reembodied, as the aforementioned British abolitionist text explains:

> The width allowed for each individual was no more than sixteen inches, and the passage between each of these rows of human packages was so small that it was impossible for a person walking by, however carefully, to avoid treading on them. Thus crammed together, like herrings in a barrel, they contracted putrid and fatal disorders, so that those who came to inspect them in a morning often had to pick dead slaves out of their rows, and to unchain their dead carcases [sic] from the bodies of their wretched fellow-sufferers to whom they had been fastened.[24]

Such horrified European and Euro-American abolitionist descriptions of slave-ship geography, and the white humanist outcry they enliven and convey, might be usefully reread in the context of Harding's interpretive framing. The death space of the slave ship, and the genocidal epoch of the Middle Passage, confined and produced bodies that were coercively displaced into the material and theoretical intersection of labor value, social death, and biological death. Less ambivalent, however, was the constitution of enslaved Africans as an emergent ontological category lurking just outside—and irreversibly, productively against—the historical telos of the European Enlightenment and modernity's humankind.

Hortense Spillers writes:

> Those African persons in Middle Passage were literally suspended in the oceanic, if we think of the latter in its Freudian orientation as an analogy on undifferentiated identity: removed from the indigenous land and culture, and not-yet "American" either, these captives, without names that their captors would recognize, were in movement across the Atlantic, but they were also *nowhere* at all.[25]

This ontological subjection, forged over a three-century span through the carceral technology of the Middle Passage, foreshadowed the enduring labor of generating the racialized unfree as the condition of possibility for the civil society of the white and free. As such, the humanist sensibility expressed by elements of the nineteenth-century European and Euro-American abolitionist movements begs the question of who, figuratively and literally, was entitled access to the domain of the "human."

Maria Diedrich, Henry Louis Gates Jr., and Carl Pederson, editors of the 1999 collection *Black Imagination and the Middle Passage*, offer a conceptualization of the transatlantic slave trade that can assist in complicating our temporal and spatial conception of the contemporary regime of imprisonment:

> The Middle Passage . . . emerges not as a clean break between past and present but as a *spatial continuum* between Africa and the Americas, the ship's deck and the hold, the Great House and the slave quarters, the town and the outlying regions.[26]

A genealogy of the contemporary prison regime awakens both the historical memory and the sociopolitical logic of the Middle Passage. The prison has come to form a hauntingly similar spatial and temporal continuum between social and biological notions of life and death, banal liberal civic freedom and totalizing unfreedom, community and alienation, agency and liquidation, the "human" and the subhuman/nonhuman. In a reconstruction of the Middle Passage's constitutive logic, the reinvented prison regime is articulating and self-valorizing a commitment to efficient and effective bodily immobilization within the mass-based ontological subjection of human beings.

Eliminations: Remapping Legacies of the Middle Passage

The contemporary prison, working within the genealogical lineage of the Middle Passage, constantly prototypes technologies premised on a respatialization of bodies and coercive reembodiment of spaces. Robert Perkinson's description of the internal geography of the Florence, Colorado, "control-unit" prison, among the first federal supermax prisons to be introduced in the early 1990s, invokes and refracts the historical image and imaginary of the slave ship's cargo hold:

Each cell contains a three-foot-wide cement bed slab, a concrete stool and desk, a steel sink and toilet, and a three-by-three shower stall. A fluorescent light panel glares from the wall, illuminating other amenities like an electric cigarette lighter, an inmate duress switch (since the cells are essentially soundproof), an air grate, and, in some cells, a small television. Double doors shrink the cells by another three feet, trapping unreachable space between bars and the outer door. Only two window slits allow external light into the cage, one on the steel door staring into the empty hallway and another body-length sliver facing an empty courtyard. The shower, along with food slots in the door, allow for total isolation. . . .

Thus, the Florence ADX's very layout determines that it can be nothing but a chamber of sensory deprivation, designed to press inmates to the brink of insanity by its very architecture. Modern electronics allow constant surveillance and supervision while prisoners themselves remain physically invisible, locked away from any direct human view or contact in compartments of solid steel.[27]

Expanding on the immobilizing logic of the Florence ADX, the September 2001 issue of *Peacekeeper* (the official publication of the California Correctional Peace Officers Association [CCPOA]), offers a propaganda piece valorizing the supermax prison's evolution into more sophisticated carceral techniques:

Imagine the ultimate Big Brother of the prison system—tracking inmates 24 hours a day, 365 days a year. Well, guess what? It exists. Big Brother has arrived at Calipatria State Prison. . . .

Every inmate wears a wrist-worn transmitter called PASS unit, which stands for Personal Activated Security Sensor. When an inmate arrives at the facility, he or she is enrolled into the system database by the system operator. The information typically entered consists of the inmates [*sic*] name, inmate identification number, housing/bed assignment and meal type. . . .

The transmitter is installed on the inmate's non-dominant wrist. It is secured with screws that are tightened with a special torque screwdriver. The clips can only be removed by breaking them. . . .

> Officer A. Felty . . . believes the system is a great deterrent. "The inmates realize they are being constantly monitored and supervised, even when the officer's eyes are not on them. . . . Basically, he knows that escape is not an option, the removal of the bracelet is not an option because he is being constantly monitored—whether the officer is watching him or not."[28]

The totalizing spatial logic of Big Brother conveys a peculiar convergence between high technologies of panoptic discipline and the banal normalization of ritualized and immanent physical violation and violence. Disciplinary biopolitical state power rearticulates through the state's self-justifying monopoly on legitimate forms of coercive and punitive bodily disintegration: far from simply inscribing a more invasive and comprehensive form of "discipline" over its captive civically dead subjects, Big Brother represents a multiplication of the potential sites and scenarios of subjection and physical punishment. This high technology remaps the "prisoner's" body onto a virtual terrain, abstracting her or his bodily movements and gestures into a computerized grid of obedience/disobedience, submission/violation. Such innovations also effect a respatialization of the prison itself, marking the extension and veritable omnipresence of the state's capacity to practice bodily domination over its "inmates."

Although such advanced technologies of imprisonment are an epochal leap from the carceral practices of the Middle Passage, as a production of power and dominion they are constituted by an analogous, and in some places materially similar, social logic and historical trajectory. Located within an extended genealogy of the slave vessel, there is a resurfaced familiarity in the prison's discursive emphasis and material production of effective mass capture, immobilization, and bodily disintegration. Spillers's meditation on the captivity of the Middle Passage illustrates a central genealogical linkage between apparently discrete and epochally distant carceral forms: "on any given day, we might imagine, the captive personality did not know where s/he was, we could say that they were culturally 'unmade,' thrown in the midst of a figurative darkness that exposed their destinies to an unknown course."[29] Jarvis Jay Masters's account of his initial entombment in San Quentin's death-row prison describes a spatial and bodily encounter with the prison's common modes of isolation and circumscription. His narrative echoes those of imprisoned African survivors of the transatlantic transfer (Cugoano, Equiano, and others),[30] while supplementing the CCPOA's rosy tribute to the high-technology prison:

> I will never forget when the steel cell door slammed behind me. I stood in the darkness trying to fix my eyes and readjust the thoughts that were telling me that this was not home—that this tiny space would not, could not be where I would spend more than a decade of my life. . . .
>
> I spread my arms and found that the palms of my hands touched the walls with ease. I pushed against them with all my might, until I realized how silly it was to think that these thick concrete walls would somehow budge. . . . The bed was bolted into the wall like a shelf. It was only two and a half feet wide by six feet long, and only several feet above the gray concrete floor.[31]

Old and new technologies of incarceration have collaborated in the emergence of the contemporary prison. Masters's description of the San Quentin cell reveals the constitutive logic that unifies "low" and "high" carceral technologies in the production of the prison regime, while invoking the captivity of the Middle Passage as living and lived memory. To absorb the geographic breadth and technological depth of the prison regime's elaboration is to come face-to-face with the unprecedented levels of autonomy granted to—and extracted by—the prison to shape the social (and carceral) worlds. It is also to find an insurgent critique of imprisonment that moves from the sometimes eloquent, though consistently displaced, theoretical languages articulated by captive radicals and revolutionaries.

Interviewed in 1970 about his first experience under state captivity, imprisoned black liberationist George Jackson recounts:

> The very first time, *it was like dying*. . . . Just to exist at all in the cage calls for some heavy psychic readjustments. . . . I never adjusted. I haven't

adjusted even yet, with half my life already spent in prison. . . . *Capture,
imprisonment, is the closest to being dead that one is likely to experience in his life.*[32]

Speaking from the experimental "High Security Unit" in Lexington,
Kentucky, some twenty years later, white anti-imperialist political prisoner Susan Rosenberg (whose sentence was commuted in 2001) echoes
Jackson's language in a manner that reveals an essential—though rarely
elaborated—facet of the prison regime. Testifying in the award-winning
1989 documentary *Through the Wire*, Rosenberg says:

> [The High Security Unit is] a prison within a prison. . . . *The High Secu-
> rity Unit is living death.* . . . I believe that this is an experiment being con-
> ducted by the Justice Department to try and destroy political prisoners
> and to justify the most vile abuse of us as women and as human beings, and
> [to] justify it because we are political. (emphasis added)

Since the time of Rosenberg's testimony, the technology of the Lexington High Security Unit has circulated and metamorphosed, virus-like,
through state and federal prisons across the country, multiplying by
the thousands those held captive within such intracarceral carcerals. On
any given day, some 2 million more are incarcerated under the more mundane and routine violence of Jackson's "cage," that is, the normative
jail/prison/detention center. Various carceral forms have astronomically
increased the numbers held captive in conditions of low-intensity physical
and psychological torture, as well as those subjected to high-intensity
punishment and state-sanctioned mental or emotional disordering.[33] In
the meantime, the expansion of youth prisons, mental health facilities,
Homeland Security and immigrant detention centers in the past decades
has been accompanied by a proliferation of conditions easily likened to
both traditional and revised definitions of solitary and mass-based torture.

Jamal al-Harath, in the aftermath of his release from the U.S. prison
camp in Guantánamo Bay, Cuba, in March 2004, surmised the logic of
his detention on flimsy suspicion of connection to Afghanistan's Taliban
and the al-Qaeda network: "The whole point of Guantánamo was to get

to you psychologically . . . . The beatings were not as nearly as bad as the psychological torture. Bruises heal after a week, *but the other stuff stays with you.*"³⁴ Echoing Jackson's meditation on captivity as an approximation of death, and detailing the indelible marks that "existing in a cage" permanently inscribes on body, soul, and psyche, al-Harath illuminates a form of subjective disarticulation that exceeds the formal temporal and spatial boundaries of imprisonment. The Guantánamo detention, he says, will always stay with him, even as he reassumes the formal status of the free person in his homeland of Britain.

The notorious routines characterizing the rise of California's Security Housing Unit (SHU) prisons further extrapolate the white-supremacist logic that persists within the spectacle of the tortured imprisoned body. The videotaped 1994 murder of black prisoner Preston Tate at Corcoran State Prison by prison guards—one of whom prefaced the fatal shooting by announcing, "It's going to be duck-hunting season"—received national attention in the mid- to late 1990s, accompanied by widespread reporting of the Corcoran guards' amused coercion of SHU prisoners into gladiator-style prison yard fights (shooting many of them under the auspices of "trying to protect another inmate or guard").³⁵ Robert Perkinson, in a somewhat furtive narrative political gesture, brings attention to the site of the SHU's unseen, where regulated regimes of bodily violence are partnered with the "application of sophisticated technology to control prisoners' routines, movements, and even thoughts more than ever before." His investigation of the SHU and federal "supermaximum-security" prisons' normative practices of psychological torture and bodily punishment illustrates a structuring, and perhaps paradigmatic, narrative for the regime's legitimated and lawful disintegration of particular racialized captive bodies:

> On April 22, 1992 . . . Vaughn Dortch was stripped naked and pulled out of his cell by a Pelican Bay SORT squad. According to court records, prison guards then carried Dortch shackled and gagged to the infirmary where six guards pressed him into a steel tub of scalding hot water for several minutes. Dortch, who is African American, told "60 Minutes" that

the guards promised to give him a "Klan bath" and scrubbed him with a bristle brush until his skin started to peel away. "Looks like we're going to have a white boy before this is through," one of the assailants joked.[36]

Similar incidents are reconstructed in mind-numbing fashion throughout the memoirs, testimonials, and correspondence of people imprisoned in SHU and supermax facilities.[37] The sheer mass and repetition of such accounts render implausible the claims, frequently voiced by official advocates and lay defendants of these punitive regimes, that such scenarios amount to isolated and exceptional episodes. The Pelican Bay "Klan bath" is an allegory of both the disavowed regularity and the white-supremacist logic of the direct bodily disarticulation—torture—that forms the primary material expression of the prison regime's immediate dominion, at the spatial site of the captive's body. In fact, recent events in the U.S. carceral occupation of Guantánamo, Afghanistan, and Iraq suggest that even the terms of "torture" may be insufficient nomenclature for this technology of immobilization and punishment as it becomes a globally produced apparatus of statecraft and warfare.

Conventional definitions of torture consider the inflicting of bodily violence to be the means to some end, whether it be extracting information, coercing confessions, or terrorizing populations. The United Nations Convention against Torture and Other Cruel, Inhuman or Degrading Treatment or Punishment, states:

> [T]he term "torture" means any act by which severe pain or suffering, whether physical or mental, is intentionally inflicted on a person *for such purposes as obtaining from him or a third person information or a confession, punishing him for an act he or a third person has committed or is suspected of having committed, or intimidating or coercing him or a third person,* or for any reason based on discrimination of any kind, when such pain or suffering is inflicted by or at the instigation of or with the consent or acquiescence of a public official or other person acting in an official capacity.[38]

There is, however, no structuring exterior or ulterior motive to the state's technology of violence and domination in the supermax prison, nor within the broader production of the prison regime. The structurally manifest political desire of the prison regime's technology of immobilizing (and deadly) violence is, in the case of Jackson's inaugural imprisonment, Rosenberg's High Security Unit, Tate's fatal SHU yard, and Dortch's Klan bath, intrinsic to the biopolitical technology of the "torture" itself: that is, the isolation, social liquidation, and immobilization of human beings on scales of flexible and racially hierarchized magnitude.

The organizing logic of the prison industrial complex writ large is echoed and embodied in the vernacular of death spoken by radical captives such as Jackson and Rosenberg. Both, among countless of their (currently and formerly) imprisoned cohorts, invoke a conception of the prison within a continuum of dying, or "being dead," that crucially expands the historical scope of the prison regime's genealogical linkages to other forms of human domination and massively structured bodily violence. In this sense the prison has become, akin to the Middle Passage, more than simply a means to an end. It is, in objective and in fact, an end in itself.

The prison, in the lineage of the slave vessel, has become essential to the production of a new social formation: the technologies of social reproduction, juridically formalized civil death, and mass-based social death converge and collapse as the durable *geographic* (spatial) production of this regime. In turn, this spatialized intersection of oppressive technologies "places" and signifies the blood work of white ("multicultural") life and subjectivity, as it is insistently and fatally *lived* against black and Third World death and ontological subjection. Kumasi Aguila (Stephen Simmons), a principal author of the 1970 Folsom Prisoners Manifesto, inhabits and theorizes the prison as a space/place of saturated and accumulated absence, death, and social irreconcilability in a series of passages from his 1969 prison letters:

> I am thinking about the days to come and yet I am in unison with many others confined and not, by being grieved, outraged, afflicted again, as all the times before, and as will be the case in the future—because bit by bit I am being destroyed.
>
> Each time one of my bro's die, a part of me dies, a part of me is

hardened, is deaf to any reasoning of compromise, toward any threat of repression, any talk of faltering and turning back. (January 17, 1969)

For too long there's been too many people in control of my destiny, dictating to my senses and restricting my movement. From prison to parole is the same transition as from slavery to free slavery. (November 28, 1969)

Presently, I am still in an adjustment unit [in] San Quentin hoping my stay is temporary so that I do not find myself in graver situations, not that one cannot handle them, it is just that such incidents are designed to liquidate us one way or another. . . . [T]o survive one battle is to be set for a second. (Undated, 1969)[39]

It is useful to meditate on Jackson's and Rosenberg's "living death," and Aguila's "liquidation," as a densely shared political vernacular organic to what Fanon might call the formative "social truth" of the prison regime. Fanon's work spurs the final theoretical connection I draw between captive radical intellectuals and the larger political imaginary of radical prison praxis.

"The Abolition of One Zone":
Imprisoned Radical Intellectuals and Social Truth

It was in the context of a revolutionary nationalist struggle for decolonization that Fanon was compelled to reject the European Enlightenment conception of truth as a transcendent philosophical ideal. In *The Wretched of the Earth* and Fanon's other writings, truth was no longer a set of ideas and moral principles abstracted from historical circumstance, but rather became the embodiment of the native's desire to be rid of the settler and, by extension, the settler society. Revolutionary decolonization, for Fanon's insurrectionist "native," offered the only viable pathway toward a historical subjectivity, that being the capacity to inscribe (or recuperate and reinscribe) an indigenous social truth:

The immobility to which the native is condemned can only be called into question if the native decides to put an end to the history of colonization—

the history of pillage—and to bring into existence the history of the nation—the history of decolonization.[40]

Foreshadowing the collective conversation of imprisoned radical intellectuals since the 1970s, Fanon writes that the native's struggle against the colonial order is fundamentally a movement against a societal structure in which the native is permanently incarcerated—in his words, "a being hemmed in" (52). This rerendering of social truth is premised on the recognition that the colonial world pivots on the native's peculiar existence as the largely immobilized object of the settler's exploitation, violence, and domination—and that in fact, *every settler benefits* from the native's continued abjection. Fanon thus asserts that, "Confronted with a world ruled by the settler, the native is always presumed guilty" (53).

The difficult and profound turn in the course of Fanon's transformation as a radical intellectual arrived on his recognition of what it meant to live in a society defined by the categorical distinction between settlers and natives. Fanon recognized that the settler/native dichotomy organized the totality of the colonial social order, and that this categorical binary was premised on the settler's capacity to wage one-sided warfare against the native's body and culture, and, more comprehensively, the native's psychic and material worlds (much like the current and virtually unilateral local-to-global "war on terror"). In this context, Fanon recognized that there was no middle ground between consent to the colonial order and radical dissent from—and at best, revolutionary action against—that very same order. This is why he writes in clearly absolutist terms:

> To break up the colonial world does not mean that after the frontiers have been abolished lines of communication will be set up between the two zones. The destruction of the colonial world is no more and no less than the abolition of one zone, its burial in the depths of the earth or its expulsion from the country. (41)

To recognize imprisonment as a regime of immobilization and disintegration, or, on a scale of greater magnitude, death and extermination, is, in this moment, to do nothing more than heed the social truth conveyed and personified by imprisoned radicals and revolutionaries. It is also to reconsider and radically reencounter Fanon's theorization of the fundamental violence at the core of the colonial order.

Civil society's structure of freedom—however endangered and superficial—is defined and reproduced through the mass incarceration of the unfree "natives," the immediate "beings hemmed in," and specifically structured against the lineage of black slave ontology and the orbiting, approximating forms of enslavement/imprisonment that it yields. Thus, working within the logic of Fanon's terms, it is crucial to absorb that *nonimprisoned ("free") people are largely constituted by "(white/multicultural) settlers" and an assimilated "native petite bourgeoisie,"* who at times disavow their political allegiance to the prison regime, yet who by their very existence—as the nominally free—define and fortify its domain. Addressing the Algerian "native intellectual" class—the colonized petite bourgeoisie whose political loyalties are cast in doubt during the movement of decolonization—Fanon posits a historically situated transformation of "truth," that is, its embodiment *in* the native and *against* the settler (and, perhaps, against the native petite bourgeoisie as well). Writing at the very genesis of the contemporary prison regime in 1971, an anonymous poet in Soledad State Prison (California) prophetically lays bare the structural antagonism of the free–unfree relation in "A Sunny Soledad Afternoon":

> come then, citizens, into the
> penal pits and claim us. come
> claim the tortured sons suffering
> toilet paper destiny. come and
> share our rue soup, zoological
> violences, and our common goals
> to nowhere but gone . . .
> come see skeletons
> tripping off the ends of monotone
> tongues and come hear the clatter
> of bones shattering on fragile

stone floors. come view the solid
wall horizon echoing empty-eyed
stare until despair drinks dry
the will to look.[41]

The overriding bitterness of the piece is a deeply principled one, the hostility toward the status of the "citizen" an expression of the political stakes at hand in the reading, interpretation, and circulation of the imprisoned poet's work by a nominally free audience (the text in which the poem was published, *Words from the House of the Dead*, was essentially a mimeographed compilation of writing and visual art smuggled from Soledad prison). This invitation to partake in a mind-numbing despair, to become intimate with living death, confronts the free person—particularly the self-identified progressive or radical activist—with the irreconcilable contradiction of embracing a freedom, or even waging a liberation struggle, that does not encompass an abolition of the poet's "sunny" Soledad. The poem's political imagery of shattering bones and empty-eyed stares recalls human holocaust while anticipating the words of imprisoned activist, writer, and political educator Viet Mike Ngo.

Ngo, during the original writing of this chapter, was punitively transferred to Avenal State Prison and threatened with an indeterminate sentence in the California SHU as retribution for his public political critiques of, and active legal actions against, the California Department of Corrections for its myriad practices of racialized violence, political retribution, and normalized torture of its captives. Speaking from this moment, he advocates an embrace of the political possibility lodged in an overwhelming condition of existence:

I see my [imprisoned] comrades sometimes . . . like everyone, our energy is low, we lose hope sometimes, and dwell in despair sometimes. A lot of times. But I feel you have to be somewhat intimate with your despair. You have to understand it, because it gives you a lot of strength. Once I no longer fear what these people can do to me, I no longer worry about the repression they put against me when I struggle. So, I don't want to dwell in my despair, but I have to be intimate with it, because some of my strength comes from this. . . . If you feel that the odds are against you, that nothing ever changes, we're fighting a mountain—always look at that and say, if that's the case, we have nothing to lose. We have nothing to lose . . . I'm doing this *because* of this feeling I have, this feeling of helplessness. I'm doing this because *this is all I have*. This is all I have. Because, I don't want to go out helpless. I don't want to go out lying in my bunk, doing nothing. . . . Win or lose, we're doing this because it's the process we need to find some meaning in our lives.[42]

Ngo clearly recognizes his condition as the embodiment of ontological death, a (non)existence formed by a fundamental social alienation and manifest in the overwhelming despair of imprisonment, a form of isolation that is at once individual and collective (note Ngo's seamless use of the "we" with the "I"). This is precisely why power and strength, that is, the activity and will to resist and perhaps disarticulate the logic of the regime, arrive through his intimacy with despair. It is Ngo's willingness, in fact his need, to be entangled in (rather than to attempt metaphysical transcendence of) the gravity and breathtaking totality of his condition that structures his liberationist praxis, a political labor that is by definition desperate both because it is borne of despair and because it is all he has. We are left asking what, exactly, Ngo "has" (possesses) in struggle, in relation to loved ones, political supporters, and extended kin in the free world. Imprisoned radical intellectuals like Ngo mediate a unique political fantasy of radical freedom, a liberation practice that refuses to be defined against, much less coexist with, coercive structures of human incarceration, immobilization, and disintegration.

Former political prisoner Ramona Africa, the sole adult survivor of the 1985 police bombing of the MOVE residence in Philadelphia, recounts an otherwise banal—even absurd—confrontation with the repressive practices that shape and articulate the regime's discursive practices of power. Meaningful to the context of her story/autobiographical allegory is that it recounts a scene from her brief, two-month jailing in 1978 for "contempt of court," rather than a moment from her seven-year

political incarceration from 1985 to 1992: with the notable exception of
Martin Luther King Jr.'s "Letter from a Birmingham Jail" (1963), most
insurgent carceral or "political-prisoner" counternarratives are authored
from the long-term incarceration site of the prison rather than the
short-term or transitory captivity of the local jail. Illustrating the forms
of life sustenance that she and other jailed MOVE women sustained as a
practice of resistance to the jail's logic of containment and isolation,
Africa recalls:

> [I]t was really something to be [imprisoned] with MOVE women for two
> months. . . . One thing we did was we fed the birds leftover food. . . .
>
> Leftover food . . . if it wasn't used, [the jail] couldn't save it accord-
> ing to their health codes, they had to toss it. The county jail is right along
> the river and there are a lot of seagulls there and the river is so polluted
> there is virtually no edible food for the seagulls, so we used to take left-
> over fish sticks, eggs or bread, different things that we figured the birds
> would eat—we had these plastic buckets and we would take the leftovers
> out [during yard time]. We would dump [the food] and walk away and the
> birds would swoop down and eat it.
>
> This one particular day, a Sunday, we had gotten the birds some
> food at breakfast and we were waiting for [yard time] so we could take the
> food out. This one sergeant, a black woman, was in a very nasty mood, she
> told us that we could not take those buckets of food out. Well, we went off.
> We told her, "What are you talking about? You were gonna throw this
> food away. Can you substantiate to us why this food should go in the trash
> when those birds could eat it? If you feel that life should not eat then apply
> it to your own self and stop eating. It's not the birds' fault they can't feed
> themselves, they don't wanna eat this slop, but man has poisoned their
> source of food. . . . You're not gonna tell us that we aren't gonna feed life."
> We went off.
>
> Well, she got all mad, she got pissed off, she called the riot squad
> over, said we were disturbing the institution, they didn't lock us in our
> cells then but that night at lock-in time they locked us in, [and] when we
> got up the next morning our cell doors were locked. . . . They had locked
> us in and gave us write-ups, misconducts. . . .

> We got found guilty . . . [and] we each got a fifty-thousand-dollar
> bail, all for taking a stand on feeding the birds. We didn't threaten anybody,
> you know, but that is the attitude of the prisons. But these are the things I
> learned from MOVE, about taking a stand for life, taking care of life.[43]

Africa's allegory signifies MOVE's praxis of "life" in and against unnatural or premature death, in this case a living death, or carceral logic of
death. The scene of this encounter crystallizes the constitutive centrality of technologies of death against life to the rigorous and relentless
shaping of the prison's everyday. As she communed with other jailed
black women through the ritual feeding of seagulls, the guard/captor
recognized that this practice was a form of intuitive antisystemic maneu-
vering and theatrical political pedagogy: amid the industrial waste and
pollution of the jail, and squarely within its (often unrecognized) sweep
of environmental poisoning and death, the civically dead expropriate the
jailer's "slop" (the leftovers of the dead) in order to preserve (defend) natural life. Africa's account enacts and animates the crux of social truth embodied by imprisoned radical intellectuals over the past three decades: a
distended passage into—and captivity within—a worldly intimacy with
death, adjoining and opposing the mundane everyday of civil society, or
the alleged free world.

Jackson, interviewed shortly before his assassination in the summer of 1971, amplifies the insurrectionist trajectory of this social truth.
Here, he conceptualizes the historical telos of the oppressed ontology as
it is entwined in a bifurcated historical possibility: massive death or total
liquidation of the existing systemic arrangement. Following Fanon,
Jackson posits the absence of middle ground in a historically embedded
condition of warfare:

> The principal contradiction between the oppressor and oppressed can be
> reduced to the fact that the only way the oppressor can maintain his posi-
> tion is by fostering, nurturing, building, contempt for the oppressed. That
> thing gets out of hand after a while. It leads to excesses that we see and the
> excesses are growing within the totalitarian state here. The excesses breed
> resistance; resistance is growing. The thing grows in a spiral. It can only

end one way. The excesses lead to resistance, resistance leads to brutality, the brutality leads to more resistance, and finally the whole question will be resolved with either the uneconomic destruction of the oppressed, or the end of oppression.[44]

This vision, and the desire to which it speaks, do not necessarily visualize a process of social transformation that is pragmatic and programmatic,

Ramona Africa, lecturing at the University of California, Riverside, 2004. Photographed by the author.

rationally procedural, or ideologically systematized. In fact, it seems that the vision of radical freedom—here, the end of oppression—is articulable only through the political possibilities that remain dormant, or that remain to be catalyzed by the creative alchemists of liberation struggle, within and outside the prison, who desire contact and kinship with their often unreachable free and imprisoned contemporaries and peers (a longing only fulfilled through actual liberation). Political possibilities previously unavailable or unknowable, as Fanon, Ngo, Africa, and Jackson remind us, may emerge as pathways to freedom in conditions of systemic crisis, disruption, or breakdown. There are times and places in which the simple, audacious act of speaking to the condition of this unknowability underlines a profound hope in the lineage of liberationist alchemies.

The substance of the "political," for imprisoned radical intellectuals, fundamentally involves an antisystemic, or system-disarticulating, logic, perhaps because, in the stronghold of the slave vessel, few political options are available other than mutiny. Henceforth springs the historical and political burden borne on (and often refused by) contemporary free-world activists, most especially self-identified radicals, revolutionaries, and liberationists, whose condition of existence (that is, their relative social, political, and bodily mobility) entails the constant immobilization of others. We can and must depart from the words of Aguila, penned in 1970 and still unfulfilled:

> When the word abolition ceases to be taken for granted then we will stop discussing impossibilities and begin our quest for victory and freedom— for the most denied and most oppressed, abolition will register as a battle cry.[45]

Acknowledgments

Forced Passages is the product of my engagement with several political and intellectual formations, most important the struggle for prison and police abolition that is, in my view, among the most urgent and life-affirming insurgencies in the current moment of U.S. global dominance. The book is grounded in my identifications and aspirations as a scholar-activist and political intellectual, and as such dispenses with the traditional pretensions of academic indifference or "objectivity," as it is traditionally conceived. It is in the spirit of such an attempted praxis that I wish to concisely acknowledge the people who have shaped and periodically transformed my desires, visions, and devotions.

The generous and critical mentorship of Angela Y. Davis and Ruth Wilson Gilmore inspired and encouraged the germination of this project in 1997, and subsequent conversations with both have deeply informed the development of *Forced Passages*. In concert with Michael Omi, Raka Ray, and Stephen Small, they allowed me the freedom to begin this project in the form of a PhD dissertation in the Department of Ethnic Studies at the University of California, Berkeley. Years of challenging intellectual exchanges with Viet Mike Ngo, Jared Sexton, Frank Wilderson III, and Andrea Smith truly forged my thinking on the links between the prison regime and the multiple vectors of human domination that we currently witness, survive, and oppose. My participation in the founding organizing collective of Critical Resistance: Beyond the

Prison Industrial Complex yielded a political education that has proved invaluable. I thank all my co-organizers for allowing me the opportunity to work alongside them in the production of the first Critical Resistance conference and strategy session in 1998. I especially acknowledge Julia Sudbury, Dorsey Nunn, Rita "B♀" Brown, Rayne Galbraith, Joyce Miller, Rose Braz, Eli Rosenblatt, Cassandra Shaylor, Janel Stead, and Suran Thrift for their periodic contributions to and interventions on my thinking.

Joy James inspired and encouraged the development of this project from its early stages. In addition to serving as my supervisor for the Ford Postdoctoral Fellowship, she provided multiple forums for the presentation of my ideas, including the conferences "Imagination, Imaging, and Memory: Racial, Gender, and Political Violence" and "Imprisoned Intellectuals: A Dialogue with Scholars, Activists, and (Former) U.S. Political Prisoners on War, Dissent, and Social Justice," both held at Brown University. James Turner and Gary Okihiro, mentors during and beyond my undergraduate years at Cornell University, have demonstrated a principled and lasting commitment to supporting my growth as a "scholar-activist," and I am thankful to them.

It has been a joy to work with Richard Morrison, my editor at the University of Minnesota Press. My colleagues and fellow activist scholars Beth Richie and Michael Hames-García read the first draft of this manuscript and, in addition to encouraging the publication of *Forced Passages*, they offered incisive and productive feedback on important sections of the book.

California Prison Focus allowed me to participate in investigative visits to the Security Housing Unit of Pelican Bay State Prison, and gave me the opportunity to speak at length with two important contributors to this book, Hugo "Yogi" Pinell and Kijana Tashiri Askari (Marcus Harrison). Yogi's testimonial narrative and Tashiri's ongoing correspondence will always remain with me. For their correspondence and critical insight, I thank the following people, all of whom are currently held captive in U.S. prisons across the country: Marshall Eddie Conway, Marilyn Buck, Jalil Muntaqim, Santino "Sonny" Enraca, Tommy Ross, Musheer Haki Gray, Yu Kikumura, Mutulu Shakur, Sundiata Acoli, Bill

Dunne, and Debbie Sims Africa. Linda Evans and Ray Luc Levasseur wrote me frequently while they were imprisoned, and I hope their release will mean freedom for more. Ramona Africa, Susan Rosenberg, Laura Whitehorn, Kumasi Aguila, and Amanda Perez have shared much regarding their struggles against and survival of the prison regime; they demonstrate a continuity of political commitment that cuts across the worlds of the "free" and "unfree."

I received incisive commentary and feedback on an early draft of chapter 6 during a panel session of the American Studies Association meeting in Hartford, Connecticut, in 2003. Gina Dent and Zachary Morgan provided key points of departure for a substantive revision of this chapter. Jenny Sharpe, Frances Hasso, and Parama Roy, my cohorts in a Rockefeller Fellows Seminar conceived and led by Leo Chavez, offered a useful critique of my first rendition of chapter 1. This seminar, in addition to other research clusters supported by the Ford Foundation Cloning Cultures Grant, took place at the Center for Ideas and Society at the University of California, Riverside. The guidance and institutional leadership of Piya Chatterjee and Emory Elliott at the Center, as well as Philomena Essed and David Theo Goldberg at the University of California Humanities Research Institute, provided a crucial space and context for the refinement of the book in its latter stages. Grants from the UCLA Institute for Labor and Employment, Ernesto Galarza Applied Research Center, and U.C. Riverside Academic Senate also facilitated important aspects of the research process.

Encouragement, political support, and research assistance from Sormeh Ayari, Greg Caldwell, Martha Escobar, and Gabriela Ocon greatly strengthened portions of the book, and their presence and friendship has changed my pedagogy immeasurably. Students at U.C. Riverside transformed many ethnic studies classes into brainstorm sessions, and their influence and support kept me upright on many days. They, along with activist attorneys Fania Davis and Charles Bonner, protected me from ugly institutional repression at crucial moments. Although I may one day write another text about that personal struggle, this short acknowledgment will have to do for now.

Among many friends, activists, grassroots organizers, and scholars, I thank the following people for their support on various facets of this project: Thandi Chimurenga, Talibah Shakir, Raman Prasad, Steve Martinot, Wayne Lum, Cynthia Young, Nerissa Balce, Rick Bonus, Roberto Labrada, Sora Han, Wesley Ueunten, Camille Acey, Connie Wun, Danny Widener, Lisa Yoneyama, Tak Fujitane, Endo Katsu, Vorris Nunley, James Kyung-Jin Lee, and Arif Dirlik. I am particularly grateful to my junior faculty colleagues in the Department of Ethnic Studies for their friendship, candor, and humor. Victoria Bomberry, Jayna Brown, Jodi Kim, Anthony Macias, and Robert Perez have been models of integrity and collegiality during my time in the department, and it is my privilege to be considered their peer.

My cousins Tony Tiongson and Derick García, and my brother Anthony Rodríguez, have embodied a healthy and consistent familial presence since the earliest moments of this project, and I have always leaned on them for companionship, moral support, and shared meals.

I am most grateful to Setsu Shigematsu for sharing her loving warrior spirit, radical feminist mind, and brilliant nonstop ideas. Her close, incisive readings of the manuscript throughout the writing, revision, and publication process were the least of her contributions to the completion of *Forced Passages*. She is truly an all-star scholar, activist, and partner. Finally, Viet Taer (Taya) Rodríguez Shigematsu has brought me the gifts of perspective, urgency, and humility (as well as countless dirty diapers). Completing this book during the first year of Taya's life was a joy exceeded only by his birth.

Notes

Introduction

1. I significantly write and act as the descendant of a contemporary Philippine and "Filipino American" educated petit bourgeoisie, a class whose genealogy invokes a particular telos of genocidal conquest, formal colonization, and neocolonial interpellation. My efforts at radical political-intellectual praxis and (racial) identification are thus at once enabled, complicated, and constituted by this history. See Dylan Rodríguez, "'A Million Deaths?': Genocide and the Subject of Filipino American Studies," in *Positively No Filipinos Allowed: Building Communities and Discourses*, ed. Antonio Tiongson Jr., Edgardo V. Gutierrez, and Ricardo V. Gutierrez (Philadelphia: Temple University Press, 2006).

2. Throughout this text, I use the term "prison" in broad categorical reference to those forms of state and state-sanctioned bodily detention that derive from the conjoined juridical and policing apparatuses and their alleged organization, mediation, and enforcement of "criminal justice." *Prison*, in this book, conceptually encompasses the statecraft and *expansive institutionality* of state-proctored human captivity, which inscribes a multiply scaled political geography of social and bodily immobilization. For purposes of analytical clarity, sociohistorical contextualization, or political emphasis, I will in places make distinctions between local jails, federal or state prisons, Immigration and Naturalization Service (INS) detention prisons, youth and children's facilities, men's and women's prisons, and prisons for the mentally disordered or ill.

3. Jill Soffiyah Elijah, "The Reality of Political Prisoners in the United States: What September 11 Taught Us about Defending Them," *Harvard Black-Letter Journal* 18, no. 129 (spring 2002): 129. By way of further example, Amnesty

International offers the following definitions of "conscientious objector" and "political prisoner": "Amnesty International (AI) considers a conscientious objector to be "all those who are imprisoned, detained or otherwise physically restricted by reason of their political, religious or other conscientiously held beliefs or by reason of their ethnic origin, sex, colour, language, national or social origin, economic status, birth or other status. Amnesty International works towards the unconditional and immediate release of prisoners of conscience."

". . . Amnesty International uses a broad interpretation of the term political prisoner so as to cover all cases with a significant political element, for example criminal offences committed with a political motive or within a clear political context. Amnesty International does not call for the release of all political prisoners within this definition, nor does it call on governments to give political prisoners special conditions. Amnesty International works to ensure that all political prisoners receive a fair trial in accordance with international standards, and Amnesty International opposes the use of torture and cruel, inhuman or degrading treatment in all cases—both criminal and political—without reservation." (*Political Prisoners in Azerbaijan and Armenia: Amnesty International's Concerns and Recommendations*, AI Index: EUR 04/001/2002, 20 January 2002). The Jericho Movement, on the other hand, suggests a more explicitly politicized definition of "political prisoner," grounded in histories of black and Third World liberation struggles: "[P]olitical prisoners are in prison today because they fought for self-determination for the people and stood up against police brutality, racism, miseducation and the unjust incarceration. The fight to free them is part and parcel of the growing effort to dismantle the entire prison industrial complex" (Jericho Movement Web site: http://www.thejerichomovement.com/aboutus.html).

Finally, the Out of Control Lesbian Committee to Support Women Political Prisoners focuses its work on women political prisoners, who "are in prison for various reasons from opposing policies of the U.S. government through revolutionary activities, participating in the Puerto Rican Independence movement, Black liberation, American Indian Movement, to anti-nuclear activities, etc." (Out of Control Lesbian Committee to Support Women Political Prisoners Web site: http//www.prisonactivist.org/ooc/#about).

4. Owusu Yaki Yakubu, "Toward Collective Effort and Common Vision: The International and Domestic Contexts of the Struggles of Political Prisoners and Prisoners of War Held by the U.S.," in *Can't Jail the Spirit: Political Prisoners in the U.S.*, 5th ed. (Chicago: Committee to End the Marion Lockdown, 2002), 13.

5. Marshall Eddie Conway was an active member and leader of the Black Panther Party (BPP) chapter in Baltimore, Maryland, during the 1960s and 1970s. Conway helped to expose and expel a key FBI COINTELPRO infiltrator into the BPP, Warren Hart. According to Conway, Hart, under government and FBI direction and protection, had actually "founded" the Baltimore chapter. Hart subsequently used his purported leadership position to gain privileged access to the inner workings of the Panther Central Committee, and reported his findings to the National Security Agency (NSA). Conway's disruption of Hart's domestic espionage operation led to his being specifically targeted by COINTELPRO for neutralization. In 1970, Conway was arrested and charged with the murder of one police officer and the attempted murder of two others. Although no physical evidence linked him to the scene of the alleged crimes, and the government was later revealed to have used a paid informant during the trial (who testified that Conway "confessed" to him), Conway was nonetheless convicted and given a sentence of life plus thirty years. There is a campaign to win his release.

6. Undergraduate ethnic studies major Sormeh Ayari, a prison and police abolitionist activist who has worked with the October 22nd Movement and other grassroots groups, posed a series of questions to Conway during this seminar/interview. Her concise and profound question, "What does it mean to be 'political?'" formed a template for the conversation between Conway and the other seminar students.

7. Interview with Marshall Eddie Conway, ethnic studies seminar (Imprisoned Radical Intellectuals and U.S. Liberation Movements, ETST 178), Riverside, California, July 6, 2004. A revised version of this interview is forthcoming in the anthology *Warfare: Prison and the American Homeland*, ed. Joy James (Durham, NC: Duke University Press, forthcoming).

8. Frantz Fanon, *The Wretched of the Earth* (1963), trans. Constance Farrington (New York: Grove Weidenfeld, 1968), 50.

9. Buck is a white anti-imperialist and antiracist political prisoner. After being imprisoned in 1973 for purchasing handgun ammunition, Buck served four years in a West Virginia federal prison. After receiving furlough, she refused to return to the prison and went underground for eight years. She was apprehended and tried in 1985 for assisting in Assata Shakur's escape from prison, and was additionally sentenced (with her codefendants Dr. Mutulu Shakur and Sekou Odinga) for conspiracy to commit armed bank robbery in support of the black liberation struggle. In 1988, Buck was sentenced to an additional decade in prison as part of the infamous "Resistance Conspiracy" case, in which she and

others were convicted of "conspiracy to protest and alter government policies through use of violence" against government and military property. (See Prison Activist Resource Center Web site: http://www.prisonactivist.org/pps+pows/marilynbuck/.)

10. Marilyn Buck, "Prisons, Social Control, and Political Prisoners," *Social Justice* 27, no. 3 (2000): 28; emphasis added.

11. Stuart Hall, "Race, Articulation, and Societies Structured in Dominance," in *Black British Cultural Studies: A Reader*, ed. Houston A. Baker Jr., Manthia Diawara, and Ruth H. Lindeborg (Chicago: University of Chicago Press, 1996), 56.

12. See, for example, Angela Y. Davis's "From the Prison of Slavery to the Slavery of Prison: Frederick Douglass and the Convict Lease System," in *The Angela Y. Davis Reader*, ed. Joy James (Malden, MA: Blackwell Publishers, 1998); Alex Lichtenstein, *Twice the Work of Free Labor* (New York: Verso, 1996); Lawrence Friedman, *Crime and Punishment in American History* (New York: Basic Books, 1993); and Paul Keve, *Prisons and the American Conscience* (Carbondale: Southern Illinois University Press, 1991).

13. For an intellectual history of racism and racial ideology, see Winthrop Jordan, *White over Black: American Attitudes toward the Negro, 1550–1812* (Baltimore: Penguin Books, 1968); George Frederickson, *Racism: A Short History* (Princeton, NJ: Princeton University Press, 2002); idem, *The Black Image in the White Mind: The Debate on Afro-American Character and Destiny, 1817–1914* (New York: Harper & Row, 1971); and David Theo Goldberg, *Racist Culture* (Cambridge: Blackwell Publishers, 1993).

14. Ruth Wilson Gilmore, "Race and Globalization" in *Geographies of Global Change: Remapping the World*, ed. R. J. Johnston, Peter J. Taylor, and Michael J. Watts (New York: Blackwell Publishing, 2002), 261.

15. In addition to the following passages from Dorothy Roberts and Andrea Smith, see Anannya Bhattacharjee, "Private Fists and Public Force," and Judith A. M. Scully, "Killing the Black Community," in *Policing the National Body: Race, Gender, and Criminalization*, ed. Anannya Bhattacharjee and Jael Silliman (Cambridge: South End Press, 2002). For a sociological examination of the crucial role of white women in contemporary white-supremacist movements and organizations, see Kathleen M. Blee, *Inside Organized Racism: Women in the Hate Movement* (Berkeley: University of California Press, 2002).

16. Dorothy Roberts, *Killing the Black Body: Race, Reproduction, and the Meaning of Liberty* (1997) (New York: Vintage Books, 1999), 22–23.

17. Andrea Smith, "Better Dead Than Pregnant: The Colonization of Native

Women's Reproductive Health," in Bhattacharjee and Silliman, *Policing the National Body*, 123–24; emphasis added.

18. The Klan's primary Web site, at http://www.kkk.bz, conspicuously displays passages from the Bible alongside gratuitous images of the Capitol building, American eagle, and U.S. flag. It is, quite literally, a classic American nationalist organization. Other white-supremacist organizations, including Patriot groups, neo-Nazis, and white militias, evince a similar commitment to the flourishing of a particular vision of American exceptionalism that draws from its core political and cultural legacies, including republicanism, "white rights," and "Christian values."

19. Ruth Wilson Gilmore, "Globalisation and US Prison Growth: From Military Keynesianism to Post-Keynesian Militarism," *Race and Class* 40, no. 2/3 (1998–99): 174. See also Gilmore's seminal book *Golden Gulag: Labor, Land, State, and Opposition in Globalizing California* (Berkeley: University of California Press, forthcoming).

20. Gilmore, "Globalisation and US Prison Growth," 176–78.

21. Linda Evans and Eve Goldberg, *The Prison Industrial Complex and the Global Economy* (San Francisco: AK Press Distribution, 1998), 5.

22. Gilmore, "Globalisation and US Prison Growth," 183.

23. Jared Sexton and Steve Martinot, "The Avant-Garde of White Supremacy," *Social Identities: Journal for the Study of Race, Nation, and Culture* 9, no. 3 (June 2003): 172.

24. The 2.5 million figure includes imprisoned populations that are almost always excluded from common carceral body counts. The most frequently quoted figures are from the United States Bureau of Justice Statistics. See, for example, Paige M. Harrison and Jennifer C. Karberg, "Prison and Jail Inmates at Midyear 2003," U.S. Department of Justice (NCJ 203947, May 2004). According to the Bureau of Justice Statistics, as of June 2003 there were 2,078,570 prisoners held in federal or state prisons and local jails. In addition, the U.S. Department of Justice's Office of Juvenile Justice and Delinquency Prevention states in its 2002 annual report that 108,931 children were incarcerated as of 1999 (*OJJDP Annual Report 2002*, NCJ 202038, 59). It is almost certain that the current population of imprisoned children exceeds this figure, especially because a growing number of youth under the age of eighteen are being sent to adult jails and prisons (statistics on incarcerated populations typically have a one- to two-year lag, because of the time expended in collecting and calculating data). Finally, the Department of Homeland Security, which bureaucratically absorbed the Immigration and

Naturalization Service (INS), reports that in 2002, there were 188,547 noncitizens held in INS prisons on an average day (memorandum from Acting Inspector General Clark Kent Ervin, "Major Management Challenges Facing the Department of Homeland Security," March 2003).

25. Jalil Muntaqim (aka Anthony Jalil Bottom), "The Cold War of the 90's," *Prison News Service*, no. 52 (September–October 1995). Jalil Muntaqim first affiliated with the Black Panther Party when he was eighteen years old, after being recruited by elementary school friends who had become Panthers. On August 28, 1971, he was captured along with Albert Nuh Washington in a midnight shoot-out with San Francisco police. It has been alleged that Muntaqim and Washington attempted to assassinate a police sergeant in retaliation for the August 21, 1971, assassination of George Jackson. Subsequently, Muntaqim, Washington, and Herman Bell—who came to be known as the "New York Three"—were charged with a host of revolutionary underground activities, including the assassination of New York City police officers, for which they were given life sentences. Muntaqim has actively worked with a wide variety of activist and educational campaigns and organizations since his imprisonment, including his founding call for the Jericho Amnesty march in 1998 (which eventually catalyzed the long-term formation of the Jericho Movement) and the National Prisoners Campaign to Petition the United Nations in 1976. See *Can't Jail the Spirit*, 136–40. Also see "The New York Three: History and Case Background," an informational essay published by Solidarity in February 2002. The essay may be obtained through Solidarity by mailing 2035 Boulevard St. Laurent, Montreal, Quebec, Canada H2X 2T3, or through the Internet at http://www.kersplebedeb.com/mystuff/profiles/ny3A.pdf.

26. Barry Goldwater, "Nomination Acceptance Speech at the 28th Republican National Convention," July 16, 1964, reprinted by the *Washington Post*, May 30, 1998.

27. Ibid.

28. Some useful background texts include Jael Silliman and Anannya Bhattacharjee, eds., *Policing the National Body: Race, Gender and Criminalization in the United States* (Boston: South End Press, 2002); Christian Parenti, *Lockdown America: Police and Prisons in the Age of Crisis* (New York: Verso, 2000); Ted Gest, *Crime and Politics: Big Government's Erratic Campaign for Law and Order* (New York: Oxford University Press, 2001); Jill Nelson, ed., *Police Brutality: An Anthology* (New York: W. W. Norton, 2000); Stuart Hall et al., *Policing the Crisis: Mugging, the State, and Law and Order* (New York: Holmes & Meier, 1978).

29. See Robert Allen, *Black Awakening in Capitalist America* (1969) (Trenton:

Africa World Press, 1990), and Jennifer Wolch, *The Shadow State: Government and Voluntary Sector in Transition* (New York: The Foundation Center, 1990).

30. For an overview of the Black Panther Party and the Black Liberation Army, see Kathleen Cleaver and George Katsiaficas, eds., *Liberation, Imagination, and the Black Panther Party* (New York: Routledge, 2001); Philip Foner, ed., *The Black Panthers Speak* (1970), 2d ed. (New York: DaCapo Press, 2002); and Charles Jones, ed., *The Black Panther Party (Reconsidered)* (Baltimore: Black Classic Press, 1998), among numerous other texts. The George Jackson Brigade's public communiqués have been published in the pamphlet *Creating a Movement with Teeth: Communiqués of the George Jackson Brigade* (Montreal: Abraham Guillen Press, 2003). Texts discussing the history and legacies of the Weather Underground include political prisoner David Gilbert's *No Surrender: Writings from an Anti-Imperialist Political Prisoner* (Montreal: Abraham Guillen Press, 2004) and Jeremy Varon's *Bringing the War Home: The Weather Underground, the Red Army Faction, and Revolutionary Violence in the Sixties and Seventies* (Berkeley: University of California Press, 2004). Mickey Melendez, *We Took the Streets: Fighting for Latino Rights with the Young Lords* (New York: St. Martin's Press, 2003), and Andrés Torres and José E. Velásquez, eds., *The Puerto Rican Movement* (Philadelphia: Temple University Press, 1998), offer political analysis and testimonial histories of the Young Lords. Information on the Chinatown-based Red Guards, I Wor Kuen, anti-imperialist and antimartial law Katipunan ng Demokratikong Pilipino, and other organizations may be obtained from Fred Ho, ed., *Legacy to Liberation: The Politics and Culture of Revolutionary Asian Pacific America* (Brooklyn: Big Red Media, 2000); Steve Louie and Glenn K. Omatsu, eds., *Asian Americans: The Movement and the Moment* (Los Angeles: UCLA Asian American Studies Center Press, 2001); and Amy Tachiki et al., eds., *Roots: An Asian American Reader* (Los Angeles: UCLA Asian American Studies Center, 1971).

31. Among other texts, see Paul Chaat Smith and Robert Allen Warrior, *Like a Hurricane: The Indian Movement from Alcatraz to Wounded Knee* (New York: New Press, 1996), and Alvin M. Josephy, Joane Nagel, and Troy Johnson, eds. *Red Power: The American Indians' Fight for Freedom*, 2d ed. (Lincoln: University of Nebraska Press, 1999).

32. In addition to the texts by Melendez and Torres and Velásquez (note 30), see the cluster of articles by and interviews with the *independentistas* in *Cages of Steel: The Politics of Imprisonment in the United States*, ed. Ward Churchill and Jim Vander Wall (Washington, DC: Maisonneuve Press, 1992).

33. See Steve Martinot's discussion of white supremacy as a cultural and

social structure in *The Rule of Racialization: Class, Identity, Governance* (Philadelphia: Temple University Press, 2003).

34. See Ward Churchill and Jim Vander Wall, *Agents of Repression: The FBI's Secret Wars against the Black Panther Party and the American Indian Movement* (Boston: South End Press, 1988); Nelson Blackstock, *COINTELPRO: The FBI's Secret War on Political Freedom*, 3d ed. (New York: Pathfinder Press, 1988); Howard Zinn, *A People's History of the United States: 1492–Present*, twentieth anniversary edition (New York: HarperCollins, 2003); James Kirkpatrick Davis, *Spying on America: The FBI's Domestic Counterintelligence Program* (New York: Praeger Publishers, 1992); and David Cunningham, *There's Something Happening Here: The New Left, the Klan, and FBI Counterintelligence* (Berkeley: University of California Press, 2004).

35. See Curt Gentry, *J. Edgar Hoover: The Man and the Secrets* (New York: W. W. Norton, 1992).

36. For recent data, see *Law Enforcement Management and Administrative Statistics, 2000*, U.S. Department of Justice, Bureau of Justice Statistics (NCJ 203350, 2004). The LEMAS program began compiling statistics on state and local police agencies in 1987. Also see *The Challenge of Crime in a Free Society: Looking Back Looking Forward* (symposium on the thirtieth anniversary of the President's Commission on Law Enforcement and Administration of Justice), U.S. Department of Justice (NCJ 170029, 1997). Christian Parenti also offers a useful overview of U.S. police expansion in *Lockdown America*.

37. Goldwater, "Nomination Acceptance Speech at the 28th Republican National Convention."

38. See William A. Williams, *Empire as a Way of Life* (New York: Oxford University Press, 1985).

39. "President Signs Homeland Security Appropriations Bill," Office of the White House Press Secretary, press release, October 1, 2003.

40. Attorney General John Ashcroft, whose reactionary tendencies at times offended even the conservative consensus that glues the Clinton–Bush axis, was among the most visible proponents of this important social project. Articulating a versatile discursive frame that ingeniously links the global policing of empire to the highly personalized security of domestic white communities, Ashcroft's announcement of a reshaped, post-911 "National Neighborhood Watch" magically rendered the "neighborhood" as the front line of antiterrorist, anticrime struggle. The populist glue of Ashcroft's appeal lay in its mobilization of white sentimentality, the shameless invoking of the time-honored melodrama of white

bodily integrity under immediate, racial threat and harm; here, it is the potentiality of violence done to white bodies that is dramatized as the essential national-cum-racial injustice and tragedy.

41. Nils Christie, *Crime Control as Industry*, 3d ed. (New York: Routledge, 2000), 22–23.

42. Cheryl I. Harris, "Whiteness as Property," *Critical Race Theory*, ed. Kimberlé Crenshaw, Neil Gotanda, Gary Peller, and Kendall Thomas (New York: New Press, 1995), 277.

43. The official name of the California Department of Corrections prison in Soledad is Correctional Training Facility at Soledad. The place is more widely known as "Soledad Prison." Viet Mike Ngo was incarcerated at age seventeen for the retaliation killing of a fourteen-year-old rival gang member. Ngo is a writer, activist, and political educator who has participated as a guest speaker and lecturer in a variety of educational and political venues. While housed in San Quentin, he petitioned the Marin County Superior Court for a writ of habeas corpus regarding the administration's illegal racial segregation of inmates in housing and discipline. See Viet Mike Ngo (with Dylan Rodríguez), "A Conversation with Mike Ngo (San Quentin State Prison, E21895): 'You Have to Be Intimate with Your Despair,'" in *NeoSlave Narratives: Prison Writing and Abolitionism*, ed. Joy James (Albany: State University of New York Press, 2005); idem, "Grave Digger" and "Red, White and Blue," *Amerasia Journal* 29, no. 1 (2003): 179–80; idem, "A Day in the Life," *Manoa: A Pacific Journal of International Writing* 14, no. 1 (2002): 22–29.

44. Ngo, "A Conversation with Mike Ngo."

45. George Jackson, *Soledad Brother: The Prison Letters of George Jackson* (1970) (Chicago: Lawrence Hill Books, 1994); Angela Y. Davis et al., *If They Come in the Morning* (New York: Third Press, 1971), which contains "prison letters" from Huey Newton, Angela Y. Davis, Ericka Huggins, Bobby Seale, Fleeta Drumgo, John Clutchette, and Ruchell Magee; News and Letters Committees, *Revolutionary Prisoners Speak! Selected Prisoner Correspondence: 1998–1999* (Chicago: News and Letters Committees, 1999). Levasseur is a white anti-imperialist political prisoner and veteran of the Vietnam War. After his return from the war in 1967, he says that he "was deeply affected by the devastation of the war on the Vietnamese people and their country." He subsequently worked with a number of organizations, including Southern Student Organizing Committee in Tennessee, Vietnam Veterans Against the War, Red Star North bookstore, and a variety of underground groups. He was captured by federal agents in 1984, and was tried and convicted for bombing U.S. military facilities, military contractors,

and corporations connected to the apartheid regime in South Africa and received a forty-five-year sentence. In 1986, he was indicted with seven others on charges of seditious conspiracy and additional charges under RICO laws. Levasseur was accused of membership in the underground Sam Melville-Jonathan Jackson Unit and the United Freedom Front. They were acquitted of the conspiracy charge, and the RICO charges were eventually dismissed. Levasseur was released on parole in August 2004. The online "Letters from Exile" site is maintained by Levasseur's friends, family, and supporters, and contains links to letters and essays, as well as "updates" on other anti-imperialist political prisoners. See http://home.earthlink.net/~neoludd/.

46. Viet Mike Ngo, correspondence, January 2002 (undated).

47. Frantz Fanon, "Letter to the Resident Minister (1956)," in *Toward the African Revolution* (1967) (New York: Grove Press, 1988), 53.

48. Georg Lukács, *History and Class Consciousness* (Cambridge: MIT Press, 1968), 83.

49. Ngo, "A Conversation with Mike Ngo."

50. Sharon Patricia Holland, *Raising the Dead: Readings of Death and (Black) Subjectivity* (Durham, NC: Duke University Press, 2000), 149.

51. Viet Mike Ngo, correspondence, January 2002 (undated).

52. Interview with Viet Mike Ngo, San Quentin State Prison (date excluded).

53. Leonard Peltier, *Prison Writings: My Life Is My Sun Dance* (New York: St. Martin's Press, 1999), 9.

1. Domestic War Zones and the Extremities of Power

1. Chapter 2 provides a more complete discussion of Alberto Melucci's conception of the "constitutive logic" of a social system in his essay "A Strange Kind of Newness: What's 'New' in New Social Movements?" *New Social Movements: From Ideology to Identity*, ed. Enrique Laraña, Hank Johnston, and Joseph R. Gusfield (Philadelphia: Temple University Press, 1994).

2. For a recent example of such a working delineation, see Leah Caldwell, "Iraqi Dungeons and Torture Chambers under New, American Trained Management," *Prison Legal News* 15, no. 9 (September 2004). See also Julia Sudbury, "Transatlantic Visions: Resisting the Globalization of Mass Incarceration," *Social Justice* 27, no. 3 (2000): 133–49.

3. Orlando Patterson, *Slavery and Social Death: A Comparative Study* (Cambridge: Harvard University Press, 1982), 31; emphasis added.

4. My use of possession, haunting, and ghostliness here is inspired by Avery

F. Gordon, *Ghostly Matters: Haunting and the Sociological Imagination* (Minneapolis: University of Minnesota Press, 1996).

5. My use of genealogy here resonates with Foucault's assertion that "One has to dispense with the constituent subject, to get rid of the subject itself, that's to say, to arrive at an analysis which can account for the constitution of the subject within a historical framework. And this is what I would call genealogy, that is, a form of history which can account for the constitution of knowledges, discourses, domains of objects etc., without having to make reference to a subject which is either transcendental in relation to the field of events or runs its empty sameness throughout the course of history" (Michel Foucault, "Truth and Power" [interview], in *Power/Knowledge: Selected Interviews and Other Writings, 1972–1977*, ed. Colin Gordon [New York: Pantheon Books, 1980], 122).

6. Patterson, *Slavery and Social Death*, 37.

7. Michel Foucault, "14 January 1976," in *"Society Must Be Defended": Lectures at the Collège de France, 1975–1976* (1997), trans. David Macey (New York: Picador, 2003), 27–28; emphasis added.

8. "Capillary," MedTerms Online Medical Dictionary, www.medterms.com.

9. "I don't want to say that the State isn't important; what I want to say is that relations of power, and hence the analysis that must be made of them, necessarily extend beyond the limits of the State. . . . [T]he State can only operate on the basis of other, already existing power relations. The State is superstructural in relation to a whole series of power networks that invest the body, sexuality, the family, kinship, knowledge, technology and so forth" (Foucault, "Truth and Power," 122).

10. Michel Foucault, *Discipline and Punish: The Birth of the Prison*, trans. Alan Sheridan (New York: Pantheon Books, 1977), 24.

11. Allen Feldman, *Formations of Violence: The Narrative of the Body and Political Terror in Northern Ireland* (Chicago: University of Chicago Press, 1991), 177.

12. J. Edgar Hoover, "Counterintelligence Program: Black Nationalist Hate Groups Internal Security," FBI memorandum, August 25, 1967. A mimeographed copy of the first two pages of this document appears in *The COINTELPRO Papers: Documents from the FBI's Secret Wars against Dissent in the United States*, ed. Ward Churchill and Jim Vander Wall (Boston: South End Press, 1990), 92–93.

13. J. Edgar Hoover, "Counterintelligence Program: Black Nationalist Hate Groups Racial Intelligence," FBI memorandum, March 4, 1968. A mimeographed copy of the first four pages of this document appears in Churchill and Vander Wall, *The COINTELPRO Papers*, 108–11; emphasis in original.

14. Hoover made this allegation in the FBI annual report for fiscal year 1969. Although few actually read this report firsthand, the statement was widely repeated or paraphrased in various corporate media outlets. The quotation here was taken from a front-page article by David McClintick in the *Wall Street Journal* titled "The Black Panthers: Negro Militants Use Free Food, Medical Aid to Promote Revolution," August 29, 1969.

15. Afro-American Liberation Army, *Humanity, Freedom, Peace* (Revolutionary Peoples Communication Network, circa 1972). Author's papers.

16. Akinyele Omowale Umoja, "Repression Breeds Resistance: The Black Liberation Army and the Radical Legacy of the Black Panther Party," in *Liberation, Imagination, and the Black Panther Party: A New Look at the Panthers and Their Legacy*, ed. Kathleen Cleaver and George Katsiaficas (New York: Routledge, 2001), 6.

17. Interview with anonymous former Black Panther Party woman, 2004 (date and location excluded). Also see Umoja, "Repression Breeds Resistance."

18. Interview with Anonymous, 2004.

19. Assata Shakur, *Assata: An Autobiography* (1987) (Chicago: Lawrence Hill Books, 1988), 241.

20. Umoja, "Repression Breeds Resistance," 4.

21. Jalil Muntaqim (on behalf of the Black Liberation Army), *On the Black Liberation Army* (1979) (pamphlet) (Montreal: Abraham Guillen Press, May 2002). This essay was first published in *Arm the Spirit* September 18, 1979. It was republished in 1997 with a new introduction by Muntaqim, and is currently available through both Abraham Guillen Press and AK Press.

22. Ibid.

23. Ibid.

24. Afro-American Liberation Army, "Interview with L.A. P.O.W.'s," in *Humanity, Freedom, Peace*, 9.

25. Muntaqim, *On the Black Liberation Army*.

26. See J. Soffiyah Elijah, "The Reality of Political Prisoners in the United States: What September 11 Taught Us about Defending Them," *Harvard Black-Letter Journal* 18, no. 129 (spring 2002): 129–37.

27. Albert Nuh Washington, "Pain," unpublished poem. This poem and others by Washington are available online through the Jericho Movement Web site at http://www.thejerichomovement.com/poetry_of_nuh_qayyum.htm.

28. An outline of the case regarding the New York Three is offered in note 25 to the introduction of this book.

29. Nuh Washington's concise autobiographical account "New Afrikan Prisoner of War—Albert 'Nuh' Washington Speaks" can be found in *Cages of Steel: The Politics of Imprisonment in the United States*, ed. Ward Churchill and Jim Vander Wall (Washington, DC: Maisonneuve Press, 1992), 200–202.

30. See Ruth Wilson Gilmore, "Race and Globalization," in *Geographies of Global Change: Remapping the World*, ed. R. J. Johnston, Peter J. Taylor, and Michael Watts (New York: Blackwell Publishing, 2002), 261–74.

31. "Call Me Nuh" (video recording) (San Francisco: Real Dragon Productions, 2000), courtesy of the Freedom Archives.

32. Discussing Frantz Fanon's philosophical rejection of ontology as it is traditionally considered, Lewis Gordon considers the problems of the European philosopher's confrontation with the black subject: "Man is ontologically prior to his conceptualization; his existence, that is, precedes his essence. Once placed in motion as an object of inquiry, however, his 'essence' is sometimes essentialized in such a way as to become a prior ontology. *Human products become human causes*" (*Fanon and the Crisis of European Man: An Essay on Philosophy and the Human Sciences* [New York: Routledge, 1995], 46; emphasis added). It is possible to transpose Gordon's critique into Nuh Washington's demystification of the category of the prisoner, and the condition of imprisonment. Washington, as well, is concerned with displacing the reification of imprisonment, and conceptualizing "the prisoner" as "preceding" her or his existence as an object of captivity and state coercion.

33. See Sundiata Acoli, "New Afrikan Prison Struggle," in *Schooling the Generations in the Politics of Prison*, ed. Chinosole (Berkeley: New Earth Publications, 1996), 67–83; Shakur, *Assata;* and interviews with Assata Shakur and Dhoruba Bin Wahad in *Still Black, Still Strong: Survivors of the War against Black Revolutionaries*, ed. Jim Fletcher, Tanaquil Jones, and Sylvère Lotringer (New York: Semiotext[e], 1993).

34. In addition to the unpublished letters and interviews compiled by legal watchdog, human rights, prison abolitionist, and prisoners' rights organizations such as Justice Now, California Prison Focus, Critical Resistance, and the Freedom Archives, a review of the post-1970s literature generated by imprisoned activists and writers clearly reveals this common language of death and disappearance. Just a few of the more profound examples of such published texts include *Words from the House of the Dead: Prison Writings from Soledad*, ed. Joseph Bruchac and William Witherup (1971) (New York: Crossing Press, 1974); articles from the *Journal of Prisoners on Prisons*, many of which have been anthologized

in *Writing as Resistance: The Journal of Prisoners on Prisons Anthology (1988–2002)*, ed. Bob Gaucher (Toronto: Canadian Scholars' Press, 2002); *Soledad Prison: University of the Poor*, ed. Karlene Faith (Palo Alto, CA: Science and Behavior Books, 1975); *Wall Tappings: An International Anthology of Women's Prison Writings*, 2d ed., ed. Judith A. Scheffler (New York: Feminist Press at the City University of New York, 2002); and Jarvis Jay Masters, *Finding Freedom: Writings from Death Row* (Junction City, CA: Padma Publishing, 1997).

35. Safiya Bukhari-Alston was a Harlem-based Black Panther Party organizer and leader from 1969 to 1973. After being subpoenaed by a New York grand jury in an attempt to coerce her testimony against fellow party members, she went underground with the Black Liberation Army until her capture on January 17, 1975. She was the first and only woman to head an armed unit of the BLA. Bukhari-Alston recounts her decision to join the BLA: "I made the decision not to go to the grand jury and I went underground in the BLA. To go underground is very difficult. Whatever made you unique as a person, you have to change all of that and become somebody totally different" (Imani Henry, "WW Interviews Safiya Bukhari," *Workers World*, July 4, 2002). Political prisoner Mumia Abu-Jamal offers a concise biography of Bukhari-Alston in his book *We Want Freedom: A Life in the Black Panther Party* (Cambridge: South End Press, 2004).

36. Safiya Bukhari-Alston, "Coming of Age: A Black Revolutionary," in *Imprisoned Intellectuals: America's Political Prisoners Write on Life, Liberation, and Rebellion*, ed. Joy James (New York: Rowman & Littlefield, 2003), 128.

37. Ibid., 130.

38. Patricia Hill Collins writes: "This dimension of Black women's standpoint rejects either/or dichotomous thinking that claims that *either* thought *or* concrete action is desirable and that merging the two limits the efficacy of both. Such approaches generate deep divisions among theorists and activists which are more often fabricated than real. . . . That Black women should embrace a both/and conceptual orientation grows from Black women's experiences living as both African-Americans and women and, in many cases, in poverty" (*Black Feminist Thought: Knowledge, Consciousness, and the Politics of Empowerment* [New York: Routledge, 1990], 28–29).

39. Foucault, *Discipline and Punish*, 14.

40. Bureau of Justice Statistics, *Prisoners in 2000* (NCJ 188207, August 2001).

41. See "Legislative Packet: Conditions inside California Women's Prisons," published by Legal Services for Prisoners with Children (2000) (available from LSPC, 1540 Market St., Suite 490, San Francisco, CA 94102).

42. See Umoja, "Repression Breeds Resistance," 15–16, and Russell Shoats, "Black Fighting Formations: Their Strengths, Weaknesses, and Potentialities," in Cleaver and Katsiaficas, *Liberation, Imagination, and the Black Panther Party*, 136.

43. Sundiata Acoli, described by supporters and allies as a New Afrikan political prisoner of war, has written of Shakur's escape: "The [1970s] ended on a masterstroke by the BLA's Multinational Task Force, with the November 2, 1979 prison liberation of Assata Shakur—'Soul of the BLA'—and preeminent political prisoner of the era. The Task Force then whisked her away to the safety of political asylum in Cuba where she remains to date" ("New Afrikan Prison Struggle," 67–83). Sekou Odinga, Mutulu Shakur, Marilyn Buck, Susan Rosenberg, Silvia Baraldini (who was repatriated to her native Italy in 1999), and others have been accused, indicted, and/or imprisoned for their alleged roles in assisting Assata Shakur's liberation. According to Ward Churchill and Jim Vander Wall, the federal Joint Terrorist Task Force, formed in 1980 as an alliance between FBI COINTELPRO agents and select New York City "red squad" detectives, has additionally credited the Revolutionary Armed Task Force with Shakur's escape (Churchill and Vander Wall, *The COINTELPRO Papers*, 309 and 411 n. 25).

44. For a detailed self-narration of Shakur's experience, see "Open Letter from Assata Shakur," *Afrikan Frontline News Service*, March 31, 1998. The letter, written in response to New Jersey Governor Christine Whitman's grandstanding public call for Shakur's extradition from Cuba, reads, in part: "On May 2, 1973 I, along with Zayd Malik Shakur and Sundiata Acoli were stopped on the New Jersey Turnpike, supposedly for a 'faulty tail light.' Sundiata Acoli got out of the car to determine why we were stopped. . . . State trooper Harper then came to the car, opened the door and began to question us. Because we were black, and riding in a car with Vermont license plates, he claimed he became 'suspicious.' He then drew his gun, pointed it at us, and told us to put our hands up in the air, in front of us, where he could see them. I complied and in a split second, there was a sound that came from outside the car, there was a sudden movement, and I was shot once with my arms held up in the air, and then once again from the back. Zayd Malik Shakur was later killed, trooper Werner Foerster was killed, and even though trooper Harper admitted that he shot and killed Zayd Malik Shakur, under the New Jersey felony murder law, I was charged with killing both Zayd Malik Shakur, who was my closest friend and comrade, and charged in the death of trooper Foerster. . . . Although he was also unarmed, and the gun that killed trooper Foerster was found under Zayd's leg, Sundiata Acoli, who was captured later, was also charged with both deaths. Neither Sundiata

Acoli nor I ever received a fair trial. . . . No news media was ever permitted to interview us, although the New Jersey police and the FBI fed stories to the press on a daily basis. In 1977, I was convicted by an all-white jury and sentenced to life plus 33 years in prison. In 1979, fearing that I would be murdered in prison, and knowing that I would never receive any justice, I was liberated from prison, aided by committed comrades who understood the depths of the injustices in my case, and who were also extremely fearful for my life."

45. Assata Shakur and Acoli were convicted of the murder of New Jersey state trooper Werner Foerster despite significant prosecutorial misconduct and fundamental inconsistencies in the alleged forensic evidence (for example, the bullets removed from Foerster's body were revolver ammunition, rather than from a pistol, the weapon said to have been found in Shakur and Acoli's car). Concise, well-researched biographies of both Shakur and Acoli are available in James, *Imprisoned Intellectuals*, and details of their legal battles are outlined in Lennox Hinds's foreword to *Assata: An Autobiography* and Evelyn Williams, *Inadmissible Evidence* (Brooklyn: Lawrence Hill Books, 1993).

46. U.S. House of Representatives Committee Hearings on H. Con. Res. 254, "Calling for the Extradition of Joanne Chesimard from Cuba," May 13, 1998.

47. Shakur, *Assata*, 166.

48. See John Blassingame, "Runaways and Rebels," in *The Slave Community: Plantation Life in the Antebellum South* (New York: Oxford University Press, 1979), 192–222.

49. Shakur, "Open Letter from Assata Shakur."

50. See, for example, Amnesty International's *United States of America: Rights for All* (1998), and *"Not Part of My Sentence": Violations of the Human Rights of Women in Custody* (1999); also see the California Prison Focus investigative report "Corcoran State Prison 2001–2002: Inside California's Brutal Maximum Security Prison" (available through California Prison Focus, 2940 16th Street #B-5, San Francisco, CA 94103).

51. Although some choose to employ the term "Euro-American" as an "ethnic" designation of whiteness, I use it here in the more literal (though still "racial") sense of the philosophical and cultural convergences between European and North American/U.S. hegemonies and modernities as white-supremacist formations.

52. Foucault, *Discipline and Punish*, 308. Although a generous reading of Foucault's later body of work reveals concern with racism and "race struggle" as part of his genealogy of war and society (see essays in *"Society Must Be Defended"*), it is worth treating his examination of "the birth of the prison" in its singularity,

as a text that has obtained significant, even foundational status in contemporary discussions of carcerality, penality, and prisons within and beyond the United States. *Discipline and Punish* may be critically reengaged as a pathway into a current, working genealogy of a regime that recalls, reinvents, and refocuses the spectacle of bodily punishment that Foucault's rendition of Euro-American modernity relegates to the dustbin of the nineteenth century. Such a critique can offer numerous points of theoretical departure for current and future activism and scholarship.

53. Joy James, "Erasing the Spectacle of Racialized Violence," in *Resisting State Violence: Radicalism, Gender, and Race in U.S. Culture* (Minneapolis: University of Minnesota Press, 1996). This section, and much of the theoretical thrust of this chapter, is an elaboration of James's essay. Ongoing conversations and correspondence with James have both inspired and transformed this attempt at framing the book's larger set of theorizations.

54. Foucault initiates his study by establishing a loose set of parameters, foregrounding an interest in how a "corpus of knowledge, techniques, 'scientific' discourses is formed and becomes entangled with the practice of the power to punish." He thus intends *Discipline and Punish* as "a correlative history of the *modern soul* and of a new power to judge; a genealogy of the present scientifico-legal complex from which the power to punish derives its bases, justifications and rules" (*Discipline and Punish*, 23; emphasis added).

55. David Theo Goldberg, *Racist Culture* (Cambridge: Blackwell Publishers, 1993), 108–9; emphasis added.

56. Ibid., 39; emphasis added.

57. Foucault, *Discipline and Punish*, 25–26.

58. Angela Y. Davis, "From the Convict Lease System to the Super-Max Prison," in *States of Confinement: Policing, Detention, and Prisons*, ed. Joy James (New York: St. Martin's Press, 2000), 66.

59. Ibid.

60. Foucault's notion of the disciplinary penitentiary is most relevant to only the most *exceptional and institutionally privileged* of the imprisoned population. "Model inmates," by definition a small minority of captives who are accorded institutional favor for various reasons, are the ones granted exclusive and coveted access to the trappings of the Foucauldian disciplinary prison: to the extent that only these privileged few are allowed entry into the prison's rehabilitation, education, and work programs, all of which compose spheres of relative departure from the normative immobilization and organized idleness of the

prison regime, these disciplinary regimens represent symbolic exceptions to the prison's modality of rule. Further, the model inmate's relative privileges are premised on the constant possibility of their instant withdrawal—the model inmate must labor to *preserve* access to the regimes of discipline and (labor) exploitation.

For an overview of the generalized marginalization of "rehabilitation" or "reintegrative" programs in the U.S. prison system, see Elliot Currie, "Alternatives III: The Justice System," in *Crime and Punishment in America* (New York: Henry Holt and Co., 1998); Joel Dyer, "The Crime Gap," in *The Perpetual Prisoner Machine: How America Profits from Crime* (Boulder, CO: Westview Press, 2000); Edgardo Rotman, "The Failure of Reform: United States, 1865–1965," in *The Oxford History of the Prison*, ed. Norval Morris and David J. Rothman (New York: Oxford University Press, 1998); and the film *The Last Graduation* (New York: Deep Dish Television, 1997).

61. Frantz Fanon, *The Wretched of the Earth*, trans. Constance Farrington (New York: Grove Weidenfeld, 1968), 38; emphasis added.

62. Sharon Patricia Holland, *Raising the Dead: Readings of Death and (Black) Subjectivity* (Durham, NC: Duke University Press, 2000), 38.

63. Foucault, *Discipline and Punish*, 254.

64. Joy James, *Resisting State Violence: Radicalism, Gender, and Race in U.S. Culture* (Minneapolis: University of Minnesota Press, 1996), 27.

65. These quotations are from Michel Foucault, "7 January 1976," in *"Society Must Be Defended,"* 7.

66. Ibid., 8–9.

67. For a brilliant analysis of the black subject as America's constitutive incoherence, and black liberation as an essentially "insatiable demand" on the ordering and political reproduction of the United States, see Frank Wilderson, "The Prison Slave as Hegemony's (Silent) Scandal," *Social Justice: A Journal of Crime, Conflict and World Order* 30, no. 2 (2002): 18–27.

2. "You Be All the Prison Writer You Wish"

1. Paulo Freire, *Pedagogy of the Oppressed* (1970) (New York: Continuum, 2000), 51.

2. José Solís Jordan, "This Is Enough!" in *Imprisoned Intellectuals: America's Political Prisoners Write on Life, Liberation, and Rebellion*, ed. Joy James (New York: Rowman & Littlefield, 2003), 290. Jordan was sentenced to fifty-one months in

federal detention in July 1999, after being convicted of participating in the bombing of a U.S. Army recruiting center in Chicago. Despite significant evidence of government conspiracy in framing Jordan—including FBI infiltration and provocation in a number of Chicago-based Puerto Rican cultural and political organizations—and the wholesale absence of any physical evidence linking him to the bombing, he served his term until his release in 2002. For additional information, see "Dr. José Solís Jordan: Puerto Rican Political Prisoner," in *Can't Jail the Spirit: Political Prisoners in the U.S.*, 5th ed. (Chicago: Committee to End the Marion Lockdown, 2002); and Michelle Foy, "José Solís and State Repression Today," *Freedom Road Magazine*, no. 3 (winter 2003). Also see the ProLibertad Freedom Campaign Web site at http://prolibertadweb.tripod.com.

3. See Antonio Gramsci's sustained discussion of the philosophy of praxis in "Notes for an Introduction and an Approach to the Study of Philosophy and the History of Culture," in *The Antonio Gramsci Reader: Selected Writings, 1916–1935*, ed. David Forgacs (New York: New York University Press, 2000).

4. Jordan, "This Is Enough!" 286.

5. Gramsci, "Notes for an Introduction and an Approach to the Study of Philosophy and the History of Culture," 332.

6. Stuart Hall, "Gramsci's Relevance for the Study of Race and Ethnicity" (1986), in *Stuart Hall: Critical Dialogues in Cultural Studies*, ed. David Morley and Kuan-Hsing Chen (New York: Routledge, 1996), 423.

7. Ibid., 431.

8. Barbara Harlow, *Barred: Women, Writing, and Political Detention* (Hanover, NH: Wesleyan University Press, 1992), 10.

9. H. Bruce Franklin, *The Criminal as Victim and Artist* (New York: Oxford University Press, 1978), xxi–xxii.

10. Founded in London in 1921, PEN (Poets, Playwrights, Essayists, Editors, and Novelists) is based on the idea of promoting world peace through fostering cooperation and communication among a "world community of writers." See the PEN American Center Web site at http://www.pen.org.

11. Bell Chevigny, "Introduction," in *Doing Time: 25 Years of Prison Writing*, ed. Bell Chevigny (New York: Arcade Publishing, 1999), xiii.

12. Chinosole, ed., *Schooling the Generations in the Politics of Prison* (Berkeley: New Earth Publications, 1996), 2.

13. Joy James, "Introduction," in James, *Imprisoned Intellectuals*, 4.

14. Paul St. John, "Behind the Mirror's Face," in Chevigny, *Doing Time*, 120–22.

15. Anonymous, "The Problems of Writing in Prison," in *Words from the House of the Dead: Prison Writings from Soledad* (New York: Crossing Press, 1974).

16. George Jackson, *Blood in My Eye* (1972) (Baltimore: Black Classic Press, 1990), 7.

17. Saidiya V. Hartman, *Scenes of Subjection: Terror, Slavery, and Self-Making in Nineteenth-Century America* (New York: Oxford University Press, 1997), 4.

18. "Constitution of the Pennsylvania Prison Society," *Journal of Prison Discipline and Philanthropy* (January 1892): cover page.

19. "One Hundred and Fifth Annual Report of the Pennsylvania Prison Society," *Journal of Prison Discipline* (January 1892): 8.

20. Ibid., 9; emphasis added.

21. See Bureau of Justice Statistics, *Women Offenders* (NCJ 175688, December 1999), *Prison and Jail Inmates at Midyear 2003* (NCJ 203947, May 2004); Amnesty International, *Not Part of My Sentence: Violations of the Human Rights of Women in Custody* (Washington, DC: Amnesty International, 1999); John Irwin, Vincent Schiraldi, and Jason Ziedenberg, *America's One Million Nonviolent Prisoners* (Washington, DC: Justice Policy Institute, 1999), and Justice Policy Institute, *The Punishing Decade: Prison and Jail Estimates at the Millennium* (Washington, DC: Justice Policy Institute, 2000).

22. Mark E. Kann, "Penitence for the Privileged: Manhood, Race, and Penitentiaries in Early America," in *Prison Masculinities*, ed. Don Sabo, Terry A. Kupers, and Willie London (Philadelphia: Temple University Press, 2001), 22.

23. Samantha M. Shapiro, "Jails for Jesus," *Mother Jones* 28, no. 6 (November–December 2003): 54.

24. Ibid., emphasis added.

25. For a basic historical overview of philanthropic practices in U.S. prisons, jails, penitentiaries, and "reformatories," see Alexander W. Pisciotta, *Benevolent Repression: Social Control and the American Reformatory-Prison Movement* (New York: New York University Press, 1994); John Pratt, *Punishment and Civilization* (London: Sage Publications, 2002); Lawrence Friedman, *Crime and Punishment in American History* (New York: Basic Books, 1993); and *The Oxford History of the Prison*, ed. Norval Morris and David J. Rothman (New York: Oxford University Press, 1998).

26. Importantly, Alexander W. Pisciotta's work provides a historiography of late-nineteenth- and early-twentieth-century U.S. prison "reform" movements as integral to the construction of new forms of psychological as well as corporal punishment. See Pisciotta, *Benevolent Repression*.

27. Martha Escobar, interview transcript, Mentored Summer Research Internship Program Thesis (unpublished), University of California, Riverside, 2002. Subsequent references are given in the text.

28. Gabrielle Banks, "Learning under Lockdown," *Colorlines* (Spring 2003).

29. "Proposal for Academic Committee," memorandum submitted to San Quentin State Prison officials, March 11, 2002, courtesy of Viet Mike Ngo (from the author's papers).

30. Eddy Zheng, "Break These Chains," *Hardboiled* 5, no. 4 (April 2002).

31. Banks, "Learning under Lockdown," and Escobar, interview transcript.

32. Banks, "Learning under Lockdown."

33. Eric Cummins, *The Rise and Fall of California's Radical Prison Movement* (Stanford, CA: Stanford University Press, 1994), 20.

34. Banks, "Learning under Lockdown."

35. Jim Doyle, "Death Row Real Estate," *San Francisco Chronicle*, November 12, 2004, F1.

36. Anonymous, "A Sunny Soledad Afternoon," in *Words from the House of the Dead: Prison Writings from Soledad*, ed. Joseph Bruchac and William Witherup (New York: Crossing Press, 1974).

37. Juanita Díaz-Cotto, *Gender, Ethnicity, and the State: Latina and Latino Prison Politics* (Albany: State University of New York Press, 1996), 161.

38. Ron Eyerman and Andrew Jamison, *Social Movements: A Cognitive Approach* (University Park: Pennsylvania State University Press, 1991), 55.

39. Ibid., 46.

40. Ibid., 60.

41. Harlow, *Barred*, 189.

42. Alberto Melucci, "A Strange Kind of Newness: What's 'New' in New Social Movements?" in *New Social Movements: From Ideology to Identity*, ed. Enrique Laraña, Hank Johnston, and Joseph R. Gusfield (Philadelphia: Temple University Press, 1994), 103.

43. Examples of such scholarship abound in the fields of radical geography, critical race theory, and (what's left of) radical criminology, but among the most widely cited texts on incarceration as social formation is Mike Davis's *City of Quartz: Excavating the Future in Los Angeles* (New York: Verso, 1990). See especially chapter 4, "Fortress L.A."

44. Melucci, "A Strange Kind of Newness," 101–2.

45. Ibid., 104; emphasis added.

3. Radical Lineages

1. Joy James offers a critical meditation on this construction in *Shadowboxing: Representations of Black Feminist Politics* (New York: St. Martin's Press, 1999). See particularly the chapter "Revolutionary Icons and 'Neoslave Narratives.'"

2. Ruchell Cinque Magee is widely acknowledged as the one of the longest-held political prisoners in the United States and the world. The Ruchell Magee Defense Fund may be contacted at: P.O. Box 8306, South Bend, IN 46660-8306 (e-mail: mathiel@michzana.org). Mumia Abu-Jamal, in his 1997 article "Ruchell Cinque Magee: Sole Survivor Still" (in SFBayView.com, August 13, 2003; sfbayview.com/081303/ruchellcinque081303.shtml) concisely summarizes the historical context of Magee's political incarceration: "Ruchell C. Magee arrived in Los Angeles, California in 1963, and wasn't in town for six months before he and a cousin, Leroy, were arrested on the improbable charges of kidnap and robbery, after a fight with a man over a woman and a $10 bag of marijuana. Magee, in a slam-dunk 'trial,' was swiftly convicted and swifter still sentenced to life.

"Magee, politicized in those years, took the name of the African freedom fighter, Cinque, who, with his fellow captives seized control of the slave ship, the Amistad, and tried to sail back to Africa. . . .

"In August, 1970, Magee appeared as a witness in the assault trial of James McClain, a man charged with assaulting a guard after San Quentin guards murdered a Black prisoner, Fred Billingsley. McClain, defending himself, presented imprisoned witnesses to expose the racist and repressive nature of prisons. In the midst of Magee's testimony, a 17 year old young Black man with a huge Afro hairdo, burst into the courtroom, heavily armed.

"Jonathan Jackson shouted 'Freeze!' Tossing weapons to McClain, William Christmas, and a startled Magee, who given his 7 year hell where no judge knew the meaning of justice, joined the rebellion on the spot. The four rebels took the judge, the DA and three jurors hostage, and headed for a radio station where they were going to air the wretched prison conditions to the world, as well as demand the immediate release of a group of political prisoners, know as The Soledad Brothers (these were John Clutchette, Fleeta Drumgo, and Jonathan's oldest brother, George). While the men did not hurt any of their hostages, they did not reckon on the state's ruthlessness.

"Before the men could get their van out of the court house parking lot, prison guards and sheriffs opened furious fire on the vehicle, killing Christmas, Jackson, McClain as well as the judge. The DA was permanently paralyzed by gun fire. Miraculously, the jurors emerged relatively unscratched, although Magee, seriously wounded by gunfire, was found unconscious.

"Magee, who was the only Black survivor of what has come to be called 'The August 7th Rebellion,' would awaken to learn he was charged with murder, kidnapping and conspiracy, and further, he would have a co-defendant, a University of California Philosophy Professor, and friend of Soledad Brother, George L. Jackson, named Angela Davis, who faced identical charges.

"By trial time the cases were severed, with Angela garnering massive support leading to her 1972 acquittal on all charges.

"Magee's trial did not garner such broad support, yet he boldly advanced the position that as his imprisonment was itself illegal, and a form of unjustifiable slavery, he had the inherent right to escape such slavery, an historical echo of the position taken by the original Cinque, and his fellow captives, who took over a Spanish slave ship, killed the crew (except for the pilot) and tried to sail back to Africa. The pilot surreptitiously steered the Amistad to the US coast, and when the vessel was seized by the US, Spain sought their return to slavery in Cuba. Using natural and international law principles, US courts decided the captives had every right to resist slavery and fight for their freedom.

"Unfortunately, Magee's jury didn't agree, although it did acquit on at least one kidnapping charge. The court dismissed on the murder charge, and Magee has been battling for his freedom ever since.

"That he is still fighting is a tribute to a truly remarkable man, a man who knows what slavery is, and more importantly, what freedom means."

3. A brief political biography of Pinell is included in the text and endnotes of chapter 6.

4. Angela Y. Davis, "Political Prisoners, Prisons and Black Liberation," in Angela Davis et al., *If They Come in the Morning* (New York: Third Press, 1971), 23–29.

5. George Jackson, *Blood in My Eye* (Baltimore: Black Classics Press, 1990), 99–100.

6. According to journalist and author Min Yee: "By the summer of 1969, mutual fears and racial animosities between blacks and whites had increased to such intensity that five (Soledad Prison) black prisoners tried to take their complaints and fears to court. Led by W. L. Nolen, a prison boxing champion who was quickly becoming politicized, the group filed civil suits against Warden Fitzharris, the Department of Corrections and several guards. . . . The Nolen suits charged that the guards were aware of 'existing social and racial conflicts'; that the guards helped foment more racial strife by helping their white inmate 'confederates' through 'direct harassment in ways not actionable in court.' Nolen meant that his charges would be hard to prove, like leaving a cell door

open 'to endanger the lives of the plaintiffs.' Also hard to prove was the fact that the guards made 'false disciplinary reports' to keep blacks on max row in the 'hole' for longer periods of time.

"... At the same time, Nolen filed a separate civil suit against Fitzharris and his subordinates, charging Soledad officials with cruel and unusual punishment. In the suit, Nolen recalled that just months earlier he had been attacked by a group of 'white Nazi-sympathizing inmates' while he was exercising on a tier corridor. He said prison guards watched the affair 'indifferently,' until they saw that he was winning. Then they jumped into the fight, pummeled Nolen to the ground and dragged the black con to a strip cell.

"... The last allegation in Nolen's suit was even more damaging to the prison. He swore that Soledad officials were 'willfully creating and maintaining situations that creates and poses dangers to plaintiff and other members of his race.' Nolen said he 'feared for his life.' The case never came to trial; four months after he wrote the petition Nolen was shot to death by an O-wing guard" (Min Yee, *The Melancholy History of Soledad Prison* [New York: Harper's Magazine Press, 1973], 34–35).

7. Interview clip in the documentary film *Day of the Gun* (dir. Ken Swartz) (San Franscisco: KRON News, 2002).

8. Angela Y. Davis, *Angela Y. Davis: An Autobiography* (1974) (New York: International Publishers, 1988), 253.

9. I have chosen not to list these people here because many are still imprisoned or on parole. Any such admitted affiliation to Jackson would (especially in California) expose them to retaliation or harassment from corrections and other state officials, who could, under current statutes, claim that such a personal link constitutes a form of (prison) *gang affiliation*. Imprisoned and paroled people who are classified as "gang-affiliated" are eligible for accelerated and enhanced forms of punishment, most notably isolation in California's Security Housing Units.

10. I am indebted to Jared Sexton and Frank Wilderson III, who in 1999 recounted their experience with the San Quentin prison "librarian" who lectured them on the significance of the plaque and the vindicating scene of state violence that it immortalized. Sexton and Wilderson, both self-identified black radical intellectuals and activists, could barely tolerate their "tour guide's" rhetorical overtures, although both maintained their composure in order to sustain their pretext of a disinterested academic fact-gathering foray.

11. Frantz Fanon, *The Wretched of the Earth*, trans. Constance Farrington (New York: Grove Weidenfeld, 1968), 222–23.

12. Jackson, *Blood in My Eye*, 182; emphasis added.

13. George Jackson, *Soledad Brother: The Prison Letters of George Jackson* (Chicago: Lawrence Hill Books, 1994), 222.

14. Ibid., 181.

15. Omer Bartov, *Murder in Our Midst* (New York: Oxford University Press, 1996), 42.

16. Ibid., 67.

17. I first heard Ruthie Gilmore use the term "industrialized punishment" during an organizing meeting in the summer of 1999, although she has also elaborated it in various articles and interviews, including the essay "Globalisation and US Prison Growth: From Military Keynesianism to Post-Keynesian Militarism," *Race and Class* 40, no. 2/3 (1998–99): 171–88.

18. Davis et al., *If They Come in the Morning*, viii–ix.

19. James, *Shadowboxing*, 120.

20. Davis, *Autobiography*, 397–98.

21. Ibid., 65.

22. Juan J. Linz, "Some Notes toward a Comparative Study of Fascism in Sociological Historical Perspective," in *Fascism: A Reader's Guide*, ed. Walter Laqueur (Berkeley: University of California Press, 1976), 39.

23. James Gregor, *Interpretations of Fascism* (New Brunswick, NJ: Transaction Publishers, 1997).

24. Roger Griffin, ed., *Fascism* (New York: Oxford University Press, 1995), 245.

25. Robert Benewick and Philip Green, eds., *The Routledge Dictionary of Twentieth-Century Political Thinkers*, 2d ed. (New York: Routledge, 1998), 183.

26. Linz, "Some Notes toward a Comparative Study of Fascism in Sociological Historical Perspective," 16.

27. Fanon, *The Wretched of the Earth*, 38, 41, 236.

28. Jackson, *Blood in My Eye*, 118.

29. Ibid., 119–20.

30. Davis, "Political Prisoners, Prisons and Black Liberation," in Davis et al., *If They Come in the Morning*, 34–35.

31. Ibid., 32.

32. Ibid., 20.

33. Angela Y. Davis, "Prison Interviews," in Davis et al., *If They Come in the Morning*, 184; emphasis added.

34. Barbara Harlow, *Barred: Women, Writing, and Political Detention* (Hanover, NH: Wesleyan University Press, 1992), 11.

35. For a sustained discussion of "Homeland," see Joy James's introduction ("Violations") to the forthcoming anthology *Warfare: The American Homeland and Prison*, ed. Joy James.

36. Ronald Takaki's widely read *A Different Mirror* (Boston: Little, Brown, 1993) is perhaps the paradigmatic example of the new liberal multiculturalism, which supplements as it competes with more traditionally white-supremacist master narratives.

37. Ward Churchill, *A Little Matter of Genocide* (San Francisco: City Lights, 1997), 432.

38. See Andrea Smith, *Conquest: Sexual Violence and American Indian Genocide* (Boston: South End Press, 2005), and Dorothy Roberts, *Killing the Black Body: Race, Reproduction, and the Meaning of Liberty* (New York: Pantheon Books, 1997).

39. See Saidiya V. Hartman, *Scenes of Subjection: Terror, Slavery, and Self-Making in Nineteenth-Century America* (New York: Oxford University Press, 1997), and Frank Wilderson III's discussion of the "absolute dereliction" of black subjectivity in context of civil society in "The Prison Slave as Hegemony's (Silent) Scandal," *Social Justice* 30, no. 2 (summer 2003): 18–27.

40. Angela Y. Davis, "Race and Criminalization: Black Americans and the Punishment Industry," in *The Angela Y. Davis Reader*, ed. Joy James (New York: Blackwell Publishers, 1998), 63.

41. Mumia Abu-Jamal, *Live from Death Row* (New York: Avon Books, 1996), 108.

42. Angela Y. Davis, "Masked Racism: Reflections on the Prison Industrial Complex," *Colorlines* 1, no. 2 (fall 1998): 12.

43. Laura Whitehorn, "Notes from the Unrepenitantary," *Prison Legal News* 9, no. 5 (May 1998): 7; emphasis added.

44. Manning Marable, *How Capitalism Underdeveloped Black America* (Boston: South End Press, 1983), 248–53.

45. U.S. Department of Justice, Bureau of Justice Statistics, *Correctional Populations in the United States, 1993*, NCJ 156241, 1995.

46. Linda Evans and Eve Goldberg, *The Prison Industrial Complex and the Global Economy* (San Francisco: AK Press Distribution, 1998), 7.

47. A concise and accessible overview of this reformation of common sense may be found in Philip McLaughlin's essay "Just Say No?" in *The Celling of America*, ed. Daniel Burton-Rose (Monroe, ME: Common Courage Press, 1998), 88–91.

48. Cultural theorist and activist Frank Wilderson III has frequently used the phrase "prisoners-in-waiting" to denote the structured imminence of the

evisceration of the black subject's nominal freedom within the despotism of white-supremacist civil society.

49. Albert "Nuh" Washington, "Message to Critical Resistance," open letter, September 1998; in author's files.

4. Articulating War(s)

1. William Appleman Williams, *Empire as a Way of Life* (New York: Oxford University Press, 1980), 14.

2. Ibid., 5.

3. Walter James, "Inside the Outside S.H.U. at Tehachapi," *Prison Focus*, no. 19 (winter/spring 2004): 15.

4. Annamarie Oliverio, *The State of Terror* (Albany: State University of New York Press, 1998), 141.

5. Jill Soffiyah Elijah, "Conditions of Confinement," in *Black Prison Movements, USA* (Trenton, NJ: Africa World Press, 1995), 140.

6. D. A. Sheldon, *Voices from Within the Prison Walls* (Chicago: News and Letters, 1998), 58–59.

7. Ibid., emphasis added.

8. J. McGhee-King, "The Many Moods of Manipulation," *Peacekeeper* (summer 2000): 13; emphasis added.

9. Ibid.

10. For a useful discussion of the discursive construction of terror and terrorism in the staging of state legitimacy and legitimated violence, see Joseba Zulaika and William A. Douglass, "Tropics of Terror: Plots and Performances," in *Terror and Taboo: The Follies, Fables, and Faces of Terrorism* (New York: Routledge, 1996).

11. Marilyn Buck, "Psychological Perspectives on Women and Repression," unpublished essay from the author's papers, March 2000.

12. Oliverio, *The State of Terror*, 55.

13. Interview with anonymous former Black Panther Party woman, 2004 (date and location excluded).

14. Allen Feldman, "Violence and Vision: The Prosthetics and Aesthetics of Terror," *Public Culture* 10, no. 1 (Fall 1997); cited in *Violence and Subjectivity*, ed. Veena Das, Arthur Kleinman, Mamphela Ramphele, and Pamela Reynolds (Berkeley: University of California Press, 2000), 49.

15. "By a *scopic regime* I mean the agendas and techniques of political visualization: the regimens that prescribe modes of seeing and visual objects, and

which proscribe or render untenable other modes and objects of perception. A scopic regime is an ensemble of practices and discourses that establish the truth claims, typicality, and credibility of visual acts and objects and politically correct modes of seeing" (ibid., 49).

16. Lewis Gordon, "Fanon's Tragic Revolutionary Violence," in *Fanon: A Critical Reader*, ed. Lewis Gordon, T. Denean Sharpley-Whiting, and Renée T. White (Cambridge, MA: Blackwell Publishers, 1996), 305–6.

17. Gregory J. McMaster, "Maximum Ink" (1999), in *Writing as Resistance: The Journal of Prisoners on Prisons, Anthology (1988–2002)*, ed. Bob Gaucher (Toronto: Canadian Scholars' Press, 2002), 64.

18. Marilyn Buck, personal correspondence, November 26, 1999; emphasis added.

19. Joy James, *Resisting State Violence: Radicalism, Gender, and Race in U.S. Culture* (Minneapolis: University of Minnesota Press, 1996), 34.

20. Kijana Tashiri Askari, personal correspondence, February 20, 2000.

21. Allen Feldman, *Formations of Violence: The Narrative of the Body and Political Terror in Northern Ireland* (Chicago: University of Chicago Press, 1991), 115.

22. Phyllis Kornfeld, *Cellblock Visions* (Princeton, NJ: Princeton University Press, 1997), 10.

23. Bill Dunne has been imprisoned since 1979. He writes in *Can't Jail the Spirit: Political Prisoners in the U.S.* 5th ed. (Chicago: Committee to End the Marion Lockdown, 2002): "I was made a prisoner of the state on October 14, 1979 in Seattle, Washington. Late that evening, I was picked up by paramedics while under the influence of police bullets near a shot-up and wrecked car containing some weapons and a dead jail escapee. According to the ensuing state and federal charges, I and a codefendant and unknown other associates of a San Francisco anarchist collective had conspired to effect a comrade's armed liberation from a Seattle jail and attempted to execute the plot on October 14, 1979. The charges further alleged the operation was financed by bank expropriation and materially facilitated by illegal acquisition of weapons, explosives, vehicles, ID and other equipment.

"After long subjection to atrocious jail conditions and three sensationalized trials, I got a 90 year sentence in 1980. I subsequently got a consecutive 15 years as a result of an attempted self-emancipation in 1983. The aggregate 105 years is a 'parole when they feel like it' sort of sentence" (196).

24. Bill Dunne, personal correspondence, November 4, 1999.

25. Ramiro R. Muñiz letters, South Texas Archives, Texas A&M University

(excerpts available online at http://www.freeramsey.com). Muñiz, an attorney, La Raza Unida Party organizer, and onetime Texas gubernatorial candidate (1972 and 1974), was indicted on federal drug conspiracy charges in 1976. In order to protect other members of La Raza Unida Party from prosecution and certain imprisonment, he pled guilty to the charge. After serving the sentence, he was relentlessly pursued and harassed by Drug Enforcement Administration agents, who unsuccessfully attempted to reincarcerate him on drug charges—these were eventually dropped (in exchange for a "parole violation") following an illegal search and seizure. In 1994, with the apparent cooperation of a *mexicano* who had been apprehended in an illegal drug deal, the DEA entrapped Muñiz and assisted in a successful prosecution that resulted in a life sentence without the possibility of parole. Ramiro "Ramsey" R. Muñiz's support committee runs a Web site at www.freeramsey.com. The site contains a biography of Muñiz as well as excerpts from his letters and essays. For a history of La Raza Unida Party, see Ignacio M. Garcia, *United We Win: The Rise and Fall of La Raza Unida Party* (Tucson: University of Arizona Press, 1990).

26. Feldman, *Formations of Violence*, 7.

27. Paul Wright, "The Cultural Commodification of Prisons," *Prison Legal News* 10, no. 11 (November 1999): 4. For a short biography of Paul Wright, published shortly after his release, see George Howland Jr., "Freed Speech," *Seattle Weekly*, January 28, 2004, 17. Wright is the cofounder and coeditor of *Prison Legal News*, which remains the only nationally circulated "prisoners' rights" journal (it is also the only such journal that is significantly authored and edited by imprisoned people). Wright has also coedited two anthologies, *The Celling of America* (Monroe, ME: Common Courage Press, 1998) and *Prison Nation* (New York: Routledge, 2003).

28. This is Chrystos's preferred self-description.

29. Chrystos, presentation at "Critical Resistance" conference/strategy session, September 25, 1999.

30. Dhoruba Bin Wahad, "Toward Rethinking Self-Defense in a Racist Culture," in *Still Black, Still Strong: Survivors of the War against Black Revolutionaries*, ed. Jim Fletcher, Tanaquil Jones, and Sylvère Lotringer (New York: Semiotext[e], 1993). Bin Wahad was a political prisoner for nineteen years. The New York Police Department, in conjunction with FBI COINTELPRO agents, apprehended and indicted Bin Wahad as part of the "New York 21" in 1969. These members of the New York chapter of the Black Panther Party were accused of more than one hundred "conspiracy" charges to assassinate police and bomb a variety of public

and corporate sites. After Bin Wahad and Michael Cetewayo Tabor went underground (jumping bail), the charges against the New York 21 (including Bin Wahad
and Tabor) were determined to be without foundation and were summarily dismissed by a jury in May 1971. The two-year incarceration of the rest of the
defendants had already decimated the leadership and organizing structure of the
Black Panther Party, however. Bin Wahad was again captured by the NYPD in
June 1971, and was accused of the attempted murder of two police officers some
two months earlier. After three trials, he was sentenced to twenty-five years to
life. A series of civil rights actions by Bin Wahad and his attorneys forced the
release of several hundred thousand declassified COINTELPRO documents,
including previously undisclosed information that a key witness had told the
prosecution that Bin Wahad did not commit the acts for which he was imprisoned. Bin Wahad won the right to a retrial in 1990. Five years after his release
from prison, the New York district attorney finally dismissed his case. See Bin
Wahad, "Toward Rethinking Self-Defense in a Racist Culture," and "Dhoruba Bin
Wahad: Biography," in *Imprisoned Intellectuals: America's Political Prisoners Write on
Life, Liberation, and Rebellion*, ed. Joy James (New York: Rowman & Littlefield,
2003), 94–95.

31. Wright, "The Cultural Commodification of Prisons," 2.

32. According to the Montreal chapter of the Anarchist Black Cross Federation
(http://www.montrealabcf.org/africa/), "The MOVE 9 are innocent men and
women who have been in prison since 1978, following a massive police assault on
MOVE Headquarters in Powelton Village, Philadelphia (seven years before the
government dropped a bomb on MOVE, killing 11 people, including 5 children).

"During the raid, MOVE adults came out of the house carrying their
children through clouds of tear gas and were immediately taken into custody.
MOVE never fired any shots and no MOVE members were arrested with any
weapons. All were viciously beaten. TV cameras filmed police brutally beating
and kicking Delbert Africa (Three of the four police were brought to trial and
acquitted despite irrefutable photographic evidence).

"One police officer was killed by 'friendly fire.' The MOVE 9 were wrongly
convicted and each sentenced to 30–100 years for the death. Janet is currently
imprisoned in Cambridge Springs, Pennsylvania."

33. Janet Hollaway Africa, "Janet Africa: MOVE Political Prisoner," in *Can't
Jail the Spirit*, 83.

34. Jack Olsen, *Last Man Standing: The Tragedy and Triumph of Geronimo Pratt*
(New York: Doubleday, 2000), 191–92.

35. Pratt's legal defense team, with assistance from private investigators, definitively proved that the FBI (largely through J. Edgar Hoover's COINTEL-PRO targeting of him and the Black Panther Party) and the Los Angeles district attorney's office conspired to hide evidence from the defense team and the jury in his original murder trial. Olsen's biography *Last Man Standing* meticulously details the seemingly endless legal machinations undertaken by ji Jaga's defense attorneys Stuart Hanlon and Johnnie L. Cochran Jr. over the course of three decades, culminating in their successful exposure of Los Angeles prosecutorial and police misconduct, as well as the targeting of ji Jaga by the FBI's Counter-intelligence Program.

36. Antonio Gramsci, *Selections from the Prison Notebooks*, trans. and ed. Quintin Hoare and Geoffrey Nowell Smith (New York: International Publishers, 1971), 229.

37. Ibid., 234.

38. Stuart Hall, "Gramsci's Relevance for the Study of Race and Ethnicity," in *Stuart Hall: Critical Dialogues in Cultural Studies*, ed. David Morley and Kuan-Hsing Chen (New York: Routledge, 1996), 427.

39. Susan Rosenberg, "Censored Women Speak," *Phoebe* 6, no. 2 (fall 1994): 98.

40. Mutulu Shakur, personal correspondence, September 9, 1999. Dr. Shakur has been a political prisoner since 1982. He has been active in the black liberation movement since the mid-1960s, working closely with the Revolutionary Action Movement (RAM), the Provisional Government of the Republic of New Afrika (RNA), the National Committee to Free Political Prisoners, and the Black Panther Party. He was cofounder and director of the National Task Force for COINTELPRO Litigation and Research. Shakur, a doctor of acupuncture, cofounded and codirected the Black Acupuncture Advisory Association of North America (BAAANA) and the Harlem Institute of Acupuncture. According to the biography composed by the Family and Friends of Mutulu Shakur, "Dr. Shakur . . . managed a detox program recognized as the largest and most effective of its kind by the National Institute of Drug Abuse, National Acupuncture Research Society and the World Academic Society of Acupuncture. . . . Many community leaders, political activists, lawyers and doctors were served by BAAANA and over one hundred medical students were trained in the discipline of acupuncture.

"By the late 1970's Dr. Shakur's work in acupuncture and drug detoxification was both nationally and internationally known and he was invited to address members of the medical community around the world. Dr. Shakur lectured on his work at many medical conferences, and was invited to the People's Republic of China. In addition in his work for the Charles Cobb Commission for Racial Justice for the National Council of Churches he developed their anti-drug program" (Family and Friends of Mutulu Shakur, "Biography of Dr. Mutulu Shakur," http://www.mutulushakur.com/who.html). In March 1982, Shakur was indicted (with ten codefendants) by a federal grand jury under the Racketeer Influenced and Corrupt Organization (RICO) Act. He was accused of conspiracy against the U.S. government through his alleged affiliations with the Black Liberation Army and New Afrikan Freedom Fighters. He was also charged with participation in the successful liberation of Assata Shakur in 1979. His son, rap artist Tupac Shakur, was killed in 1996.

41. Leonard Peltier, *Prison Writings: My Life Is My Sun Dance* (New York: St. Martin's Press, 1999), 33.

42. Feldman, *Formations of Violence*, 5.

43. Marilyn Buck, personal correspondence, September 23, 1999.

44. Peltier, *Prison Writings*, 28.

45. Ray Luc Levasseur, personal correspondence, October 2, 1999.

5. "My Role Is to Dig or Be Dug Out"

1. Michel Foucault, *Discipline and Punish: The Birth of the Prison*, trans. Alan Sheridan (New York: Pantheon Books, 1977), 217.

2. See chapter 2, "The Spectacle of the Scaffold," in Part I, "Torture," in ibid.

3. As mentioned earlier, the work of activist and radical theorist Joy James has been influential to the development of this argument. See Joy James, "Erasing the Spectacle of Racialized State Violence," in *Resisting State Violence: Radicalism, Gender, and Race in U.S. Culture* (Minneapolis: University of Minnesota Press, 1996).

4. Foucault, *Discipline and Punish*, 201.

5. The state proclaims its incarceration techniques conspicuously in its public self-narrations. See, for example, "Pelican Bay State Prison: Security Housing Unit," California Department of Corrections Web site (http://www.corr.ca.gov/InstitutionsDiv/INSTDIV/facilities/fac_prison_PBSP.asp), 2004.

6. John H. Morris III, "It's a Form of Warfare: A Description of Pelican Bay State Prison" (1991), in *Writing as Resistance: The Journal of Prisoners on Prisons Anthology (1988–2002)*, ed. Bob Gaucher (Toronto: Canadian Scholars' Press, 2002), 349–50.

7. In September 1999, twelve Puerto Rican *independentistas* were granted conditional clemency through presidential order. Eleven were released immediately,

and Juan Segarra Palmer was released in January 2004. The twelve freed are Palmer, Alicia and Ida Luz Rodríguez, Elizam Escobar, Ricardo Jiménez, Adolfo Matos, Dylcia Pagán, Luis Rosa, Carmen Valentín, Alberto Rodríguez, Alejandrina Torres, and Edwin Cortés ("11 Puerto Rican Nationalists Released from Prison," CNN, September 10, 1999). Susan Rosenberg and Linda Evans, white anti-imperialist antiracist political prisoners, both had their sentences commuted in January 2001 through presidential order.

8. A 1988 court decision declared that imprisonment in the Lexington High Security Unit had violated the women's constitutional rights. See generally "Follow Up," *Nation*, October 24, 1987, 436. This editorial was written about three weeks after director of the Federal Bureau of Prisons, J. Michael Quinlan, had agreed to shut down the HSU "within nine months."

9. Lorna A. Rhodes, *Total Confinement: Madness and Reason in the Maximum Security Prison* (Berkeley: University of California Press, 2004), 3. Rhodes's text is a critical ethnography of "control units" that offers a useful and rigorous overview of the prison's institutional discourses of law, logic, reason, and rationality over and against its production of regimented bodily violence, performative irrationality, and "madness." Rhodes examines control units and "mental health facilities" in comparative fashion, pointing out convergences and distinctions in their modalities of institutional rule.

10. *Through the Wire* (video recording), dir. Nina Rosenblum (Daedalus Productions, 1990).

11. The Prison Activist Resource Center, based in Oakland, California, defines control unit prisons as follows: "A control unit prison is a prison or part of a prison that is in a state of permanent lockdown, a usually-temporary condition used to control and suppress disruptions within a prison by severely restricting prisoners' rights. In theory, control units warehouse the 'worst of the worst,' the most violent prisoners who threaten the security of guards and other prisoners. This once temporary condition has been increasingly adopted as the new model for US prisons" (http://www.prisonactivist.org/control-unit/).

12. For a detailed history on the emergence of control unit prisons in the United States, see *From Alcatraz to Marion to Florence—Control Unit Prisons in the United States* (pamphlet), published by the Committee to End the Marion Lockdown (1992).

13. Kijana Tashiri Askari, personal correspondence, September 24, 2000.

14. Kijana Tashiri Askari, personal correspondence, February 20, 2000.

15. Kijana Tashiri Askari, "The Legalization of Genocide: Genocide as a

Common Practice," unpublished essay from the author's papers, January 5, 2004. This essay was written as a public correspondence, and has since been circulated as required reading for several college-level courses.

16. Kijana Tashiri Askari, personal correspondence, September 24, 2000.

17. Tyrone Love, ADX prison (Colorado), "Supermax Prisons," The Learning Channel.

18. Jay Thompson, Westville Prison (Indiana), "Supermax Prisons," The Learning Channel.

19. Christy Marie Camp, "Inside Valley State Prison for Women," *North Coast Xpress* (winter/spring 2001): 5. See also "Sexual Molestation Policy Stopped," *Prison Focus*, no. 19 (winter/spring 2004): 10–11.

20. See, for example, *Prison Masculinities*, ed. Don Sabor, Terry Kupers, and Willie London (Philadelphia: Temple University Press, 2001), and Christian Parenti, *Lockdown America: Police and Prisons in the Age of Crisis* (New York: Verso, 2000).

21. Christy Marie Camp, "Inside Valley State Prison for Women"; emphasis added.

22. Daniel Burton-Rose, "Our Sister's Keepers," *Prison Legal News* 10, no. 2 (February 1999): 1.

23. Kijana Tashiri Askari, personal correspondence, January 7, 2001.

24. Rhodes, *Total Confinement*, 56.

25. Robin Wagner-Pacifici, *Theorizing the Standoff: Contingency in Action* (New York: Cambridge University Press, 2000), 9.

26. Michael Dorrough, "Reflections on the Madrid Decision," in *Extracts from Pelican Bay*, ed. Marilla Argüelles (Berkeley: Pantograph Press, 1995), 35.

27. Sally Mann Romano, "If the SHU Fits: Cruel and Unusual Punishment at California's Pelican Bay State Prison," *Emory Law Journal* 45, no. 3 (summer 1996): 1130; emphasis added.

28. Terry Kupers, *Prison Madness: The Mental Health Crisis behind Bars and What We Must Do about It* (San Francisco: Jossey-Bass Publishers, 1999), 56–57.

29. Wagner-Pacifici, *Theorizing the Standoff*, 98.

30. Rhodes, *Total Confinement*, 112.

31. Keith R. Lansdowne, "Choosing Sanity," in *The Funhouse Mirror: Reflections on Prison*," ed. Robert Ellis Gordon (Pullman: Washington State University Press, 2000), p. 40–41.

32. "The Attica Rebellion: Eyewitness Accounts" (audio recording) (New York: Radio Free People, 1971).

33. John Edgar Wideman, "Introduction," in Mumia Abu-Jamal *Live from Death Row* (New York: Avon Books, 1996), xxx.

34. Cassandra Shaylor, "Four Years in Solitary Confinement," *San Francisco Chronicle*, April 9, 2000, 4.

35. Ibid.

36. Arthur Kleinman, "The Violences of Everyday Life: The Multiple Forms and Dynamics of Social Violence," in *Violence and Subjectivity*, ed. Veena Das, Arthur Kleinman, Mamphela Ramphele, and Pamela Reynolds (Berkeley: University of California Press, 2000), 238.

37. Anonymous, interviewed September 2000.

38. Marilyn Buck and Susan Rosenberg, "Censored Women Speak," *Phoebe* 6, no. 2 (fall 1994): 99.

39. Wagner-Pacifici, *Theorizing the Standoff*, 60.

40. Raymond Luc Levasseur, "Trouble Coming Everyday: ADX—the First Year," *North Coast Xpress* (winter/spring 2001): 24.

41. Wagner-Pacifici, *Theorizing the Standoff*, 137–38.

42. "The Attica Rebellion: Eyewitness Accounts" (audio recording).

43. Wagner-Pacifici, *Theorizing the Standoff*, 19.

44. Interview with Hugo "Yogi" Pinell, Pelican Bay State Prison (California), April 19, 2001 (interviewed by the author and Georgia Schreiber, California Prison Focus). Pinell has been imprisoned in the Pelican Bay SHU since 1990. His supporters run a Web site on his behalf at www.hugopinell.org.

45. Ibid, emphasis added.

46. Avery F. Gordon, *Ghostly Matters: Haunting and the Sociological Imagination* (Minneapolis: University of Minnesota Press, 1996), 179.

47. Interview with Hugo "Yogi" Pinell, April 19, 2001.

48. Gordon, *Ghostly Matters*, 19.

49. Interview with Hugo "Yogi" Pinell, April 19, 2001.

50. Viet Mike Ngo, "Grave Digger," *Amerasia Journal* 29, no. 1: 180.

6. Forced Passages

1. Alex Lichtenstein, *Twice the Work of Free Labor* (New York: Verso, 1996), 188–89.

2. Angela Y. Davis, "From the Prison of Slavery to the Slavery of Prison: Frederick Douglass and the Convict Lease System," in *The Angela Y. Davis Reader*, ed. Joy James (Malden, MA: Blackwell Publishers, 1998), 75–76.

3. Ibid., 75.

4. See the Campaign Against Prison Slavery, which is fighting to end "forced labor" in British prisons (http://www.enrager.net/hosted/caps/); Lorenzo Komboa Ervin, "Prison: Corporate Slavery?" *Green Left Weekly* (online edition), April 19, 2000 (http://www.greenleft.org.au/back/2000/419/419p23.htm); idem, "Prison: The New Slavery?" *Touchstone* 10, no. 4 (September/October 2000); Drug Policy Alliance, "A New Slavery," 2004 (http://www.drugpolicy.org/communities/race/anewslavery/); and Ky Henderson, "The New Slavery," *Human Rights* 24, no. 4 (1997).

5. See David Garland, "The Rationalization of Punishment," in *Punishment and Modern Society: A Study in Social Theory* (Chicago: University of Chicago Press, 1990), and Edgardo Rotman, "The Failure of Reform: United States, 1865–1965," in *The Oxford History of the Prison*, ed. Norval Morris and David J. Rothman (New York: Oxford University Press, 1998); Kijana Tashiri Askari, "The Legalization of Genocide: Genocide as a Common Practice," unpublished essay from the author's papers, January 5, 2004. Community organizer Dorsey Nunn, during organizing meetings for the 1998 conference "Critical Resistance: Beyond the Prison Industrial Complex," repeatedly asserted that he had borne a lifetime of witness to the emergence of the prison regime as a form of low-intensity "genocide" for poor black and brown people in the United States. Nunn's claim presented a vexing, if consistently deferred political problem for the otherwise smooth functioning of these organizing sessions. His insistence on resituating a radical critique of the prison industrial complex as *a confrontation with black/brown death* could only be met with a deafening, if respectful, silence from most of his co-organizers, many of whom were attorneys, academics, salaried activists in progressive nonprofit organizations, and other professionals who lived at a fundamental distance from the reality about which Nunn, a former prisoner, spoke. The gravity of his political vernacular was inescapable, invoking a historical lineage of black and Native struggles against varieties of state and state-sanctioned mass killing, and illuminating the theoretical entanglement between mass imprisonment and human liquidation. Nunn is a founding organizer of the "All of Us or None" movement, a national alliance composed of current and former prisoners struggling for "the human and civil rights of prisoners, former prisoners, and their families." See Virginia Vélez, "All of Us or None," *The Fire Inside*, no. 24, (summer 2003) (published by the California Coalition for Women Prisoners).

6. Sharon Patricia Holland, *Raising the Dead: Readings of Death and (Black) Subjectivity* (Durham, NC: Duke University Press, 2000), 15.

7. Frank Wilderson III, "The Prison Slave as Hegemony's (Silent) Scandal," *Social Justice* 30, no. 2 (summer 2003): 18–27.

8. A Federal Prisoner (anonymous), "A Mount Everest of Time" ("Sunday Punch" section, 2), *San Francisco Chronicle*, October 7, 1990.

9. See Orlando Patterson, *Slavery and Social Death: A Comparative Study* (Cambridge: Harvard University Press, 1982). Here, my material genealogy of the slave ship resonates with—while critically departing from—Paul Gilroy's well-known conceptualization of the ship as "a living, micro-cultural, micro-political system in motion." "Ships immediately focus attention on the middle passage, on the various projects for redemptive return to an African homeland, on the circulation of ideas and activists as well as the movement of key cultural and political artifacts" (Paul Gilroy, *The Black Atlantic: Modernity and Double Consciousness* [Cambridge: Harvard University Press, 1993], 4). Although Gilroy's conception of the Black Atlantic has been well-noted and heavily critiqued by black feminist/womanist scholars for its attachment to masculine or masculinist conceptions of mobility and cultural production, I am critically revisiting the slave ship through a different genealogy that recenters the sometimes ambiguous gendering of bodies in sites of mass capture. For useful critical meditations on Gilroy's conception of the Black Atlantic (as well as his use of the ship as "chronotope"), see Julia Sudbury, "From the Point of No Return to the Women's Prison: Writing Spaces of Confinement into Diaspora Studies," *Canadian Woman Studies* 23, no. 2 (winter 2004): 154–63; Jacqueline Nassy Brown, "Black Liverpool, Black America and the Gendering of Diaspora Space," *Cultural Anthropology* 13, no. 2 (1998): 291–325; Laura Chrisman, "Journeying to Death: Gilroy's 'Black Atlantic,'" *Race and Class* 39, no. 2 (1997): 51–65; Ronald A. T. Judy, "Paul Gilroy's 'Black Atlantic' and the Place(s) of English in the Global," *Critical Quarterly* 39, no. 1 (April 1997): 22–30.

10. Eric Williams, *Capitalism and Slavery* (1944) (Chapel Hill: University of North Carolina Press, 1994).

11. David Eltis, "The Volume and Structure of the Transatlantic Slave Trade: A Reassessment," *William and Mary Quarterly* 58, no. 1 (January 2001): 17–31. Outlining the historical debate over this figure, Eltis, David Richardson, and Stephen D. Behrendt write that the empirical research that followed publication of Curtin's classic text "focused on the two centuries after 1660 when the transatlantic traffic in Africans peaked, [and] has used archival shipping data unavailable to Curtin. Usually interpreted as more reliable than Curtin's, the new findings have nevertheless tended to corroborate rather than challenge Curtin's original

estimates of the totals involved" (David Eltis, David Richardson, and Stephen D. Behrendt, "Patterns in the Transatlantic Slave Trade, 1662–1867," in *Black Imagination and the Middle Passage*, ed. Maria Diedrich, Henry Louis Gates Jr., and Carl Pederson [New York: Oxford University Press, 1999], 21). By way of reflection on this debate among historians over the human volume of the transatlantic slave trade, Joseph Inikori and Stanley Engerman wrote in 1992: "Inikori has suggested a global figure of 15.4 million. This figure has been contested by some scholars, and while the process of revision continues, it seems probable that the ultimate figure is unlikely to be less than 12 million or more than 20 million captives exported from Africa in the transatlantic slave trade" (Joseph Inikori and Stanley Engerman, eds., *The Atlantic Slave Trade* [Durham, NC: Duke University Press, 1992], 6). Paul E. Lovejoy, a decade earlier, arrived at a figure remarkably close to both Curtin's and Eltis's, suggesting a figure of 11,698,000 "exported" enslaved Africans between 1450 and 1900, with approximately 9,778,500 surviving the transatlantic transport (Paul E. Lovejoy, "The Volume of the Atlantic Slave Trade: A Synthesis," *Journal of African History* 23, no. 4. [1982]: 477–78).

12. In addition to the books and articles already mentioned, it is worth noting the following texts for the purposes of providing a broad historical overview of the scholarship addressing the trade in enslaved Africans and the Middle Passage: Philip D. Curtin, *The Atlantic Slave Trade: A Census* (Madison: University of Wisconsin Press, 1969); Johannes Postma, *The Atlantic Slave Trade* (Westport, CT: Greenwood Press, 2003); David Northrup, ed., *The Atlantic Slave Trade* (Lexington, MA: D. C. Heath and Company, 1994); David Eltis and James Walvin, eds., *The Abolition of the Atlantic Slave Trade: Origins and Effects in Europe, Africa, and the Americas* (Madison: University of Wisconsin Press, 1981); Herbert S. Klein, *The Middle Passage: Comparative Studies in the Atlantic Slave Trade* (Princeton, NJ: Princeton University Press, 1978); Henry C. Carey, *The Slave Trade: Domestic and Foreign* (1853) (New York: Augustus M. Kelley Publishers, 1967); George F. Kay, *The Shameful Trade* (London: Frederick Muller, 1967); Tommy L. Lott, ed., *Subjugation and Bondage: Critical Essays on Slavery and Social Philosophy* (New York: Rowman & Littlefield, 1998); Patrick Manning, ed., *Slave Trades, 1500–1800: Globalization of Forced Labour* (Brookfield: Ashgate Publishing, 1996); Vincent Harding, *There Is a River: The Black Struggle for Freedom in America* (New York: Vintage Books, 1983); John W. Blassingame, *The Slave Community: Plantation Life in the Antebellum South* (New York: Oxford University Press, 1972); Lerone Bennett Jr., *Before the Mayflower: A History of Black America*, 5th ed. (New York: Penguin Books, 1984).

13. Hortense Spillers, "Mama's Baby, Papa's Maybe: An American Grammar Book," in *Black, White, and in Color: Essays on American Literature and Culture* (Chicago: University of Chicago Press, 2003), 215. The essay first appeared in *Diacritics*, 17, no. 2 (summer 1987).

14. The full passage reads as follows: "Because slaves were valuable investment property, ship captains kept careful records in logbooks and mortality lists of the dates and causes of death. . . . These records survive for about one-fifth of the documented slave voyages and are now accessible through the Cambridge University Press Database. They show that on average 12 percent of the enslaved did not survive the ocean crossing, though there was considerable variation from one transport to another. Before 1700, death rates tended to be higher, averaging more than 22 percent. They decreased to about 10 percent by the end of the eighteenth century, but rose again to nearly 12 percent during the years of illegal trading in the mid-nineteenth century" (Postma, *The Atlantic Slave Trade*, 43–44).

15. Stephen D. Behrendt, "Crew Mortality in the Transatlantic Slave Trade in the Eighteenth Century," in *Routes to Slavery*, ed. David Eltis and David Richardson (London: Frank Cass, 1997), 66; also quoted in Postma, *The Atlantic Slave Trade*, 47.

16. Curtin, *The Atlantic Slave Trade*, 282–83.

17. Richard H. Steckel and Richard A. Jensen, "New Evidence on the Causes of Slave and Crew Mortality in the Atlantic Slave Trade," *Journal of Economic History* 46, no. 1 (March 1986): 59–60. Postma writes that the slave-ship crew's voyages "consisted of five stages: Europe to Africa, African coastal stay, Middle Passage, American port call, return voyage" (Postma, *The Atlantic Slave Trade*, 47).

18. Esther Copley, *A History of Slavery, and Its Abolition* (London: Houlston & Stoneman, 1839), 124. Postma's 2003 survey of the historical data similarly notes: "Most slaves were crammed into their designated spaces like loaves of bread on a shelf, with an average of six to seven square feet and rarely more than two or three feet of head space" (Postma, *The Atlantic Slave Trade*, 23).

19. Ottobah Cugoano, "Thoughts and Sentiments on the Evil and Wicked Traffic of the Slavery and Commerce of the Human Species" (1787), in *Thoughts and Sentiments on the Evil of Slavery and Other Writings*, ed. Vincent Carretta (New York: Penguin Books, 1999), 15.

20. Ibid., 15–16.

21. Saidiya V. Hartman, *Scenes of Subjection: Terror, Slavery, and Self-Making in Nineteenth-Century America* (New York: Oxford University Press, 1997), 42.

22. Harding, *There Is a River*, 10–11.

23. Olaudah Equiano, *Equiano's Travels: The Interesting Narrative of the Life of Olaudah Equiano, or Gustavus Vassa the African* (1789), abridged and ed. Paul Edwards (New York: Praeger Publishers, 1966), 27.

24. Copley, *A History of Slavery*, 124.

25. Spillers, "Mama's Baby, Papa's Maybe," 214–15.

26. Maria Diedrich, Henry Louis Gates Jr., and Carl Pederson, "The Middle Passage between History and Fiction," in Diedrich, Gates, and Pederson, *Black Imagination and the Middle Passage*, 8; emphasis added.

27. Robert Perkinson, "Shackled Justice: Florence Federal Penitentiary and the New Politics of Punishment," *Social Justice* 21, no. 3 (1994): 124–25.

28. Nichol Gomez, "Big Brother Is Watching," *Peacekeeper* (September 2001): 39.

29. Spillers, "Mama's Baby, Papa's Maybe," 215.

30. In addition to Cugoano and Equiano, narratives that articulate an autobiographical or generational memory of the Middle Passage may be found in such collections as *Pioneers of the Black Atlantic: Five Slave Narratives from the Enlightenment, 1772–1815*, ed. Henry Louis Gates Jr. and William L. Andrews (Washington, DC: Counterpoint, 1998). The narratives of Mary Prince (1831), Old Elizabeth (1863), Mattie J. Jackson (1866), Lucy A. Delaney (1891), Kate Drumgoold (1898), and Annie L. Burton (1909) are compiled in *Six Women's Slave Narratives*, ed. Henry Louis Gates Jr. (New York: Oxford University Press, 1988). The narratives of James Albert Ukawsaw Gronniosaw (1772), William Wells Brown (1847), Henry Bibb (1849), Sojourner Truth (1850), William and Ellen Craft (1860), Harriet Ann Jacobs (1861), and Jacob D. Green (1864) are anthologized in *Slave Narratives* (New York: Library of America, 2000). The autobiography and other narratives of Frederick Douglass are gathered in *Narrative of the Life of Frederick Douglass*, ed. Henry Louis Gates Jr. (New York: Library of America, 1994).

31. Jarvis Jay Masters, *Finding Freedom: Writings from Death Row* (Junction City, CA: Padma Publishing, 1997), 4–5.

32. Min S. Yee, *The Melancholy History of Soledad Prison* (New York: Harper's Magazine Press, 1973), 121; emphasis added.

33. According to a 1994 article in the *Progressive*, the opening of California's Security Housing Unit in 1989 at Pelican Bay State Prison led to thirty-six other states following suit over the next two years: "California Governor George Deukmejian said, in 1989, that Pelican Bay would serve as 'a model for the rest

of the nation.' Unfortunately, he was right. At least thirty-six states have already built 'super-maxi' prisons like it, according to a 1991 report by Human Rights Watch" (Paige Bierma, "Torture behind Bars: Right Here in the United States of America," *The Progressive* 58, no. 7 [July 1994]: 21).

34. "Brit Tells Tale of Torture at Guantánamo," *Windsor Star* (Canada), March 13, 2004, A17; emphasis added.

35. There is a significant body of reporting on the Corcoran incidents and the subsequent criminal trials of several guards, and the following articles offer a clear overview of the fundamental issues: the comprehensive 2002 California Prison Focus (CPF) report "Corcoran State Prison 2001–2002: Inside California's Brutal Maximum Security Prison," obtainable at the CPF Web site: www.prisons.org; Jerry Bier and Mike Lewis, "Eight Correctional Officers Indicted: Corcoran State Prison Officials Accused of Orchestrating Inmate Fights as Entertainment," *Fresno Bee*, February 27, 1998, home edition, A1; Tom Kertscher, "Controversy at Corcoran Prison is 10 Years Old: First Inmate Shootings Occurred Nine Months after Facility Opened," *Fresno Bee*, February 27, 1998, home edition, A16; Pamela J. Podger, "Corcoran Whistle-Blower Deals with Consequences Two Years Later: Richard Caruso Is Suing the State Department of Corrections," *Fresno Bee*, November 3, 1996, home edition, A16; Associated Press, "FBI Probes Fatal Shootings of Prison Inmates by Guards: Seven Convicts Killed at Corcoran Facility since 1988," October 28, 1994.

36. Perkinson, "Shackled Justice," 121.

37. I have refrained from extensively quoting such texts here for the sake of space, as well as to protect the anonymity of those who have a possibility of obtaining parole, but a significant collection of personal and legal correspondence, as well as untranscribed audio recorded interviews, has been amassed by California Prison Focus in the process of its interviews with people imprisoned in SHU facilities. California Prison Focus may be reached at 2940 16th Street #B-5, San Francisco, CA 94103; phone: (415) 252-9211; e-mail: info@prisons.org. Similar material is being gathered by the organization Justice Now, which focuses its work on the conditions of women's prisons. Justice Now may be contacted at 322 Webster Street, Suite 210, Oakland, CA 94612; phone: (510) 839-7654; e-mail: cshaylor@earthlink.net.

38. Convention against Torture and Other Cruel, Inhuman or Degrading Treatment or Punishment, United Nations Office of the High Commissioner for Human Rights, adopted December 10, 1984; emphasis added.

39. Kumasi Aguila, correspondence (1969), from the author's papers. Letters

provided courtesy of Aguila. The Folsom Prisoners Manifesto was reprinted and widely circulated in Angela Y. Davis et al., *If They Come in the Morning* (New York: Third Press, 1971).

40. Frantz Fanon, *The Wretched of the Earth*, trans. Constance Farrington (New York: Grove Weidenfeld, 1968), 50; subsequent references are given in the text.

41. Anonymous, "A Sunny Soledad Afternoon," in *Words from the House of the Dead: Prison Writings from Soledad*, ed. Joseph Bruchac and William Witherup (New York: Crossing Press, 1974).

42. Viet Mike Ngo, interview, May 24, 2002.

43. Ramona Africa, interview (transcribed by Sormeh Ayari), Riverside, California, April 16, 2004. Ramona Africa is the only adult survivor of the May 13, 1985, police bombing of the MOVE organization's home in West Philadelphia. The FBI, in collaboration with the city of Philadelphia, detonated a C4 bomb, killing all occupants except for Ramona and Birdie Africa. Both survivors remember that after the explosion, as MOVE family members fled the inferno, they were immersed in automatic gunfire by waiting police and FBI agents. Eleven MOVE family members were burned alive. Ramona Africa was charged with conspiracy, riot, and numerous counts of simple and aggravated assault. She served seven years in prison, and is currently an internationally recognized activist and lecturer. She was given a two-month jail sentence for "contempt of court" after she became a supporter of the MOVE Nine during their trial. See Michael Vitez, Vanessa Williams, and Craig R. McCoy, "Memories of the MOVE Bombing," *Philadelphia Inquirer*, April 20, 1993, A11.

44. "Remembering the Real Dragon: An Interview with George Jackson, May 16 and June 29, 1971," interviewed by Karen Wald, in *Cages of Steel: The Politics of Imprisonment in the United States*, ed. Ward Churchill and Jim Vander Wall (Washington, DC: Maisonneuve Press, 1992), 178.

45. Kumasi Aguila, correspondence from Folsom State Prison (California), January 12, 1970, author's papers.

Prison Activism and Support Resources

All of Us or None
http://www.allofusornone.org/

Alvaro Luna Hernandez National Freedom Coalition
http://www.freealvaro.org

American Friends Service Committee
http://www.afsc.org

Anarchist Black Cross Network
http://www.anarchistblackcross.org/

Critical Resistance
http://www.criticalresistance.org/

Free Mumia Coalition
http://www.freemumia.org

Human Rights Watch Prison Project
http://www.hrw.org/prisons/

International Friends and Family of Mumia Abu Jamal
http://www.mumia.org

The Jericho Movement
http://www.thejerichomovement.com/

Leonard Peltier Defense Committee
http://www.freepeltier.org/

Malcolm X Grassroots Movement
http://www.mxgm.org

Out of Control Lesbian Committee to Support Women Political Prisoners
http://www.prisonactivist.org/ooc

Prison Activist Resource Center
http://www.prisonactivist.org/

Ramsey Muñiz Defense Committee
http://home.earthlink.net/~aou/

Index

abolitionism, 235, 236, 238, 239
Abu Ghraib, 40
Abu-Jamal, Mumia, 35, 36, 142, 207–8, 282n2
Acoli, Sundiata, 61, 63–64, 275–76nn43,44,45
affective alienation: and free/unfree relations, 33–34, 168–69; and methodology, 30; and SHU regimes, 188; and state terror, 168–69; and subjective disarticulation, 228–29; and technologies of imprisonment, 65; and temporality, 212–13; and white civil society as threatened, 97–98. *See also* civic death; subjective disarticulation
Africa, Janet Hollaway, 171
Africa, Ramona, 251–53, 254, 302n43
agency. *See* prisoner as subject
Aguila, Kumasi (Stephen Simmons), 246–47, 255
al-Harath, Jamal, 243–44
alienation: and Middle Passage,

231–33; and prison praxis, 76, 77, 110, 159–60; and prison regime as standoff, 209; and subjective disarticulation, 228–29. *See also* affective alienation; civic death; subjective disarticulation
Al-Jaami, 102
All-African People's Revolutionary Party, 51
"All of Us or None" movement, 296n5
American Civil Liberties Union (ACLU), 189
Amistad, Kombozi, 59
Amnesty International, 189, 261–62n3
antiblack racism: and chattel slavery, 228; and incorrigibility, 48; and methodology, 30; and prison regime as standoff, 207
Ashcroft, John, 268–69n40
Askari, Kijana Tashiri, 30, 161–62, 163, 191–94, 197, 227

Dylan Rodríguez is a Pinoy scholar-activist who works with a variety of radical social-justice and liberationist movements. He is a founding member of the Critical Resistance organizing collective and has been engaged in the struggle for prison and police abolition since 1997. He is assistant professor of ethnic studies at the University of California, Riverside.